The CANADIANS

GEORGE WOODCOCK

Fitzhenry and Whiteside

Fitzhenry and Whiteside Limited
150 Lesmill Road
Don Mills, Ontario M3B 2T5

Canadian Cataloguing in Publication Data

Woodcock, George, 1912-
The Canadians

Includes index
ISBN 0-88902-571-1

1. Canada — History. 2. Regionalism — Canada.
3. Canada — Civilisation. I. Title.

FC97.W66 971 C79-094777-3
F1027.W66

Editorial/Sarah Reid
Design/David Shaw & Associates Ltd.
Picture Research/Sue Dickin

The publisher gratefully acknowledges the assistance
of the Ontario Arts Council.

Printed and bound in Canada
by T.H. Best Printing Company Ltd.

Contents

Introduction 7

I Canadian Origins

The Earliest Immigrants 11
The Explorers 27
Region and Nation 47

II A Pattern of Regions

Newfoundland: Where the Empire Began 75
Atlantic Canada 95
Quebec: Remembrance of Things Past 115
Ontario 137
The Prairie Provinces: Canada's Third World 161
British Columbia: Beyond the Great Divide 193
The Vulnerable North 219

III A Canadian Identity

Unity Without Uniformity 241
The Life of the Arts 253
Canadians at Leisure 277
Canada: Identity Crisis 291

Introduction

The popular image of Canada, especially outside that country, is still that of a land of farmers and outdoorsmen. Yet the average modern Canadian, unlike his grandfather (in the uncertain event of his grandfather having lived in Canada), is likely to be an urban man, and only a tiny minority of the inhabitants of our country are now dependent on the golden wheat fields or the apple orchards or the traplines that once seemed to provide the very foundation of the land's existence.

Even so, the mystique of rural living is remarkably present in the Canadian consciousness; almost equally strongly the mystique of the wilderness lingers there also. Vast lands impress the mind in different ways from small lands, and the difference is more than merely one of size. Large countries which lack the intimacy of close and ancient settlement seem always, as Canada does, to project on the minds even of people who have retreated into the growing cities a sense of geographical void, a feeling of ambient and compelling solitude like that which a century ago induced a wandering English officer, William Francis Butler, to call his book on the Canadian west *The Great Lone Land.*

In the 1970s Canada is still physically a great land — the second largest in the world — and a lone land, for only a twelfth of its 3,852,000 square miles is utilized by men in their settlements and their farms. The rest is still forest and mountain, tundra, muskeg and rock; all this wild land encircling — in its 290,000 square miles of lakes and rivers — more than half the fresh-water surface of the whole world. It is not surprising that this sheer vastness of terrain, so menacing, so inspiring and at times so boring in its monotonous extent, should have become a constant factor in the Canadian consciousness, emerging to dominate poetry and fiction and the visual arts. Perhaps more than in any other country, this vastness has shaped the sharply variant regional characteristics of the people who live across the four thousand miles' breadth of the country and across its northward extension from the American border at 49 degrees to the tip of Ellesmere Island at more than 83 degrees north — almost a thousand miles beyond the Arctic Circle and only about four hundred miles south of the Pole. (The magnetic Pole, as distinct from the geographic Pole, is actually in Canadian territory.) Northrop Frye, the shy dean of Canadian critics, talked often of a "garrison mentality" among Canadians of the colonial period, and even today, though few people of this country any longer regard the wilderness as an enemy against which they must defend themselves, the great unsettled solitudes still dominate their view of the land and condition their images of themselves. The vastnesses still call, and the call is often answered, even if the answerer travels in a camper or a speedboat instead of in the *canot de maître* of the exploring fur trader.

But if Canadians show themselves often in their vacations and in their arts, to which they are increasingly attached, as a geographically preoccupied people, they have also become far more deeply concerned than their ancestors with history. Less than thirty years ago, when I returned from Europe to Canada, which I had left as a small child, I rejoined a people still largely immersed in the pioneer frame of mind, for whom the past was elsewhere and the urgency of immediate tasks meant that the here was always the now. During the decades following the Second World War, as life drew away from the hard and present realities of the frontier existence, a radical change of attitude towards the past took place in the minds of Canadians. It peaked around 1967 (the centennial year of Confederation) in a passionate interest in both national and local history that manifested itself not only in an unparalleled multitude of books about a past hitherto largely unexplored, but also in an awareness among Canadians in general that they were no longer timeless pioneers, but people with a record interesting in itself and meaningful in terms of their personal identities. To be a Canadian no longer meant being a colonial, dependent on some other country's history; it meant being a member of an autonomous historical continuum.

Canadians, in other words, have largely discovered themselves in place and time; and if, at this point in the late 1970s, they sometimes appear bewildered and directionless, it is largely because they have not yet understood how to apply the newly acquired self-knowledge; the knowledge — among other things — that the sharply particular attachment to region and locality which so many of them possess is counterposed to a wide historic unity based on common experiences and perils, and that the two urges, the regional and the national, must be brought into a complementary rather than a conflicting relationship if Canada and the sense of being Canadian as something specific and valuable in the world are to survive. Centralization, embodied in the outdated nineteenth-century European concept of the nation-state which unfortunately still hypnotizes many of our political leaders, is alien to the Canadian genius, but the full possibilities of a true federalism based on an awareness of the historic and geographic realities of Canada's regions have yet to be thoroughly explored.

This book is intended as a contribution, verbal and visual, to that exploration. Its fourteen chapters are divided into three parts which represent stages in the process of enquiry.

The three chapters of Part I, "Canadian Origins," are devoted to posing an alternative to the familiar theory of Canada as the product of the actions of two "founding races" or "founding peoples," the French and the British. What I pose is a three-stage chart of origins, beginning with the native peoples, Canada's first immigrants, proceeding to the fur traders who also explored and mapped the country and established the lines of communication we have since used, and ending with the settlers who slowly filled in the maps, in the process establishing our political and social patterns. The basic classification of Europeans as trader-explorers and settlers, in my view cuts across the traditional racial and linguistic lines; the Sieur de la Vérendrye and Alexander Mackenzie, engaged in their westward discoveries, had far more in common than either of them would have had with a Québec *habitant* or a Prairie homesteader, who have their own areas of similarity in life and aspirations which override their differences of language or original homeland.

A corollary of the emphasis on settlement being the important factor in determining Canadian political and social patterns leads us to the regional nature of Canada. It is less language than unique combinations of historical and geographical circumstances that mould cultures, and hence — given its size — Canada is a country where the regions are all-important. The seven essential Canadian regions, in my view, are Newfoundland; the three Atlantic provinces (Nova Scotia, New Brunswick and Prince Edward Island); Québec; Ontario; the three Prairie provinces (Manitoba, Saskatchewan, and Alberta); British Columbia; and the North, consisting of the Northwest Territories and the Yukon Territory. In Part II of this book, "A Pattern of Regions", I devote a chapter each to examining the special history and character of the people who inhabit these regions, how their environments have helped condition their lives and attitudes, and what they contribute to the general Canadian pattern.

For all their regional differences, and largely because of them, Canadians have a common area of distinctiveness in comparison with other peoples, including their American neighbours. This is the subject of the four chapters comprising Part III, "A Canadian Identity", which explores common moral, political, and social attitudes, the shared economic background, the arts and leisure activities of the people, and finally comes to the crucial question of what we mean by a Canadian identity. What is a Canadian — as distinct from a British Columbian or a Québecois or a Newfoundlander — in his own eyes, the eyes of his fellow countrymen, the eyes of the world?

I Canadian Origins

The landing of Icelanders on Canadian soil moved from saga into certainty in 1958 when Helge Ingstad discovered the remains of a Norse settlement at L'Anse aux Meadows in Newfoundland.

CHAPTER ONE

The Earliest Emigrants

The awareness that survives — because it is recorded — of the soil we call Canada and of the first Canadians begins at the point when history emerges from the prehistoric and preliterate past: the point when literate Europeans reach the country and encounter the native peoples. The first to arrive were the Vikings. Their ancestors had left Norway to settle the sparse pastures among the volcanoes of Iceland, and their fathers had pushed westward under Eric the Red to make their precarious settlements on the shores of Greenland. The first European to sight the coast of North America was the seaman Bjarni Herjolfsen, blown off his course on the way from Iceland to Greenland. Not long afterwards, about 1000 AD, Eric the Red's son, Leif, set out on an exploratory voyage, and the sagas describe how he found the lands which he called Helluland and Markland and Vinland. Helluland was probably Baffin Island, and Markland, which was described as "level and wooded, with broad beaches of white sand and a gentle slope to the sea," was probably Labrador. In Vinland, where Leif found wild grapes and felled timber for use in Greenland, the dew was sweet to the taste, there were bigger salmon than the Norsemen had ever seen before, and, as the sagas remarked, "there was such abundance that it seemed as though cattle would need no winter fodder, since the grass hardly withered in winter, while the days and nights were more equally divided than in Greenland or Iceland." It is now virtually certain that Vinland was Newfoundland, since it was here, at L'Anse aux Meadows, that Helge Ingstad in 1961 and later years discovered the remains of a Norse settlement of eight houses and four boatsheds; this must have been the place where Leif wintered and to which his brother Thorvald returned in the following year.

As far as we know, Thorvald was the first European to meet any of the native people of the American continent. He and his men were attacked by "Skraelings" who came in a multitude of skin boats; the Skraelings had bows and shot arrows at the Norsemen, and Thorvald alone was hit. "I have a wound under my arm," he said, "an arrow came between the gunwale and my shield. It will be my death." And indeed it was.

On this, or perhaps a later occasion, for the sagas vary in their accounts, Freydis, the brave and cruel illegitimate daughter of Eric the Red, turned the tide in a battle with the Skraelings by rushing forward,

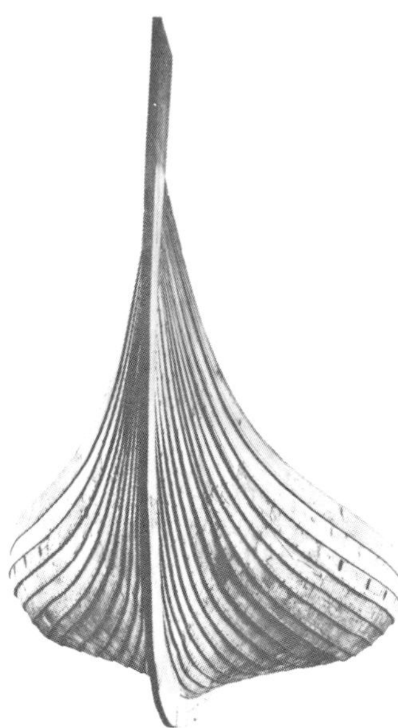

It was in high-prowed vessels like the Gokstad ship, discovered on the shore of Oslo Fjord in 1880, that the Norsemen sailed the north Atlantic and eventually came, via Iceland and Greenland, to the shores of Baffin Island, Labrador and Newfoundland.

loudly exhorting the men of her own side and beating a sword on her naked breasts. The same Freydis was later responsible for a gruesome treachery; she and a number of Greenlanders accompanied to Vinland a group of Icelanders who had a large trading ship and wished to cut timber. Freydis persuaded the Greenlanders to slaughter the thirty Icelanders and seize their ship; when the men refused to kill the Icelandic women, Freydis slew them herself.

Who the Skraelings were is uncertain. Their hide boats make one think of Inuit craft, but they used the bow, which Inuit did not then possess. The sagas describe them as "dark, ugly men who wore their hair in an unpleasant fashion. They had big eyes and were broad in the cheek," while one of their chiefs was described as "of large size and fine bearing." They probably belonged to one of the Algonkian tribes who inhabited this region in historical times; it does not seem likely that they were Beothucks, since there is no reference to the strange colouring which struck the English and Breton fishermen who first encountered these people in the fifteenth century. "These Indians are called *Red*," recorded Captain George Cartwright in 1770, "from their custom of painting themselves, and everything belonging to them, with red ochre, which they find in great plenty in various parts of the island." It was because of this Beothuck custom, not because of skin colouring, that North American native people were first called Red Indians, but it seems evident that the Norsemen saw no people of this kind.

In the years immediately after Thorvald's death the Norsemen returned twice to the Vinland settlement and again encountered the Skraelings, but after that the settlement was abandoned and there are no records to tell us whether any further contacts were made between the Vikings and the ancestors of the native Canadians. One historian, Tryggvi Oleson, has suggested that the Norsemen encountered and interbred with the Eskimo of Baffin Island, and that in this way a cultural link was established that would explain some of the technological features of the so-called Thule culture which appeared in this region round about 1000 AD, at the period of the Norse settlement of Greenland. The explorer Vilhjalmur Stefansson encountered, in 1910 on Victoria Island in the central Arctic, a tribe he called the Copper Eskimo, who were tall and inclined to be blond, and he decided the most likely hypothesis to explain their unusual physical and mental attributes was that they were partly descended from Norsemen who had found their way from Greenland into the Arctic Archipelago. All this, of course, is conjecture, supported by no firm evidence, but if it were true it would mean that the Vikings were not merely fleeting visitors to Canada, but actually contributed through extensive and intimate mingling with the Inuit to the mixture of peoples we now call Canadians.

Since we know that European fishermen had reached the Great

In La Grande Hermine, *here represented by a replica now kept in the Parc Cartier-Brébeuf at Québec, Jacques Cartier sailed from St. Malo in 1535 and ascended the St. Lawrence to the Iroquois village of Hochelaga on the site of Montréal.*

Banks of Newfoundland and had even penetrated the Gulf of St. Lawrence before the French explorer Jacques Cartier first appeared there in 1534, it is likely that already, by the time of his arrival, there had been contacts and trade at least with the Micmacs of Nova Scotia and possibly even with the Iroquois who then lived on the banks of the St. Lawrence River. But Cartier was the first traveller actually to describe the Indians of the Canadian mainland, and he provided a direct contact between the two worlds by taking two Indians with him when he returned to France in 1534. In the following year, 1535, he ascended the St. Lawrence and visited the considerable Iroquois settlements of Stadacona and Hochelaga which then stood on the sites of present-day Quebec City and Montréal.

These places were no nomadic camps. They were settled villages, around which the forest had been cleared by burning to provide garden land on which the Indians grew corn and beans, and varieties of squash, as well as sunflowers whose seeds they had learnt to press for the oil. Built

No authenticated portrait of Jacques Cartier (1491-1557) exists; this is one of a number of imaginary sketches based on artists' conceptions of his personality.

of poles and thatched with bark, the communal houses were often sixty yards long and might be inhabited by as many as a dozen families. Though Cartier may never have learnt of it, the Iroquois had a complex ceremonial life and a religion of Manichean duality, conceiving a universe in which two Great Spirits, one good and the other evil, waged perpetual conflict. The description of Cartier's arrival at Hochelaga which became part of the chronicle of his voyages presents a striking example of the joy and goodwill that so often marked the first encounters of the native peoples of Canada with those who now — rather oddly — we call the "founding races," the French and the British.

> And on reaching Hochelaga, there came to meet us more than a thousand persons, both men, women and children, who gave us as good a welcome as ever father gave to his son, making great signs of joy; for the men danced in one ring, the women in another, and the children also apart by themselves. After this they brought us quantities of fish, and of their bread which is made of Indian corn, throwing so much of it into our longboats that it seemed to rain bread. Seeing this, the captain, accompanied by several of his men, went on shore; and no sooner had he landed than they all crowded about him and about the others, giving them a wonderful reception. And the women brought their babies in arms to have the captain and his companions touch them, while all held a merry-making which lasted more than half an hour. Seeing their generosity and friendliness, the captain had the women all sit down in a row and gave them some tin beads and other trifles; and to some of them he gave knives. Then he returned on board the longboats to sup and pass the night, throughout which the Indians remained on the banks of the river, as near the long-boats as they could get, keeping many fires burning all night and dancing and calling out every moment *aguyase,* which is their term of salutation and joy.

So rapidly did this dawn of trust fade that a mere seventy-four years later, in 1609, the second great French explorer of Canada, Samuel de Champlain, was busily engaged against the Iroquois, shooting them down with his arquebusiers to promote an alliance with a rival group of Indians, the Ottawas, and thus setting going a strife between races that may have changed its forms but has remained to this day a shadow on the life of Canadians.

With Cartier's arrival, the native peoples of Canada move on stage. For many generations they were known to history only as the white men first saw them; in Québec and the Maritimes during the sixteenth century, on the Prairies in the seventeenth and early eighteenth centuries, on the Pacific coast at the very end of the eighteenth century, and in parts of the high Arctic not until the twentieth century. Since then archaeology

Already, by the time Samuel de Champlain completed his voyages by the early seventeenth century, the French fur traders known as coureurs de bois *were living among the native people in the forests of the Québec hinterland. In this print one of them is shown with three types of the Indians, from whom he has learnt the art of snowshoe travel.*

During the seventeenth century many European mariners entered the Arctic seas in search of the North West Passage, and artists in Europe represented their observations of northern life in drawings like this, depicting the drying of fish and the trapping of foxes.

has, to a certain extent, stretched out the temporal perspective, so that we know the human species in none of its forms actually evolved in the New World of the Americas. Like their white successors, the native peoples of Canada were immigrants. They wandered into the continent as nomads crossing the land-bridge where the Bering Strait now runs. Genetically they are related to Siberians, Mongols, and Tibetans, the Central Asian peoples whose primeval shamanistic religion they shared. The ancestors of the various Indian peoples came so long ago — some of them perhaps as early as 20,000 BC — that no people now living in Asia speaks anything that resembles their languages. The Inuit who spread over the Arctic regions from Alaska to Greenland, including almost all of Canada north of the tree line, came so much later — around five thousand years ago — that they still have identifiable Asian relatives in far eastern Siberia, where about two thousand Inuit reside under Russian rule.

There are many distinctions we can make — in Canada and elsewhere — between the cultures we call civilized and those we call primitive. None of them implies innate superiority or inferiority in moral or intellectual terms; rather they reflect the extraordinary adaptability to circumstances which is one of the universal human traits. Two of these distinctions are important in the present context. The first concerns the existence of records. The second concerns the relationship of Man to the natural world.

By records I do not mean only the written documents, ranging from inscriptions on stone or baked clay to fragments of papyrus or paper or vellum, on which literate peoples set out their transactions. Some sophisticated peoples, who used ephemeral record systems to operate elaborate political systems, like the knotted strings of the Incas, left no such written documents, but they did build cities and roads and fortifications of lasting materials like stone or brick, and in the debris of their houses and palaces and temples they left enduring fragments of their lives, such as stone carvings or expressively designed pottery or objects of metals that did not quickly oxidize. From such relics, taken in connection with the narratives of the earliest travellers or conquerors, it is often possible to create a quite elaborate picture of the past before history, such as we possess in the cases of the Egyptians or the Aztecs of Mexico.

When Captain James Cook reached Vancouver Island in 1778, the people of Nootka had for centuries been carving the masks of animal spirits, which the chiefs wore when they danced to welcome the first white explorers who landed on their beaches.

Primitive peoples, on the other hand, rarely maintain permanent settlements. They are always on the move, in search of game or — if they have reached the stage of herding or agriculture — of new pastures or unexhausted land. They do not build monumentally in enduring materials, and often, apart from stone implements, they use very little in their daily lives that is not perishable. The Indians of Canada were peoples of this kind. Even when, as among the Coast Indians of western Canada, they achieved high levels of artistic and technical accomplishment — building wooden houses 1,500 feet long like that which Simon Fraser reported seeing near the Fraser estuary in 1807, and carving giant canoes as long as the ships of the Spanish explorers of the 1770s — their work would usually be done in some easily workable but perishable material like wood, rather than stone, which demands a relatively complex technology. Back before the vital meeting time with the first white visitors, their relics are slight and laconic in what they tell us; human and animal bones, some primitive tools and weapons, modest ornaments, the ashes of fires, and the traces of foundation holes. Their houses, their boats, their wooden artifacts, their woven fabrics, rarely survive. Since carbon 14 dating and various modificatory techniques came into being, it has at last become possible to date prehistoric sites with relative accuracy, which is why we now know that the Indian peoples first came to Canada about twenty millenia ago. But we can only scantily reconstruct their physical lives in prehistory, and it is only in their surviving myths, which are partly objective history in symbolic form and partly subjective fantasy, that we can approach an understanding of their mental lives.

This woman of Nootka Sound, encountered by sea traders at the end of the eighteenth century, is wearing the wet-weather clothing of the Coast Indians — a cape of cedar-bark fibres and a hat of woven spruce root. The hat is decorated with designs representing the hunting of the whale, which was the privilege of Nootka chiefs.

Early travellers in the Canadas encountered many unaccustomed species of the animal world, some of which were recorded by Charles de Granville, who illustrated the manuscript, Les Raretés des Indes. *Here he presents the perilous beauty of the rattlesnake.*

This print from Lahontan's New Voyages to North America *(English translation, 1735) shows the regular townplanning of Indian villages of woven sapling houses along the St. Lawrence.*

It is these myths of the Indian and Inuit peoples that reinforce the second of the two distinctions I make between the cultures we call civilized and the cultures we call primitive. They differ profoundly in their attitude to and their working relationship with the natural world. A "civilized" people seeks to dominate and transform the natural world in order to exploit it in support of a basically unnatural way of life. A "primitive" people seeks to ensure survival by living in as close a harmony with the natural world as any natural predator.

The myths of the Canadian Indians and of the Eskimo (or Inuit, meaning "The People", as they prefer to call themselves) illustrate this point admirably, for they show how the hunter sought to propitiate the spirits of the animals he pursued; how the fisherfolk of the Pacific Coast did honour to the salmon and the oolichan that came as guests to their rivers before catching them; how the young man in search of his spirit guardian went into the wilderness, the very heart of the natural world, and in the solitude encountered the beings in animal form who would give him his vocation and would guide him for the rest of his life. Such animal spirits, as well as supernatural beings of a more fantastic kind, were also associated with the secret society rituals of peoples like the Ojibway in eastern Canada and the Kwakiutl on the west coast which provided the nearest thing to both religious ritual and drama among the

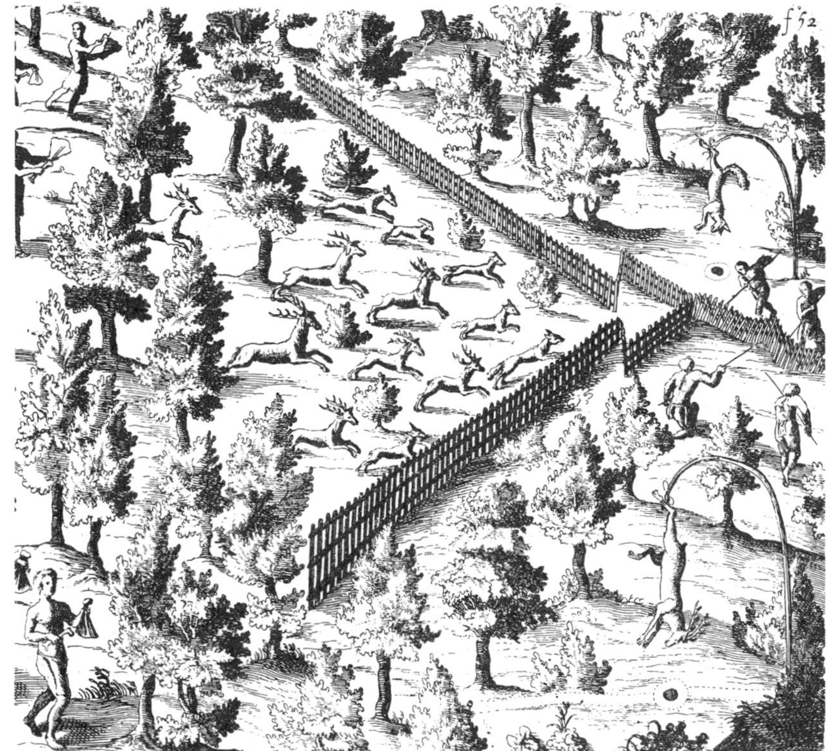

An illustration from Champlain's Voyages *shows the elaborate methods by which the Indians of early Canada trapped wild game and drove deer into fenced pounds where they could be killed with ease.*

native peoples of Canada. The Winter Dances of the Kwakiutl went on for weeks and focused around the Hamatsa Society, devoted to the spirit known as the Great Cannibal from the North End of the World. When the festival time came the whole life of the village was centred around it, the sacred whistles blew in the forests to announce the coming of the supernatural beings, and novices who had fasted in the woods were initiated in ceremonials which included the ritual eating of the flesh of corpses. The members of other societies clowned and performed extraordinary illusionist tricks, in which dancers would appear to be decapitated and voices would speak from the fires. Central to Indian mythology were the great trickster figures who were animal in form, like Raven among the Pacific Coast Indians and Coyote inland. These tricksters were also benefactors, fulfilling the same role as Prometheus in Greek legend; one of the most widely spread stories about Raven tells how he stole the light from an evil spirit for the benefit of mankind, who up to this time had lived in darkness. Some myths presented human beings as animals who had lost their skins, and among the Pacific Coast Indians it was thought that when the salmon kings and the chiefs of the killer whales returned to their underwater houses, they doffed their animal shapes and looked like men. According to the legends of the Skeena river in northern British Columbia, the Gitksan hunters of Temlaham of-

The Iroquois custom of killing their captured enemies by torture struck deeply into the imagination of seventeenth century Europeans (whose own forms of punishment were barbaric by modern standards), and artists freely exploited the horrors of such occasions.

OPPOSITE:
Joseph François Lafitau, a Jesuit born at Bordeaux, served for six years in the mission at Sault St. Louis, now known as Caughnawage, where he learnt from the aged missionary Joseph Garnier (who lived sixty years among the Indians and knew all their languages and dialects) the lore which on his return to France in 1717 enabled him to write Les Moeurs des Sauvages. *The book was garnished with many illustrations like these, which represent respectively prisoners tied down while their captors sleep and later being paraded into the victors' village holding tortoiseshell rattles and wearing the head-dresses of defeated tribes.*

fended the mountain goats by hunting them in a cruel manner. One captured kid was subjected to inhumane abuses by all but one man who treated it kindly and allowed it to escape to its mountain home. Later, disguising themselves as human chiefs, the goats invited the Gitksan hunters to a potlatch. There the goat who had once been persecuted as a kid assumed his animal form and danced up an earthquake which destroyed all the hunters except the one who had befriended him. Significantly, his supernatural powers were linked with his animal form.

In the myths, the human and animal worlds were in fact coterminous and in constant interpenetration, and in actual life this viewpoint was paralleled by an extraordinary adaptability to the environment. Most Canadian Indians and all the Canadian Inuit took the land as they found it and wandered nomadically over its surface, gaining food, clothing, shelter, as well as supernatural favours, from the wild animals and the

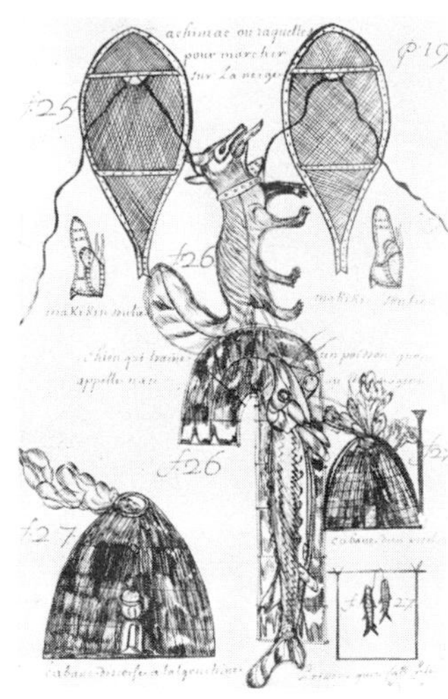

The artist of Les Raretés des Indes *was interested in strange techniques as well as strange animals, and here he represents means of transport (snowshoes and dog sleigh) and methods of preserving fish (smoking and drying).*

Among the Hurons, as among most primitive peoples, great stress was laid on the ceremonials connected with death, and the final disposal of the remains of a chief was an occasion for oration and feasting.

wild plants of forest and prairie and tundra. Only the Iroquois had begun to transform and dominate the natural environment by introducing agriculture, which necessitated the destruction of the forest, and there is no doubt that this relatively dependable and man-fostered resource was one of the main reasons why the Iroquois remained such a power for so long on the borderlands of Québec and such a peril to the rural settlement of New France. Even though they were good cultivators, the Iroquois remained superb woodsmen, expert in their own kind of guerilla warfare. "They come like foxes through the woods," said the Jesuit Father Lalement in 1659. "They attack like lions. They take flight like birds, disappearing before they have really appeared." Manor houses, farmhouses, missions in New France; all were subject to the depredations of the Iroquois, who, as allies of the British, continued to harass the French settlers well into the eighteenth century.

One of the results of the remarkable adaptation to their environment by the Indian and Inuit peoples of Canada is that their languages and their origin myths are less reliable guides to cultural patterns than the kind of terrain in which they lived and moved. An Atlantic pattern of sea-fishing and hunting characterized the Beothuk of Newfoundland and the Micmac and Malecite of the area which is now Nova Scotia and New Brunswick. The agrarian culture of the Iroquois — including the Huron — occupied the St. Lawrence valley and the areas around the more easterly of the Great Lakes. The vast boreal woodland region stretched from Labrador across the Canadian Shield to the taiga, the area of small trees and brush stretching west of Hudson's Bay as far as the Mackenzie and the Yukon, and here flourished a nomadic hunting culture, featuring such marvellously adapted forms of transport as the light and portable birchbark canoe and the snowshoe. South of the boreal woodlands and west of the Shield, stretched the great plains which we commonly call the Prairies, and here wandered a group of hunting peoples who depended on the vast migratory herds of buffalo — the North American bison — moulding their seasonal and ceremonial lives around the animals' movements. The prehistoric Prairies were in this way as much a one-crop region as they later became when white immigrants turned them into gigantic wheat fields after the great herds had died; the whole economy of the plains Indians was dependent on the buffalo, whose carcass provided fresh meat and pemmican for storage, rawhide for the great tents or lodges and for clothing, robes for blankets, sinews for thread, and bone and horn for all kinds of implements. When the Hudson's Bay man Antony Henday reached the Prairies on foot in 1755, the tribes were already adapting their way of hunting by using horses that had spread northward through the midwest from the Spanish posts in New Mexico. This acquisition of a domestic animal even more useful than the dog, which they already had, might have led the Plains Indians to dominating rather than adapting to their environment if the influx of the white men had not brought an end to the indigenous prairie culture in the 1870s.

Beyond the Prairies, in the series of mountain ranges between the Rockies and the coast, wandered a number of peoples who hunted the mountainsides and the valley forests and fished in the rivers and lakes, while on the shores of the Pacific and on the great westward flowing rivers such as the Fraser, the Skeena and the Nass, lived the most prosperous and artistically sophisticated of all the Indian peoples of Canada, the group of tribes generally called the Coast Indians. These had been able, through the abundance of the great annual salmon runs, to establish settled villages and to develop a ceremonial and cultural life unrivalled among other food-gathering peoples anywhere in the world. All summer long they collected and preserved food, sun-drying salmon and clams, stamping oil out of the rich flesh of the oolichan or candlefish which came in great migrations up some of the rivers, gathering and drying berries of many kinds, stripping off the inner bark of the hemlock which served as a kind of bread and digging the bulbs of the blue-flowered camas and the knobbly roots of clover which provided them with starch. This great summer gathering of wealth provided the food for a winter of leisure, and the capital needed for the spiritual and artistic and social activities of that season. The great carved poles which the Coast Indians erected before their houses, the splendid masks and rattles and other ceremonial paraphernalia which they carved and painted, place them at the very peak of primitive artistic traditions; their winter ceremonials were long and complex rituals verging on true drama, their giving-feasts or potlatches displayed the immense wealth which the chiefs were able to gather and to use in the validation of the crests and titles they proudly claimed, and one tribe at least — the Nootka — hunted the grey whale from canoes for glory rather than blubber.

Finally, to the north, lay the sharp line where the boreal woodland came to an end and the treeless tundra began, stretching north to the great islands of the Arctic Archipelago. This was the territory of the Eskimo or Inuit, traditional enemies of all Indians (who for the most part feared the land beyond the tree line, the relentless Barren Land). Some of the Inuit lived mainly by following the great migratory herds of caribou that wandered over the Barren Land, while those of the Arctic Sea and its islands lived mainly on marine mammals — such as seal, walrus, narwhal and beluga — and fish. With their kayaks and umiaks, made of skin stretched on light frames; with their dog-drawn sleighs and warm houses built of ice — the famous igloos; with their highly specialized techniques for hunting and fishing during the Arctic winter the Eskimo were perhaps the most superbly adapted of all indigenous Canadians to their harsh and inhospitable world.

Each region of Canada before the white men came and history began

to be recorded had its own culture that, with variations, was strikingly homogenous throughout its natural bounds, but this was far from meaning a parallel homogeneity of language or of tradition. What little we know of the Beothuks (they were extinct by the early nineteenth century from white mens' sicknesses and the loss of their fishing grounds and from plain massacre by the early settlers; only scanty records of their language have survived) suggests that they fitted into the Algonkian family of languages that spread as far as the Rockies, and included sea-verge peoples like the Micmac, woodsmen like many of the Cree, and plains hunters like the Blackfoot. Those who spoke the Iroquian languages inhabited a relatively small area around the St. Lawrence and the Great Lakes. Athabaskan was the language group of the peoples of the boreal forests west from Hudson's Bay and into the northern interior of British Columbia, but at least one Athabaskan people, the Sarcee, had become so completely assimilated into the plains culture that it was admitted into the Blackfoot Confederacy. Finally, despite the extraordinary homogeneity of the Coast Indian culture, where such customs as the potlatch were universal and art styles blended into each other over great distances of coastline, there were no less than five distinct groups of languages in this area — Haida, Tlingit, Tsimshian, Wakashan, and Salish, and though there are faint clues suggesting links between Haida and Tlingit and the Athabaskan languages, the time of parting must have been so many centuries ago that all traditions suggesting any connection have vanished. Indeed, the one body of evidence that points to an original common culture among the Indians of the far west, and links them still to their Asian homeland, is the shamanic cult, which in surprisingly minute details has remained unchanged, so that, in Indian villages where the old ways have survived or revived, the shaman will still suck the sickness out of his patients with drumming and tranced dancing, and will mime the journey into the underworld in search of the souls whose loss causes certain illnesses, just as the shamans of Siberia did long ago and still do.

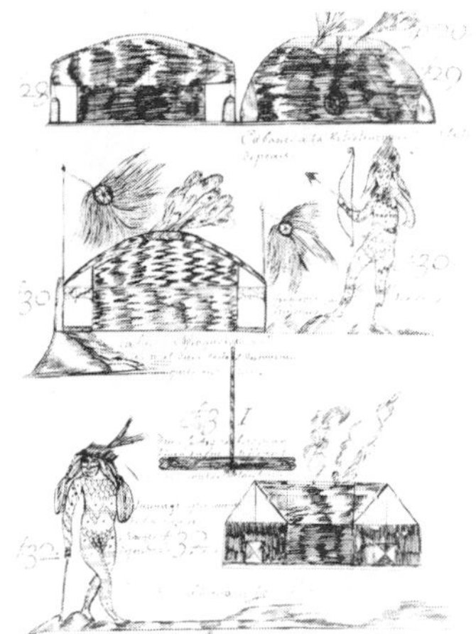

de Granville, the artist of Les Raretés des Indes *was less concerned than Lafitau with classical artistic proprieties, and his sketches of Indian dress and dwellings give a sense of fresh and direct observation.*

The sicknesses like smallpox and syphilis, influenza and measles, which came with the white men; the hunger brought about by white invasion of age-old hunting and fishing grounds; and the cultural disruption brought about when missionaries and administrators sought to suppress customs essential to Indian societies, were all forces that reduced the Indians in numbers and played havoc with their traditions and their self-respect. Already, early in the nineteenth century, the Saulteaux chief Peguis complained about the changes in the Red River region:

> Before you whites came to trouble the ground, our rivers were full of fish and our woods of deer. Our creeks abounded with beaver and our plains were covered with buffalo. But now we are brought to poverty. Our beavers are gone for ever; our buffalo have fled to the lands of our enemies. . . . The geese are afraid to pass over the smoke

OPPOSITE:
In these illustrations to Lafitau's Moeurs des Sauvages, *which represent Indians trading among themselves, the classical influence of French seventeenth-century painting is evident; it militates against complete authenticity.*

> of our chimneys and we are left to starve while you whites grow rich on the dust of our fathers, troubling the plains with the plough, covering them with cows in summer and in winter feeding your cattle with hay from the swamps whence our beavers have been driven.

The tendency to imitate French peasant art spread rapidly among Indians who were taught by the priests and nuns of New France, and the result was a hybrid style of decoration; the design of this Iroquois cradle board was derived from a typically European bird and vine pattern.

Worse was to come after the buffalo were finally destroyed through the introduction of firearms and the coming of the white hunters. Starving, the Indians were thrust into reservations where they languished and declined for decades. Even the prosperous potlatch-givers of the west coast felt the effect of the white invasion that began when Captain Cook sailed into Nootka harbour in 1778. Chief Joe Capilano's lament in 1911 was even more devastating than that of Peguis, because it showed the near-death of a culture as well as a people.

> We have lost our lands, our forests, our game, our fish; we have lost our ancient religion, our ancient dress; some of the young people have even lost their fathers' language and the legends and traditions of their ancestors. We cannot call these old things back to us; they will never come again.

In every respect that decline has been halted in recent decades. There are now more Indians than the 250,000 which historians estimate were here when Cartier arrived. Accompanying this demographic revival there has been an upsurge of pride in Indian traditions, a resurgence of native arts among the Indians and the Inuit, and an assertion of claims to ancestral lands which shows the native peoples turning from the half-forgotten vestige they seemed to many people a generation ago, into a vital factor in Canada's social life, demanding and receiving attention.

CHAPTER TWO

The Explorers

This sixteenth century astrolabe was typical of the instruments early explorers like Cartier and Champlain used for navigation and surveying.

To the explorers, whose achievements extended over more than four centuries from the late fifteenth to the twentieth, Canadians owe not only the possession of their land, but also much in their way of perceiving it. The original Canada — the colonies that came together in Confederation and for long formed the heartland of the country — comprised the regions touched by the first recorded travellers by sea since the Norsemen — Nova Scotia and Newfoundland, first sighted by John Cabot in 1498; and Québec, originally New France and later divided into Lower Canada and Upper Canada, which Jacques Cartier set foot on when he raised his cross on the Gaspé Peninsula in 1534. Cartier invented one of the enduring Canadian images of the north country when, in the same year, he sighted the mainland shore of Labrador facing Newfoundland and remarked, as his Elizabethan English translator put it, "To be short, I beleeve that this was the land that God allotted to Cain." The name that shore now bears commemorates another and scantily remembered early explorer, the "lavrador" (or landowner) João Fagundes who voyaged in the waters off Greenland (and possibly farther south) in the 1490s.

But neither Cabot nor Cartier was in fact, the first voyager to the regions. Of the humble Breton and Portuguese and west-of-England fishermen who appear to have preceded Cabot to the Great Banks of Newfoundland and Cartier into the Gulf of the St. Lawrence, we know very little, largely because they chose to remain secretive about the discovery of such plentiful resources in fish and furs. However, Dr. John Dee, Queen Elizabeth's astrologer and one of the most learned men of his age, noted on a chart that around 1494 — several years before Cabot's arrival — Newfoundland had been discovered by two Bristol merchants, Thorn and Eliot, and it is certain that throughout the middle ages the lore of the far lands discovered by Leif Ericsson was current in the North Sea ports of Europe.

Adam of Bremen, a priest living in Hamburg, recorded in 1070 that King Swen Estridson of Denmark told him of "a land, discovered by many in that ocean, which is called Vinland," and that beyond Vinland there was "intolerable ice" an "awful gulf" where King Harald the Ruthless of Norway had voyaged and seen "the bounds of the earth grow dark before his eyes." Obviously this is a reference to the long Arctic night, and these and other facts and rumours about the Canadian north

From the time when the skraelings *returned to Europe with 'packs wherein were grey furs, sables and all kinds of peltries', until the early years of the nineteenth century, drawings of fur-bearing animals of the Canadian wilderness depended more on exaggerated reports and the artists' imaginations than on first-hand observation. The sketches of Charles de Granville, dating from around 1701, are among the more lively exceptions.*

OPPOSITE:
Huronia was an area lying between Lakes Huron, Couchiching and Simcoe which in the seventeenth century was inhabited by Huron Indians converted by the Jesuits. For its time it was the farthest westward expansion of European influence; in 1648-9 the mission villages were destroyed by the Iroquois, the missionaries were slaughtered, and the Hurons — many of whom died — virtually ceased to exist as a nation.

continued to circulate among the Hansa merchants and the sea captains of French and English towns so that several years before Cabot's voyage the cartographer Martin Baheim could note on a map near what we now know is Baffin Island the remark: "Here one catches white falcons."

Of course, the fishermen and merchants who were really the first fifteenth-century explorers of Canada did not think of themselves as explorers, and, unlike Cartier and later Champlain, they had no thought of annexing territories for their kings or of making converts for their Church. They came in their dour fishermen's way in search of goods for which they knew there was a market in Europe, and in so doing they established a strong tradition in Canadian exploration, only a small part of which has been entirely detached from the mercantile impulse.

New France itself was in the beginning a fur-trading colony, and even at the end, when it was lost to England, Madame de Pompadour, the reigning mistress of the French King Louis XV, dismissed it with the remark, "Canada is useful only to provide me with furs." The Basque traders had established themselves before the end of the sixteenth century at Tadoussac where the Saguenay enters the St. Lawrence, and Quebec City was founded in 1608 as a royally sponsored centre of the trade which attracted the men from northern France, from Brittany and Normandy, whose descendants would form the majority of the inhabitants of French-speaking Canada; in the beginning there were many Huguenots, but later on Protestants were forbidden entry into the colony.

The *coureur de bois*, the woodsman who combined fur trading and trapping and penetrated into the forest regions which he called the *pays d'en haut*, was more typical of the earliest French culture in Canada than the *habitant*, the man who settled beside the great thoroughfare of the St. Lawrence to cultivate the soil. The first farmer — and also the first *seigneur* or ennobled landowner, broke soil at Port Royal in Acadia in 1606 and again in 1617 at Quebec City after a period in France. He was the apothecary Louis Hébert. Hébert used a spade but the first plough began to work a Canadian field in 1628. That was long after the first cod were fished and the first furs were traded. Hébert, it is interesting to note, began his farming a year before the first settlers arrived in 1607 at Jamestown in what became the American colonies.

The farmers were pioneers, tied to the land once they had appropriated it; the fur traders were explorers. In the interests of their commerce, they followed the example of Etienne Brulé, the early traveller who had discovered Lake Ontario in 1615 and Lake Superior a few years afterwards. They lived among the Indians, learning their languages, adopting their habits, and becoming absorbed into their lives, most in a somewhat less extreme and literal way than Brulé did when he became the main dish in a Huron cannibal feast about 1633.

When royal edicts in the seventeenth century, intended to restrict the supply of furs to keep up prices in Europe, recalled the *coureurs de bois*

HVRONVM EXPLICATA TABVLA
OÑENDITIAQVI
OENTARONE LACVS
TIONONTATE pp
Seu Natio Vulgo del tabaco
lacus Ontario
Scala leucarum francicarum horariarum
Scala Millar. Italicarum Communium vel Mediocrium
LACVS SVPERIOR
MARE DVLCE
ALGOM
CHINI
ONTARIO lacus seu SANCTI LVDOVICI
GĀSISTA GVE
NOVVM BELGIV
NOVA SVECIA
Erie populi
VIR GI NIA
Concilium

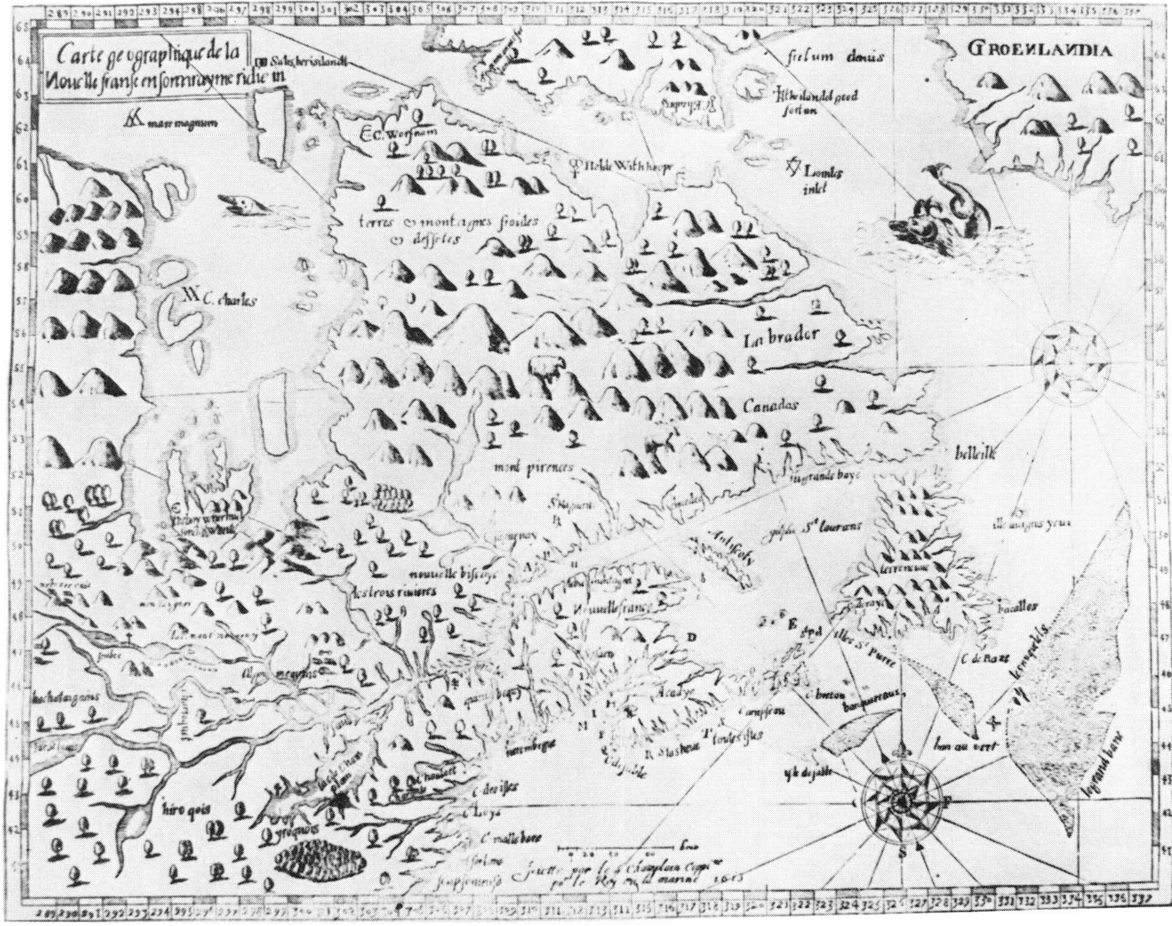

By 1613 the efforts of French navigators and fur traders had resulted in enough knowledge of the terrain of New France for this kind of moderately accurate map to be drawn for inclusion in Champlain's account of his explorations.

from the *pays d'en haut*, many of them remained, choosing to trade with the Dutch and later the British on the Hudson River rather than abandon their forest life. The most celebrated of these disaffected *coureurs* were Pierre-Esprit Radisson and the Sieur des Groseillers, who, after years of trading and exploration around the Great Lakes, transferred their loyalties to England and in 1668 led the first expedition to Hudson's Bay that was sponsored by the London merchants who later formed the Hudson's Bay Company.

The *coureurs de bois* were successful in penetrating the unknown land because they were willing to learn and adapt to their own uses the techniques the native peoples had developed for living off the land. The comparatively light and easily portable birchbark canoe enabled them to travel quickly through the network of lakes and rivers that stretched west from the St. Lawrence waterway, carrying the craft over land portages where the streams did not connect. Later, on reaching the great plains, the fur traders utilized another Indian invention; pemmican, or buffalo meat preserved in its own fat, enabled them to travel long distances without having to halt for hunting and also made it possible to winter more easily in the wilderness, a matter of necessity when the trade routes extended into the far northwestern country beyond the Prairies.

The kind of life which the *coureurs de bois* and their successors, the *voyageurs*, lived at the height of the fur trade is portrayed in the recollections of an old French Canadian whom Alexander Ross knew on the Red River early in the nineteenth century.

> I have now — he told Ross — been forty-two years in this country. For twenty-two I was a light canoeman. No portage was too long for me; all portages were alike. Fifty songs a day were nothing to me. I could carry, paddle, walk and sing with any man I ever saw. No water, no weather, ever stopped the paddle or the song. I have had twelve wives in the country and was once possessed of fifty horses and six running dogs. I beat all Indians at a race, and no white man passed in the chase. I wanted for nothing. Five hundred pounds twice told have passed through my hands, although now I have not a spare shirt to my back nor a penny to buy one. Yet were I young I should glory in commencing the same career again. There is no life so happy as a *voyageur*'s life; none so independent; no place where a man enjoys so much variety and freedom as in the Indian country. *Huzza, huzza pour le pays sauvage!*

Sir Humphrey Gilbert established the English presence in Canada by claiming Newfoundland in the name of Queen Elizabeth I when he landed there on the 5th August 1583 from his ship, the Squirrel, *on which he was seeking the entrance to the North West Passage. On the way home, at midnight on the 9th September, his ship sank in heavy seas and he was drowned. Earlier in the same day, Sir Humphrey was heard to shout: "We are as near to heaven by sea as by land."*

The early travels of the *coureurs de bois* in Indian country prepared the way for the later and more ambitious explorations sponsored by the French colonial authorities, such as those of the Sieur de la Salle, who travelled down the Mississippi to its mouth, and the Sieur de la Vérendrye, who in the 1730s reached the Prairies near where Winnipeg is today. Later, de la Vérendrye's son, Louis-Joseph, would explore the lower reaches of the Saskatchewan River.

As a result of these early eighteenth-century expeditions the fur trade which centred on Montréal was extended beyond the forest country of the Canadian Shield, north of the Great Lakes, and into the Prairies. Hector St. John Crévecoeur, who travelled through Montréal in 1782, remarked that: "Most of the merchants and young men of Montreal spend the greatest part of their time in trading with the Indians, at an amazing distance from Canada; and it often happens that they are three years together absent from home." The European fashion for hats of beaver felt, which lasted many generations, created such a demand that the beaver population was quickly depleted by Indians who had little idea of conserving fur-bearing animals when they could earn trade goods by killing them, and this in turn led the fur traders constantly to seek new sources of supply.

In the 1760s after the conquest of Québec, the fur trade was taken over by English-speaking entrepreneurs. Most of these were Highland Scots, and in banding themselves into the Northwest Company they

By the time this drawing of Québec was printed in 1699, 91 years had passed since the foundation of the city by Samuel de Champlain, and the fur-trading post of 1608 had become a place of churches, mansions and monasteries.

created an aggressive competition to the Hudson's Bay Company, the consortium of English merchants founded in 1670 and based on Hudson's Bay. Over the decades between 1760 and 1820 the Northwesters and their French Canadian canoemen or *voyageurs* followed the westward thrust of Canadian waterways until they had created channels of communications that reached to the extremities of the land that eventually became Canada. As the historian Harold A. Innis remarked, "Canada emerged as a political entity with boundaries largely determined by the fur trade. These boundaries included a vast north temperate land area extending from the Atlantic to the Pacific and dominated by the Canadian Shield."

Among these Northwesters were some of Canada's greatest explorers, mentally and physically tough fur traders who combined a desire for large profits with a zest for the adventure of penetrating unknown country with their small canoe-borne expeditions. Peter Pond pushed northwest from the Prairies over the Methye Portage in 1778 to discover Lake Athabaska. He may have reached Great Slave Lake, and he

Much of the exploration of Canada was carried on by "peddlar" traders who would barter their blankets and other manufactured goods with the Indians for furs and for the pemmican made of dried buffalo meat which served as a convenience food for travellers in the old West.

Portages linked the waterways across Canada into a network that in the end stretched all the way from Montréal to the Pacific and the Arctic oceans. Goods were carried on the backs of the voyageurs *from one landing to the next, and the light birchbark canoes were borne on their shoulders.*

Alexander Mackenzie was not the most industrious of Canadian explorers. Undoubtedly David Thompson, of whom no portrait survives, covered and charted more territory during his long travels at the end of the eighteenth century. But Mackenzie carried out two explorations which changed men's conceptions of North American geography and opened up ways between three great oceans. His aim was to find a way by land from the St. Lawrence to the Pacific Ocean. In these terms his first expedition in 1789 was a failure, though in any other terms it was a success, for it led him to discover the Mackenzie River and follow it to the Arctic Sea. It was on his second great journey, in 1793, that he crossed the Rockies and descended the Bella Coola to Pacific salt water. Born in Stornoway in 1764, Mackenzie emigrated to Montreal in 1779 and joined the North West Company in 1787. In 1802 he helped found the breakaway XY Company, but after that soon retired from the fur trade and spent most of his remaining life, up to his death in 1820, in Britain. The narrative of his great journeys — *Voyages from Montréal* — was published in 1801 and he was knighted in 1802.

certainly put into Alexander Mackenzie's mind the idea of exploring as far as the western ocean.

Mackenzie's first great journey in 1789 led him from the Great Slave Lake down a river which he thought would empty into the Pacific; instead it took him to the great delta where he saw the tidal throb of the Arctic Sea. Though Mackenzie was unaware of it, the end of his down-river journey coincided with the fall of the Bastille. Failing to reach the great *Mer d'Ouest*, he christened the great stream up which he started on his return voyage the "River of Disappointment," though later generations renamed it the Mackenzie in his honour. Starting again in 1793 from Fort Chipewyan, he crossed the Rockies from the Peace River and descended the Bella Coola River, staying in the Indian villages and marvelling at the well-carpentered and commodious cedar houses, to arrive on salt water at Dean Channel. "I now mixed some vermilion in melted grease, and inscribed in large characters, on the South-East face of the rock on which we had slept last night this brief memorial — 'Alexander Mackenzie, from Canada, by land, the twenty-second of July, one thousand seven hundred and ninety-three'."

Mackenzie's route had been an arduous one, impractical for fur brigades to follow, and his successors spent a great deal of effort in finding a practicable way to carry trade goods through the series of great mountain ranges between the Rockies and the sea. The estuary of the Columbia had already been discovered by sea, and when Simon Fraser moved south in 1808 from the post he had founded at Fort George (on the site of present-day Prince George), he thought he was actually following the same river. The story of his journey through the Fraser Canyon is one of the epics of Canadian travel. Fraser remarked that not in all his experience of the Rocky Mountains had he encountered country such as that which he and his twenty-three men now had to traverse.

> We had to pass where no human being should venture. Yet in those places there is a regular footpath impressed, or rather indented, by frequent travelling upon the very rocks. And besides this, steps which are formed like a ladder, or the shrouds of a ship, by poles hanging to one another and crossed at certain distances with twigs and withes, suspended from the top to the foot of the precipices, and fastened at both ends to stones and trees, furnished a safe and convenient passage to the Natives — but we, who had not the advantages of their experience, were often in imminent danger, when obliged to follow their example.

There were times when Fraser risked the water rather than the land, but this involved shooting the most frightening rapids any of them had ever experienced:

Rivalry between fur traders in gaining Indian goodwill existed from the beginning, first between the French and the Hudson's Bay Company, and later, particularly in the Athabaska country, between the Hudson's Bay men and the Scottish traders of the North West Company. At first it was competition in pleasing the Indians with gifts and treats (including "regales" of rum or brandy); later it turned into physical conflict which ended only when the companies were united in 1821 in an enlarged Hudson's Bay Company.

Most of the fur trading posts were small establishments like that which the Hudson's Bay Company established on the Rivière aux Rats (named after the abundance of muskrats), which ran into the St. Maurice about 80 miles inland from Three Rivers.

Largest and most formidable of all the fur-bearing animals was the grizzly bear, whose combination of cunning and strength was admirably captured by the artist of Les Raretés des Indes.

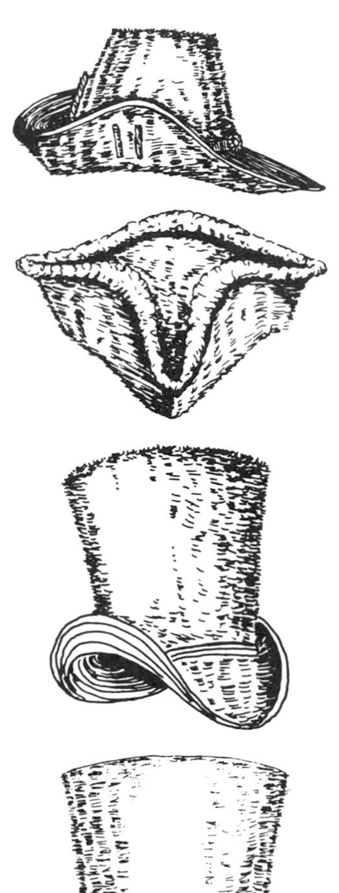

For many generations the Canadian fur trade was based on the use of the long guard hairs of the beaver's pelt to make felt for beaver hats, but though the basic material remained constant, styles changed, until finally in the second quarter of the nineteenth century the beaver hat was replaced by the silk topper, which caused a crisis in the fur trade.

> It being absolutely impossible to carry the canoes by land, yet sooner than to abandon them all hands without hesitation embarked, as it were *à corps perdu* upon the mercy of the Stygian tide. Once engaged the die was cast, and the great difficulty consisted in keeping the canoes in the medium, or *fil d'eau*, that is to say, clear of the precipice on one side, and of the gulphs formed by the waves on the other. However, thus skimming along like lightning, the crews cool and determined, followed each other in awful silence. And [when] we arrived at the end we stood gazing on our narrow escape from perdition. After breathing a little, we continued our course to a point where the Indians were encamped.

Reaching the river's estuary, where he found the Musqueam Indians dangerously hostile, Fraser realized that he too had been following a "river of disappointment," for the latitude was clearly not that of the mouth of the Columbia. He too is remembered by the river having been given his name.

It was David Thompson, another Northwester and a fine surveyor, who finally identified the headwaters of the Columbia and explored its course to the sea. He reached the sea on July 15, 1811, hoping to claim the river for Britain by establishing one of his Company's forts. He was too late; the American Fur Company's employees had arrived in March and had already built Fort Astoria. This delay of a few weeks had a great influence on the history of the Pacific Northwest, since it gave the United States a plausible claim to the lower valley of the Columbia, and was the reason why, when the boundary west of the Rockies was finally settled in 1846 on the forty-ninth parallel, the present state of Washington was lost to Canada.

But Thompson's failure on this occasion was balanced by the vast and diligent labour which he put into mapping for the first time the great terrain traversed by the Northwesters. He was able to say with justifiable pride:

> Thus I have fully completed the survey of this part of North America from sea to sea, and by almost innumerable Astronomical Observa-

This gentleman fur trader travels comfortably in a cariole, escorted by an Indian guide (with trade musket and trade blanket) and a stylishly attired canadien *to drive the dogs. (Note the handwoven* ceinture flèché *and the plumed hat, fashions the* voyageurs *carried with them from Québec to the Red River.)*

> tions have determined the positions of the Mountains, Lakes and Rivers, and other remarkable places on the northern part of this Continent; the Maps of all of which have been drawn and laid down in geographical position, being now the work of twenty-seven years.

More than any other single person David Thompson is the man to whom we owe our maps of Canada.

In penetrating the barrier of the Rockies and exploring such great rivers as the Mackenzie, the Fraser, and the Columbia, the Northwesters established a record of discovery that — like the general style of these daring and often ruthless traders — was more spectacular than the slow-but-sure ways of the Hudson's Bay Company with its London-based caution. From the beginning the practice of the Northwesters had been to go to the Indians from whom they hoped to purchase furs and to set up forts or posts among them, from which each year the brigades would bring the furs to the great depot at Fort William on Lake Superior, whence other brigades would carry them via Sault Ste. Marie to Montréal. The rival company, having established its forts on the shores of Hudson's Bay and James Bay, at first followed a policy of waiting for the Indians to bring them their furs. It was only at the end of the eighteenth century that the fierce competition of the Northwesters forced them to set up their depots in the hinterland and to organize their brigades of Orkneymen to transport the furs.

Yet some extraordinary journeys of exploration were in fact under-

M.Vander Gucht Scul:

taken by Hudson's Bay Company men with a view to establishing contact with tribes who, it was hoped, would visit the Bay. While the Northwesters travelled in style, with one or more large canoes, crews of *voyageurs*, and often attendant bagpipers, the most successful travellers from the Hudson's Bay Company were those who got nearest to the land by attaching themselves to parties of nomad Indians and sharing their lives for fairly long periods. In 1690 "the boy Henry Kelsey" (no-one knows for certain quite how old he was at the time) carried out some notable explorations by joining a wandering band of Chipewyans and spending two winters and a summer with them. Kelsey reached the Canadian Prairies forty years before the Sieur de Vérendrye. He was the first white man to kill a grizzly bear, and the first to encounter the Plains Indians with whom he took part in one of the great hunts in which the buffalo were driven into a pound for slaughter. Kelsey was also the first would-be poet to journey on the Prairies, writing a doggerel prologue to his journal in which he described the strange beasts he encountered:

Thus it continues till you leave ye woods behind
And then you have beast of severall kind
The one is a black a Buffillo great
Another is an outgrown Bear wch. is good meat
His skin to gett I have used all ye means I can
He is mans food & he makes food of man
His hid they would not let me it preserve
But said it was a God and they should starve.

OPPOSITE:
One of the great Canadian explorers was the Sieur de la Salle, who in 1679 launched the Griffon *on the Niagara River and in 1682 set out southward from Michilimackinac, to follow the Mississipi to its mouth and to claim the country for France as Louisiana. This illustration imaginatively presents his landing in 1684 to found a French colony in Texas, where in 1687 he was murdered by his men.*

Frances Ann Hopkins was an English amateur painter who married the secretary of Sir George Simpson, Governor of the Hudson's Bay Company. Between 1858 and 1870 she travelled with her husband over western Canada, sketching Indian life and fur trade scenes, like this drawing of voyageurs *rising at dawn from their makeshift beds in the lee of upturned canoes.*

The surviving portrait of Samuel Hearne, which represents an elegantly dressed Georgian gentleman, gives little sense of his real qualities. Hearne was the first white man to reach the Arctic Ocean by land, and he did so, after two failures, by learning painfully to observe the Indians and live off the land as they did. Hearne originally served in the Royal Navy, and after joining the Hudson's Bay Company was deputed to travel from York Factory in search of the deposits from which the Indians obtained their copper. After two failures, he finally reached his objective in 1771-2. He built the Hudson's Bay Company's first inland post, Cumberland House, in 1774, and it was he who defended Fort Prince of Wales against the French in 1782 and finally surrendered it to the great navigator La Pérouse, who let Hearne go free on condition that he publish his journal. Hearne retired from the fur trade in 1787 and spent his remaining years writing his classic *Journey . . . to the Northern Ocean.*

In the journal itself he described the beliefs of the Plains Indians and wrote with a fair degree of accuracy on the practices and pretensions of their medicine men. Sixty-odd years afterwards, in 1754, Anthony Henday made a similar journey; he got within sight of the Rockies, encountered the formidable Blackfoot, and found that in the interval since Kelsey's journey they had acquired horses from the tribes farther to the south.

Undoubtedly the most remarkable of these Hudson's Bay Company explorers was Samuel Hearne, who undertook three journeys from Prince of Wales Fort on the Bay to find the source of the virgin copper that passed in trade among the Indian bands of Keewatin. Twice, in 1769 and 1770, he failed to get anywhere near his objective, and he was successful only through meeting a Chipewyan chief, Motanabee, who befriended him and told him the reasons for his earlier failures.

> He attributed all our misfortunes to the misconduct of my guides, and the very plan we pursued, by the desire of the Governor, in not taking any woman with us on this journey, was, he said, the principal thing that occasioned all our wants: "for," said he, "when all the men are heavy laden, they can neither hunt nor travel to any considerable distance; and in case they meet with success in hunting, who is to carry the produce of their labour?"

Hearne joined Motanabee's band when they set off for the north. Though he does not say it in so many words, there seems little doubt that he was adopted by Motanabee and given a wife for the journey, which lasted from December 1770 to June 1772. Otherwise it is difficult to explain the unfailing comradeship that the Indians displayed towards him in contrast to the atrocious cruelty they showed towards their traditional enemies, the Inuit, in a treacherous attack that Hearne describes with a vividness projecting not only his own horror as a witness and an unwilling participant, but also the deep mutual hostilities that divided the native peoples of early Canada. He describes the rituals with which the Indians prepared themselves, and then proceeds to the attack itself:

> By the time the Indians had made themselves thus completely frightful, it was near one o'clock of the morning on the seventeenth; when finding all the Esquimaux quiet in their tents, they rushed forth from their ambuscade, and fell on the poor unsuspecting creatures, unperceived till close at the very eves of their tents, when they soon began the bloody massacre, while I stood neuter in the rear.
>
> In a few seconds the horrible scene commenced; it was shocking beyond description; the poor unhappy victims were surprised in the midst of their sleep, and had neither time nor power to make any resistance; men, women and children, in all upward of twenty, ran out of their tents stark naked, and endeavoured to make their escape;

The elaborate maps of eighteenth century surveyors were often decorated with imaginary scenes from fur trading life; in this example, the brandy keg assumes a suitably central position.

The original structure at Fort Prince of Wales was built in 1689 and burnt down before completion. The massive, star-shaped masonry fortress in this engraving was built over a long period between 1733 and 1771. It still stands, across the river from the modern town of Churchill on Hudson's Bay; it is the oldest surviving Canadian building west of the province of Québec.

York Fort was built in 1684 by Pierre-Esprit Radisson on behalf of the Hudson's Bay Company. Later it became known as York Factory, and from 1713 onwards it was the most important fur trading depot on Hudson's Bay. It remained in use until 1957, and its site is now a National Historic Park.

> but the Indians having possession of all the landslide, to no place could they fly for shelter. One alternative only remained, that of jumping into the river; but, as none of them attempted it, they all fell a sacrifice to Indian barbarity!
>
> The shrieks and groans of the poor expiring wretches were truly dreadful; and my horror was much increased at seeing a young girl, seemingly about eighteen years of age, killed so near me, that when the first spear was stuck into her side she fell down at my feet, and twisted round my legs, so that it was with difficulty that I could disengage myself from her dying grasps. As two Indian men pursued this unfortunate victim, I solicited very hard for her life; but the murderers made no reply till they had stuck both their spears through her body, and transfixed her to the ground. They then looked me sternly in the face, and began to ridicule me, by asking if I wanted an Esquimaux wife, and paid not the smallest regard to the shrieks and agony of the poor wretch, who was twining round their spears like an eel!

Finally, Hearne found himself forced to ask one of the Indians to kill the girl, which was done with a spear blow to the heart.

> My situation and the terror of my mind at beholding this butchery, cannot easily be conceived, much less described; though I summed up all the fortitude I was master of on the occasion, it was with difficulty that I could refrain from tears; and I am confident that my features must have feelingly expressed how sincerely I was affected at the

In 1812 the North West Company trader David Stuart founded the first Fort Kamloops. It was soon abandoned, and by 1862 a fourth fort had been built. This last fort is probably the one here illustrated; it is typical of the wooden bastions erected at the trading posts in New Caledonia, as mainland British Columbia was then named.

> barbarous scene I then witnessed; even at this hour I cannot reflect on the transactions of that horrid day without shedding tears.

A sense of unity of interests between Indians and Inuit, or even between different groups of Indians, was rare indeed before the Europeans came, and political leagues of warrior democracies like the Blackfoot Confederacy and the Iroquois Six Nations were so unusual as to excite special attention and admiration. The idea of the Indians of Canada — or the Inuit for that matter — as forming a single nation is as much a product of rule by Europeans as the idea of India as a single state was a product of the British Raj.

Hearne's relationship with his Indian companions survived the shock of the Inuit massacre; he needed them and they felt no guilt once they had performed their purification ceremonies. He visited the Coppermine River and he was the first white man to reach the Arctic Sea by land. His *Journey to the Northern Ocean* is a remarkable book for its narrative and descriptive skill, for its appealing self-portrait, and for its vivid account of Indian life seen intimately and day by day over a long period.

Yet, in the long run perhaps the most important fact about Hearne's journey as part of the history of Canadians is that it formed a practical education in the arts of survival. Hearne did more than accept and adapt Indian inventions like the birchbark canoe and the snowshoe and the quickly constructed birchbark wigwam; he learned to live off the bare tundra, one of the harshest regions in the world, using methods evolved by the Indians over the millenia. There is a symbolic factor here; it was explorers like Hearne — rather than the early settlers with their attempts

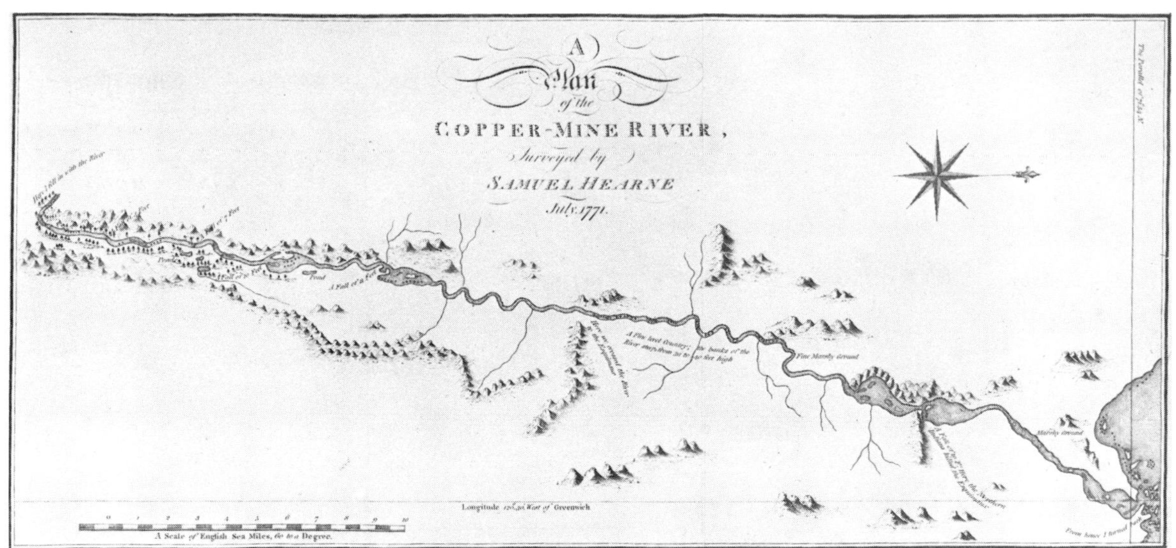

It is to the surveys of fur traders during the eighteenth century that we owe the earliest reasonably accurate maps of the great Canadian rivers, like this of the Coppermine prepared by Samuel Hearne in 1771.

to reproduce European societies in a wild country — who first began to accept Canada as the vast untamed and untapped continent it was and to break down the restrictions of the garrison mentality that regarded the wilderness as a natural enemy: but there were also practical consequences. During the nineteenth century, as the Prairies and the boreal forest became less productive as a fur-gathering area, the Hudson's Bay Company began to turn its attention towards the far north and the islands that stretched towards the Pole. A generation of superb explorer-traders developed, whose methods of travel in the high Arctic were based on a maximum reliance on the resources the land offered and minimum use of imported equipment.

The virtues of this characteristically Canadian kind of Arctic exploration were to be shown very dramatically during the 1850s, the period of the great search for Sir John Franklin's vanished ships. Franklin set off with two ships, the *Erebus* and the *Terror*, in 1845, and got caught in the ice off King William Island. Franklin, whose earlier experience of the Arctic should have taught him better, was an exponent of the kind of highly organized expedition which the British Admiralty thought appropriate for voyages of discovery. He always led well-manned, well-disciplined, and well-supplied expeditions, but his men were never trained in the arts of Arctic survival; when their stores ran out they were doomed. His early expeditions in the 1820s were semi-disasters, resulting in great suffering and much death, and it was evident when he went again in 1845 he had learnt very little from the past. When his ships were trapped the tragedy in which he and all his men died was almost inevitable.

The great contrast to Franklin was the man who eventually discovered the grisly truth about the British explorer's fate. Dr. John Rae was a Hudson's Bay Company man who learnt so well from Hearne's experience that in 1846-47, travelling with few men and few supplies, but with a thorough knowledge of the techniques of survival, he led the first expedition of white men to winter north of the tree line, and later — without losing a single man from scurvy or starvation — carried out a number of notable explorations of the Arctic coastline. Perhaps the greatest of all the explorers who continued this specifically Canadian tradition of exploration was Vilhjalmur Stefansson, a descendant of Vikings, who was born in a Manitoba Icelandic settlement. Stefansson lived among the Inuit and by foot and sleigh during the early years of the present century explored vast areas of the Arctic Archipelago and described it in a series of splendid books such as *My Life with the Eskimo* and *The Friendly Arctic.* Stefansson was a scientific explorer and a fine anthropologist, but the ways of living and travel he adopted were those that the fur-trader explorers had developed through their intelligent observation of native ways of survival. With vivid humour, Stefansson justified his method of exploration in the remark: "One of the advantages of skin clothing over woollens in Arctic exploration is that you can eat them in an emergency. . . . This puts actual starvation off by a week or two."

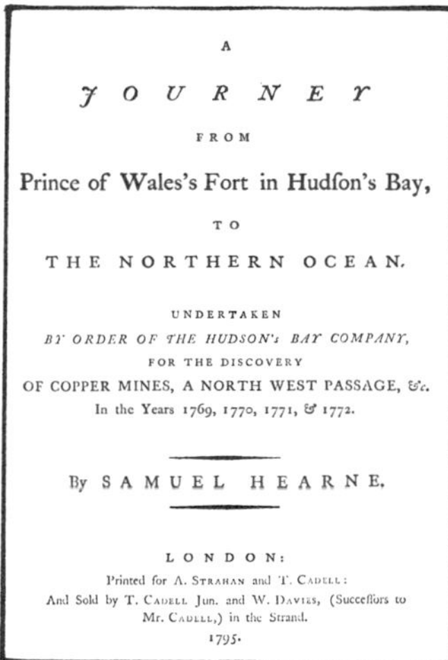

A

JOURNEY

FROM

Prince of Wales's Fort in Hudſon's Bay,

TO

THE NORTHERN OCEAN.

UNDERTAKEN

BY ORDER OF THE HUDSON's BAY COMPANY,

FOR THE DISCOVERY

OF COPPER MINES, A NORTH WEST PASSAGE, &c.

In the Years 1769, 1770, 1771, & 1772.

By SAMUEL HEARNE.

LONDON:

Printed for A. STRAHAN and T. CADELL:

And Sold by T. CADELL Jun. and W. DAVIES, (Succeſſors to Mr. CADELL,) in the Strand.

1795.

Hearne's Journey . . . to the Northern Ocean *was the first of the great Canadian exploration narratives, and provides an admirable account of life among the Indians of the northern forest. The title page of the book is a record of Hearne's persistence; his efforts in 1769 and 1770 were abortive, but in 1771-2 he finally attained his objective, and reached the Arctic waters that are part of the North West Passage.*

But a technique of survival and an attitude of accepting rather than rejecting the realities of a wild land were by no means the only contributions the fur traders made to the life of Canadians. The very pattern on which Canada was populated and became a nation is their creation. The great railways linking the St. Lawrence Valley with the Pacific Coast and physically uniting the country follow routes which were first discovered by trader explorers and developed by the amphibious brigades of the Northwesters and the Hudson's Bay Company men. Many important Canadian cities, Winnipeg, Edmonton, Victoria, Thunder Bay, Brandon, Kamloops and Prince George among them, began as fur-trade posts while Quebec City and Montréal owed their early development to the export of beaver skins collected in the *pays d'en haut.* Without the fur trade New France would not have survived its first decades, and the Prairies and British Columbia would never have been declared British territory as a prelude to becoming Canadian. The Hudson's Bay Company, chartered by Charles II in 1670 as a commercial enterprise that was also a political entity, since it involved the rudimentary governing of a territory, provided a model for the curious intermingling of public and private enterprise which has characterized Canadian life from the early days of European settlement.

Finally, the fur trade left its imprint on the very composition of Canada's population. It first introduced the Scots as an important — almost a dominant — mercantile element in the country's life, while it brought into existence one very distinct group of Canadians. These are the Métis, the people who came into being when French *coureurs de bois*

For long this was regarded as a portrait of Captain George Vancouver, who sailed to Vancouver Island with Cook in 1778 and in 1791 returned to chart the Pacific coastline of Canada. Now the experts at the National Portrait Gallery in London, where the original hangs, doubt the authenticity of the attribution, and describe it as "Portrait of an Unknown Gentleman."

and *voyageurs* and Scottish traders took Cree and Saulteaux and Sarcee wives in common-law marriages according to "the custom of the country," and founded lines of sturdy hunters and rebels.

To be sure, the coasts of Canada were explored by sea voyagers; from the Norse, French, and Portuguese on the eastern seaboard, to the maritime explorers of the west — the Spaniards who sailed these coasts from 1755 onwards, and their better remembered English rivals like James Cook (who in 1778 was the first white man to set foot on Canada's Pacific coast), and George Vancouver (who in the 1790s traced the intricate shores of British Columbia). But it was the fur traders who — after the native peoples — were the real discoverers of the vast continental mass whose four thousand miles of breadth divided the two oceans. It was they who brought Canada into history by proving that Europeans could learn to survive and prosper even in the "land that God gave Cain," provided they were willing to meet its challenges, learn from its rigours, and realize its abundance in material riches and the means to a free life.

This map of the British possessions in North America was evidently drawn between the loss of the thirteen colonies that became the United States in 1783 and Vancouver's charting of the Pacific coast in the name of Britain during the early 1790s.

CHAPTER THREE

Region & Nation

The scale and impetus of exploration in Canada were sub-continental. The discoverers started in the east, around the Gulf of St. Lawrence, and their westward and northward progress was virtually uninterrupted until, about eight hundred years after the Icelanders landed in Newfoundland, Alexander Mackenzie marked his arrival at the Pacific in 1793; more than a century after that, in his great expedition of 1913-18, Stefansson charted the last unexplored islands of the Arctic Archipelago, and all that remained was, by land and aerial survey, to fill in the corners which the original travellers had passed by. Almost all the influences leading towards the unification of Canada into the peculiar kind of nation it has become, have been developments of that original exploratory urge. First patterns of transport and communication, then habits of settlement followed the east-west line whose direction was pointed by Cartier when he sailed up the St. Lawrence to the Indian towns of Stadacona and Hochelaga, and by the *coureurs de bois* when they followed the scent of furs into the westerly *pays d'en haut* that became upper Canada. The great national institutions — the railways and airlines, the CBC and the RCMP, even Confederation itself — were foreshadowed by men going in birchbark canoes from the settlements into the wilderness, learning its ways, and eventually annexing it.

But for most of Canada's history the settlers and their heirs have been more numerous, and ultimately more powerful than the explorers, whose usefulness expires when the land is entirely discovered. After Cardinal Richelieu came to power in France, a serious policy of settlement was initiated in New France and in 1627 the first peasant farmers were brought from Normandy and Brittany to become the pioneer *habitants*, establishing their strip farms running long and narrow inland from the St. Lawrence and the Richelieu. It was even hoped, vainly as it turned out, to incorporate the native people into a settled society, and in 1671 Louis XIV's minister Colbert wrote to Jean Talon, the Intendent of New France:

> Always endeavour by every possible means to encourage the clergy . . . to bring up in their communities as many Indian children as possible, so that being educated in the maxims of our tradition and our customs they, along with the settlers, may evolve into a single nation and so strengthen the colony.

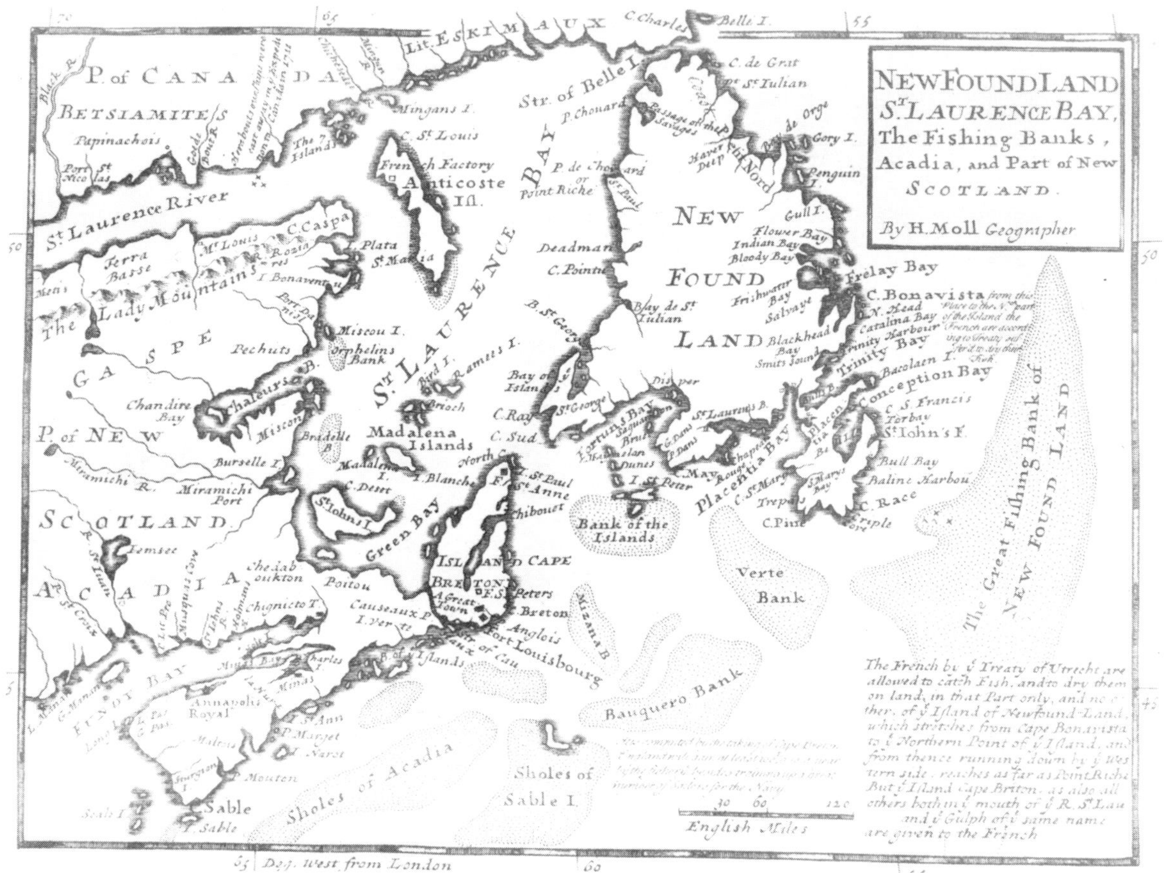

This early seventeenth century map of Newfoundland and the neighbouring coasts shows the importance attached to fishing, but also indicates the settlements that were surviving along the coasts of the island colony.

At the same time the first durable British settlements on what eventually became Canadian soil were established in Newfoundland by Sir George Calvert (later Lord Baltimore) and David Kirke, who were trying, with some disregard for the infertile soil and climatic rigour of Newfoundland, to establish plantation colonies like those of Virginia in which something like the English pattern of rich landowners and tenant farmers could be transferred to the New World. The greater part of Nova Scotia became British in 1713 under the Treaty of Utrecht, but the French kept Cape Breton Island where they built the great fortress of Louisbourg. It was only after Louisbourg was captured by the New Englanders in 1745 that English-speaking settlement on the Canadian mainland was seriously attempted with the foundation of Halifax.

Throughout the early centuries of Canadian history there was strong, often bitter opposition between settled farmers and wandering fur traders and fishermen. The fishing interests in Newfoundland and the fur-trading interests in New France were both opposed to the pioneer farmers, and the same pattern continued in the west. There the fur traders realised that settlement always meant a diminution in fur supplies, since the wild animals retreated before the advance of cultivation. They therefore attempted to discourage farmers from entering the country they themselves had explored, though — ironically — it was fur traders who proved the viability of agriculture in the west by cultivating gardens and small farms around their own forts. The Northwesters were so bitterly opposed to Lord Selkirk's early nineteenth-century introduction of landless Highland Scots into the Red River valley that they encouraged the Métis to attack them, and the massacre of Seven Oaks in 1816, when Governor Semple of Assiniboia and twenty settlers were butchered, was the most dramatic episode in this long Canadian rivalry between exploring traders and pioneer settlers. It manifested an attitude that continued in the far west until 1858, when the arrival of miners in British Columbia during the Fraser valley gold rush brought about the end of the fur-trading hegemony in the regions that a few years later — in 1871 — would become part of the newly created Dominion of Canada.

Tecumseh was an American Indian who became a Canadian hero. A chief of the Shawnee, he led a coalition that resisted the westward penetration of the Americans after 1783, and during the war of 1812 he and his warriors supported the British. He took part in the capture of Detroit, and fought bravely at the head of his Indian troops until, in 1813, he was killed in the Battle of the Thames.

It was the settlers in whose minds developed the garrison mentality that Northrop Frye found dominant among early Canadian writers. Most early settlers would have agreed with Mackenzie King's remark that "if some countries have too much history, we have too much geography," and throughout their literature there runs a distrust that often approaches hatred of the unsettled wilderness. Joshua Marsden, writing in 1816 in New Brunswick, caught the sense of sheer horror that sometimes struck in the wilderness when he wrote: "There is a solitary loneliness in the woods of America to which no language can do adequate justice. It seems a shutting out of the whole moral creation." His feelings were not far removed from those of Standish O'Grady, whose poetry had much to say about the tribulations of the emigrant settler. In 1841, in his poem "Winter in Upper Canada," O'Grady wrote:

Thou barren waste, unprofitable strand
Where hemlocks brood on unproductive land,
Whose frozen air on one bleak winter's night
Can metamorphose *dark brown hares into white.*

While the fur traders depended on the continuing inviolability of the wilderness and adapted to it as best they could, the settlers sought to destroy the wilderness and to replace it with a humanized landscape like that of nineteenth-century Europe. Only when the land was tamed could a man farm successfully and feel secure in his house and his community. The inhabitants of the wilderness, Indians and wild beasts, were the settler's enemies, and for generations the French farms and hamlets along the St. Lawrence were vulnerable to the attacks of the Iroquois.

To the settlers, in fact, the wilderness itself was at once alien and attractive, so that one of the perpetual anxieties of the *habitants* was that their sons might desert the plough to become *coureurs de bois*. In later generations, during the nineteenth century, many farmers in Upper and

Laura Secord was a Loyalist from New England who emigrated to Canada as a child. In 1813, when invading American soldiers were billeted on her farm, she heard them talking of a planned attack, and walked 19 miles to warn Lieutenant James FitzGibbon. FitzGibbon had already learnt of the American plans from his Indian spies, but whether Laura Secord was first with the news or not, hers was a courageous act, the stuff of Canadian myth.

Lower Canada and also in the Maritimes would satisfy their ambivalent feelings towards the untamed forest by spending certain seasons away from home as lumbermen, an occupation that enabled them to answer the call of the wilderness at the same time as they helped to destroy it and to clear the woodlands for farmers like themselves to settle.

On a smaller scale, the same ambivalence survives among modern urban Canadians, whose ordinary occupations may well be directly or indirectly destructive of the natural environment, yet who like to get away into the pine-smelling wilderness for the routine canoeing or fishing trip, or spend the summer months in a cabin on some far lake of the Pre-Cambrian Shield or the Cariboo.

It was these settlers who provided the strong regional loyalties that explain the centrifugal tendencies that have existed in Canadian political life ever since the country was unified a century ago. The basis of Canadian life has always been local and regional, determined by linguistic differences and also by cultural and geographical divisions.

Canadians who speak English and Canadians who speak French are not identical; that is obvious enough. But to see the national pattern of variations in terms of language alone is a naïve oversimplification. The French of Québec and the Acadians of New Brunswick speak roughly the same language, but they have different pasts and even different cultures (as a comparison of Québecois and Acadian poetry will clearly show), and they do not especially like each other. Old Maritime cultures with deep British roots, like those of Newfoundland and Nova Scotia, are profoundly different from those of Americanized Ontario, or the multiracial Prairies, or British Columbia with its Pacific Rim allegiances. And geographical barriers like the Shield and the Rockies are as much psychological as physical. They have a mentally insulating effect.

The explorers, to be sure, charted the main lines of Canada as a country, pioneered its routes of travel and communication, and in so far as we think of Canada as a unit they are responsible for it. But that unity is a strange and paradoxical thing. As the economist Kenneth Boulding said in 1957, long before we became greatly concerned over the matter, "Canada has no cultural unity, no linguistic unity, no religious unity, no geographic unity. All it has is unity." The unity, one might almost say, depends paradoxically on the diversity, and Canada, socially and politically as much as geographically, is the diverse country which the settlers created out of their differences of origin as well as of environment.

In a vast country like Canada, where Maritimers live nearer to London, England, than they do to Vancouver, communication is always difficult; understanding is inevitably tenuous. The places where people live and the local worlds in which they grow up are at least as important as any precarious pattern of national union; test the priorities of the inhabitants of Canada in 1978, and you will find an amazing number who think of themselves as Québecois and even as Newfoundlanders or

A *Loggers' Camp, Vancouver Island,* E. Sandys

A View of Château Richer, Thomas Davies

Red River Carts on a Prairie Road, Adrian Neison

The war of 1812 was carried on by water as well as by sea. The British and the Americans both maintained miniature navies on the Great Lakes, and there were frequent battles like that between the American sloop General Pike *and the British corvette* Wolfe. *The action was indecisive.*

The battle of Queenston Heights was one of the decisive actions of the war of 1812. The Americans invaded across the Niagara River, and gained an early advantage. In attempting to dislodge them the British Commander Sir Issac Brock, was killed leading his troops, but General Roger Sheaffe drove the invaders from the Heights and won the day for the combined forces of British regulars and Canadian militia.

The attack on Fort George, May 27, 1813, was one of the successful American actions of the War of 1812. Led by General Winfield Scott, the invaders captured the Fort and occupied it for seven months. General McClure abandoned it in December, 1813, in the face of a strong British advance.

British Columbians before they think of themselves as Canadians. To think of oneself as Canadian is important abroad; not always so important at home where the realities of life, which are mainly local realities, are close and pressing.

Kildare Dobbs once made the very astute remark that "Canada is a society rather than a nation," and in the sense that it has never successfully become a centralized nation-state on the classic European model, this is quite true. Such an insight also makes one conscious that regional and local loyalties are social even more than political; they have to do with neighbours and neighbourhoods, and they operate on many other levels of human intercourse than simply the political. The attraction of a congenial setting, the support of a sympathetic circle of friends, the opportunity to carry on one's chosen vocation, can be just as important in shaping a local loyalty as childhood memories or economic advantages. I have found that some of the most fervent British Columbian local patriots are not even Canadian by birth and some of the most passionate defenders of the rights and interests of the Maritimes were born in Toronto and Vancouver.

This, of course, is much in keeping with the social nature of Canada, which has always been a country not only of settlement, but also of migration, whether from abroad or inside its own vast expanses; a sixth of those inhabiting Canada today were born abroad, and a much higher proportion have shifted from province to province, from country to city, or vice versa. These are the threads that make Canada, as Kildare Dobbs has said, a *society*, united organically rather than institutionally, and perhaps the most notable characteristic of that society is its local variability. For this reason a considerable part of this book has to be devoted to considering Canadians as inhabitants of the definable Canadian regions.

It is when we consider how these notably different regions fit together that we move out of the social and into the political sphere. For the essential task of Canadian politics, applied to the nation as a whole rather than to its separate parts, has been to reconcile the two heritages — the explorer and the settler. Are we to see Canada in terms of its regions primarily? Or are we to see it in the sub-continental terms of the fur traders and the CPR and the CBC and the machinery of central government? Which is the true federalism? And are the two standpoints irreconcilable, as often they are made to seem? And if they are not, what compromise, to talk of a concept beloved of Canadians (though they use the word itself less frequently nowadays) must be envisaged?

The imperatives that unite Canadians are not simple. There was the original geographical imperative that led the explorers and united the great plains and the mountains and coast of British Columbia into the fur-trading empire that was linked to the original Canada through Montréal, and to Britain through the sea route to Hudson's Bay. There was the secondary drive to the west when settlement surged out at the end of the nineteenth century to fill the Prairies and flood over the mountains to the Pacific. There was the fact that the provinces of Canada had all originally been colonies which differed from the thirteen other colonies to the south in choosing to remain under the symbolic aegis of the British crown and to follow the parliamentary traditions of Westminster rather than the republican innovations of Washington. This choice was confirmed in two wars — 1775-76 and 1812-14 — when Canadians of all origins, French and English, Indian and white, rebuffed the arrogant certainty of American leaders like Thomas Jefferson who, in 1812, remarked:

> The acquisition of Canada this year, as far as the neighbourhood of Quebec, will be a mere matter of marching, and will give us experience for the attack on Halifax the next, and the final expulsion of England from the American continent.

And here, of course, we have the final and perhaps the most important factor that has contributed to Canada's precarious unity. The threatening presence of an expansionist United States, full of triumphant belligerence at the end of the Civil War, was what finally led the distrustful and often mutually antagonistic colonies to subordinate their differences and unite in the Confederation of 1867, and it has been as much the presence of the United States as any other factor that has kept together

John George Lambton, Earl of Durham, was sent to Canada in 1838 to investigate the causes of the rebellions of 1837. Nicknamed Radical Jack, he was sympathetic to the reformers, and his famous Report on the Affairs of British North America, *written after five months in Canada and published in 1839, is regarded as a major Canadian constitutional document for its recommendation of responsible government. Durham perceived the problems inherent in a bicultural country, but unfortunately he thought they could be solved by anglicizing Québec, and for this reason the* Report *aroused alarm and hostility among French Canadians.*

our loose and straggling country. "There are two miracles of Canadian history," the poet F. R. Scott once said. "The first is the survival of French Canada, and the second is the survival of Canada." Yet Canada is now an old country in world terms; older than most members of the United Nations, older even than great European countries like Germany and Italy.

The very idea of Canada — Canada as a concept in the mind — is dependent on the fact of settlement, and it has changed as men have moved out and occupied the land. It has not always meant the great country stretching, as its motto says, *A mari usque ad mare*, from sea even unto sea. When Cartier first used the word *Canada* in the account of his voyage in 1535, he applied it to the region along the St. Lawrence near Quebec City, and he may have derived it from misunderstanding an Iroquois word, *kanata*, meaning a village or community. The word became popular in France through another misunderstanding on Cartier's part when, on his voyage of 1541-42 he found "stones like Diamants, the most faire, pollished, and excellently cut that it is possible for a man to see." When he took them back and presented them at the French court they turned out to be quartz crystals, and the saying "as false as the diamonds of Canada" came into being.

After the settlement of New France, Canada became the locally used name for the colony, and the *habitants* began to call themselves *canadiens*. In this exclusive sense the word is still used by the farmers of the older villages along the St. Lawrence, who do not describe themselves by the currently fashionable term *québecois* but still use the word *canadien* as a narrow description for those descended from the original

In 1849 a controversial measure, the Rebellion Losses Bill, was introduced in the legislative assembly of the Province of Canada. It compensated those who had suffered losses in the suppression of the Rebellions of 1837. Its opponents argued that it rewarded former rebels, and when it was passed a mob burned the Parliament buildings in Montréal.

settlers in New France. Even the Acadians are not included in this traditional definition, and all other Canadians are lumped together as *anglais*.

In spite of its incendiary consequences, the Rebellion Losses Bill was a crucial event in Canadian political history. Lord Elgin, the incumbent Governor-General, was the son-in-law of Lord Durham and shared his viewpoint. He disagreed with the Bill, but when the Assembly passed it by a majority he gave his assent and so established the principle of responsible government.

The general application of the terms *Canada* and *Canadians* began to expand after the conquest. At first New France was designated the Province of Québec but in 1791 it was divided at the line of the Ottawa River, and the name *Canada* was revived as the new provinces became Upper Canada and Lower Canada, roughly corresponding to the present Ontario and Québec.

There were striking changes in the population of Canada that brought about this readjustment. At the time of the conquest of New France about 65,000 French-speaking Canadians decided to remain, and until the American Revolution they and their descendants comprised the vast majority of the population. The success of the Revolution resulted in the emigration to Québec and to Nova Scotia of between 50,000 and 60,000 Loyalists who refused to accept the new dispensation. It was to accommodate their desire for self-government that the new provinces of Upper Canada and New Brunswick were created, the latter in 1784 by the division of Nova Scotia. The Loyalists came as the first wave of the great flood of settlers that continued to pour in through the nineteenth century and ended the dominance of the trader-explorers.

More than that, the coming of the Loyalists permanently shifted the ethnic balance of population in Canada, and created the cultural dualism of the English and the French, who—ignoring the prior claims of Indians and Inuit — are curiously referred to as the "founding peoples" or "founding races." In later years, as we shall see, the ethnic origins of

When the Loyalists came northward after the establishment of American independence, many of them settled in the part of Nova Scotia which later became New Brunswick. One of their principal settlements was Saint John, which was chartered as a town in 1785.

The Place d'Armes in Montréal as it appeared in 1830.

Canadians again shifted to such an extent that the most recent full census (1971) revealed that almost twenty-five per cent of our population is now neither British nor French by descent. But the two original languages have remained dominant, and establish the most prominent of Canada's many cultural divergences.

There were many ways, other than the coming of the Loyalists, in which the proximity of the young United States — during the century before Canadian Confederation in 1867 — helped to change and broaden the scope of Canada and the consciousness among its inhabitants of being Canadians, whatever else they might be in terms of regional or cultural loyalty.

Even after the last of the Loyalists had arrived, the United States remained a reservoir of settlers to help fill the empty lands of Upper Canada. Many of those who were counted in later Canadian censuses as British in ethnic origin were, in fact, descended from American settlers who filtered over the border into Upper and Lower Canada and the Maritimes after 1783, helping to shift the balance of population until, by the first census after Confederation, held in 1871, there were 2,110,000 people of "British" origin as against 1,083,000 of "French" origin (out of a total population of 3,486,000).

Direct emigration from Britain into the Canadas and the Maritime colonies did not reach high proportions until after the Napoleonic Wars had come to an end in 1815. This meant that when war broke out in 1812 between Britain and the United States, the population of the two Canadas, against which American hostilities were principally directed, consisted mainly of the *canadiens* of Lower Canada, the Loyalists of Upper Canada and the Eastern Townships, and the considerable number

One of the first buildings in a new settlement in Upper Canada would be the grist mill, like this which George Keefer established at Thorold in 1827. Eventually, in 1917, it was converted into a pulp mill.

From early Victorian days, one of the favourite scenic spots in eastern Canada was Le Rocher Percé in the St. Lawrence estuary off Gaspé.

One of the earliest Canadian industrial establishments was the Forges on the St. Maurice River, nine miles from Three Rivers. From 1743 it was operated by the French Crown, and after the conquest went through many hands before it ceased operation in 1883. The manager's house, shown in this print, dated from the French period.

Victorian artists loved to embellish and enhance, as is shown in this lithograph of the Main Block of the Parliament Buildings in Ottawa, executed in 1873. Note the steepening of roofs, the heightening of towers, the luxuriance of detail.

The fur trading explorers looked upon the landscape in a utilitarian way. How many furs could it produce? And what were the best ways of access? The Victorian sensibility reacted to the grandeur of scenes like the Ouimet Canyon near Thunder Bay.

of non-Loyalist American farmers whose loyalty to the British crown was regarded as highly precarious. (Though there were also many American settlers of dubious allegiance in the Maritimes, the problem did not materialize there, since the New Englanders did not approve of or effectively support the war, which they regarded as bad for trade).

In the event, there was little attempt by American settlers even in Upper Canada to support the invaders, and a combination of Loyalist and *canadien* militias, of Tecumseh's Indian columns and of red-coated British regulars, held off the invaders and wrote in action one of the finest of Canada's national myths. The battles of the War of 1812 may have been small compared with those in Europe at the same period, when Napoleon was making his disastrous invasion of Russia, but actions such as the capture of Detroit, and the victories of Lundy's Lane, Crysler's Farm, Queenston Heights, and Chateauguay (where *canadien voltigeurs* fought under de Salaberry), became part of the folk history of Canadians. The participants of those battles — General Brock, Laura Secord and the great Tecumseh for example — became heroes among us. The events of the War of 1812 convinced Canadians that they had a land worth defending and a varied way of life they did not wish to see submerged; these events also gave them a collective pride in themselves and a sense not only of their powers but also of their rights. Here again

Sir John A. Macdonald, first Prime Minister of the Dominion of Canada, combined audacity with procrastination in an extraordinary degree, and was without doubt the most witty of all Canadian politicians. Born in Scotland in the year of Waterloo, he came to Canada in boyhood. His family settled in Kingston where he trained as a lawyer and which in 1844 he represented as a Conservative in the assembly of the Province of Canada. He began thus a political career that lasted until his death 47 years later. He first held office as Receiver-General in 1847, and from that time was constantly in and out of cabinets, becoming Prime Minister in 1857 in the Macdonald-Cartier ministry. In 1864 he entered into coalition with his Grit opponents to solve the political deadlock that had arisen, and out of this alliance came the proposals for Confederation. If Macdonald was not the only architect of Confederation, he was the first among equals, and it was just that when it came about in 1867 he should become Prime Minister. Except for an interlude of five years from 1873-1878 (after he had been defeated following a scandal over contracts for the Canadian Pacific Railway), he remained Prime Minister from Confederation until his death 24 years later, and presided over the implementation of the National Policy to develop Canadian industry through high tariffs. Macdonald's most controversial act was his insistence on the execution of Louis Riel in 1885; it meant the end of Conservative influence in Québec and gravely affected Tory strength in Canada as a whole.

the importance of settlement, which is the theme of this chapter, emerges. When men owned land and created a way of life, they were ready to risk their lives in defence of what they had against foreign invaders, but also against domestic tyrants.

And from this point the definition and defence of rights became urgent issues not only for Lower and Upper Canadians, but in all the colonies that formed what was then called British North America, a loose grouping of provinces that had few links except their relationship to the British crown and the imperial government in Westminster. The Loyalists may have rejected the republican form of government which the Thirteen Colonies had established, but they remained Americans in their desire for local self-government. It was their arrival that forced Britain in 1791 to introduce representative assemblies not only in Upper Canada but also in the lower province where, since the conquest of 1760, the *canadiens* had been ruled in an authoritarian way not different in kind, even if distinct in structure, from that to which they had been subjected by the French governors and intendants under the *ancien régime*. The French Canadians quickly learnt how to utilize British parliamentary institutions, and soon, in both Canadas as well as in Nova Scotia, there emerged a demand for the end of the dual system of an elected assembly that passed laws and voted funds and an appointed executive of governor and council responsible not to the peoples of the British North American colonies, but to the imperial government in Westminster.*

It was as much out of this struggle, as out of the perennial threat of American domination, that the peculiar amalgam of regions and the unique coalition of peoples that form modern Canada and the modern Canadians came into being. Responsible government was not given without a fight. Canada's few armed rebellions, like the battles on its borders, have been physically small events with gigantic consequences. In 1837, despairing of the slow workings of British political processes, Upper Canadian farmers and Lower Canadian *habitants* were prompted by leaders like William Lyon Mackenzie and Louis-Joseph Papineau to declare war on the authoritarian regimes of British officials and local patricians, known as the Family Compact in Upper Canada and the Château Clique in Lower Canada. These rebellions were essentially settlers' movements which drew their support from the farmers and local craftsmen who resented the arrogance of what Anna Jameson, a sharp-eyed English traveller of the time, referred to as "a petty colonial

*Since this is not meant as a political history, but as an account of the Canadian people — a kind of collective biography — I have skipped much of the detail of these events; readers wishing a fuller background might consult my larger book, *Canada and the Canadians* (revised edition, 1973) and *Who Killed the British Empire* (1974), and Ramsay Cook's excellent *Canada: A Modern Study* (revised edition, 1977).

The St. Lawrence Hall, a neo-classical building designed by William Thomas and built on King Street in 1850, was the cultural centre of mid-Victorian Toronto. It fell into decay at the turn of the century, but in 1967 it was restored as a centennial project and now it is the home of the National Ballet of Canada.

When the first travellers crossed them, the Prairies were clothed with high buffalo grass and embroidered with a myriad wild flowers. Settlement imposed its geometry on wild nature, and the rectangular formations of the land conform in spirit with the mechanization of modern harvesting methods.

As Canada burgeoned during the progressive decades of the nineteenth century, the habitant *communities of Québec, like Sainte-Jean d'Arc, showed little visible change.*

oligarchy, a self-constituted aristocracy, based upon nothing real, nor even upon any thing imaginary. . . ."

Mackenzie's ill-armed supporters, assembled at Montgomery's Tavern for the invasion of Toronto, fled in disorder when Colonel Allan McNab led a hastily assembled column of militia and loyal citizens up Yonge Street to defend the established regime. The Patriotes in Lower Canada resisted more stubbornly, and there were pitched battles on the Richelieu River and even a renewal of fighting in 1838. But most Canadians, though many of them were sympathetic with the rebels in their fight against arbitrary power, still in the last resort preferred the curious English combination of hierarchy and democracy to American republicanism, and that preference has lasted to this day, when Canadians are willing to accept the domination of elites, provided always that the elites are Canadian.

Nevertheless, the rebellions of 1837-38 indicated very clearly that a danger point had been reached beyond which the patience of Canadians and Maritimers could not be relied on indefinitely. Many who had not supported the rebellions were disturbed by the repressive measures that followed. When Samuel Lount and Peter Matthews, two of the leaders of the Upper Canadian Rebellion were hanged, Egerton Ryerson's brother

The colonial baroque grandeur of the British Columbian Parliament Building, overlooking the little harbour of Victoria, is only one example of the versatile genius of the young English architect, Francis Mawson Rattenbury, who left an indelible mark on Vancouver as well as Victoria. Rattenbury was only thirty when the Parliament Building was completed; he had designed it when he was 27. He was one of the colourful tragic characters of whom so many have gravitated to the Canadian Pacific coast; he was murdered in 1935 by his chauffeur, who was his wife's lover.

John recorded: "Very few persons present, except the military and the ruf scruff of the city. The general feeling is total opposition to the execution of these men."

In 1838 Lord Durham — known as Radical Jack for his democratic sympathies — came out as a special commissioner of Queen Victoria's government and wrote his famous Report. While the Durham Report was astonishingly imperceptive in its argument that the French culture of Canada must eventually be absorbed into the dominant English-speaking culture of North America, it also recognized two basic truths of the situation: the colonies of British North America could resist absorption only if their peoples felt they were controlling their own destinies (which could only be achieved by responsible government), and if they achieved some form of defensive unification. Most Canadians and most Maritimers at that time would have agreed with the first proposition; experience had to teach them the virtue of the second.

Yet it was the second that — in a wrong-headed and arbitrary way — was first imposed, when the two Canadas were united by the British Parliament's Act of Union (1840) into the Province of Canada, a legislative union in which Upper and Lower Canada (now become Canada West and Canada East) shared a single parliament with equal numbers of seats for the two sections of the province. The plan was designed to keep the French Canadians in a permanent minority, since the representatives of Upper Canada plus those of the English-speaking Eastern Townships in Lower Canada could always outvote them in a racial confrontation. It did not at first work out in this way, since the English-speaking reformers of Upper Canada, led by Robert Baldwin, allied themselves with the French-speaking reformers of Lower Canada, led by Hippolyte Lafontaine, to press for responsible government. A similar movement appeared in Nova Scotia led by Joseph Howe. The imperial government finally surrendered, and responsible government came into being, first in Nova Scotia (1848) and than in Canada (1849), not by statute but through the creation of precedents by colonial governors who called on parties with elected majorities to form governments.

At this point the peoples of British North America gained self-government, at least internally. They were citizens of autonomous communities, even if they remained British subjects and even if their loyalties were sometimes diluted by nostalgia for the countries from which want and tyranny had driven them, a nostalgia that on occasion produced haunting poetry like the anonymous "Canadian Boat-Song:"

From the lone shieling of the misty island
    Mountains divide us, and the waste of seas —
Yet still the blood is strong, the heart is highland,
    And we in dreams behold the Hebrides.

But still there lingered the feeling that such autonomy was precarious

OPPOSITE:
As settlement moved westward, the people who arrived began to desire the political maturity which the people of Red River had gained when the province of Manitoba was created in 1870. In 1905 the Northwest Territories south of the 60th parallel were divided into the new provinces of Saskatchewan and Alberta, and in Edmonton the new legislative assembly was housed in this building, designed by A.M. Jeffers and completed in 1912.

The Bonsecours Market was one of the centres of Montreal life in the early Victorian era. Designed by John Footner and begun in 1844, it served not only as a market hall, but also as a place of assembly; functions of many kinds went on in its two public halls.

The expansiveness of the opening Canadian west found its expression in many ways, and architecture was one of them, as is shown in the Winnipeg City Hall, which was built in 1886 and shows all the extravagance of design which in that era was thought to exemplify prosperity. Unfortunately this extraordinary period piece was demolished in 1962.

While Canada moved into the expansiveness of the 1890s, Newfoundland, which had refused to enter Confederation in 1867 and remained an autonomous colony, was still largely a country of deserted shorelines.

while the colonies remained disunited and hence vulnerable to either British or American domination. The kind of close union which the Province of Canada represented had become stifling and stultifying by the 1850s, when a renewed strife arose between French and English over what George Brown of the *Globe* called — "rep by pop" — representation by population. Now that the English were in a majority they were no longer willing to accept the equal representation in the Assembly for each section of the province that had seemed ideal when they were in a minority. Alliances shifted, governments lasted a few months, a few weeks, and in 1864, when it was obvious that the present system was unworkable, Brown dramatically offered to set aside his partisanship and join in a coalition to explore a new way, through confederation.

Meanwhile the Maritime colonies — Newfoundland, Nova Scotia, New Brunswick, Prince Edward Island — were exploring the idea of a smaller confederation. In September 1864 their leaders were to meet in Charlottetown to discuss this idea. The Canadians decided to gatecrash the conference and put their own proposals, and they chartered the steamship *Queen Victoria* in Quebec City. John A. Macdonald, George Brown, and six other Canadian ministers formed the delegation; they were accompanied on board by champagne valued at $13,000. Their arrival at Charlottetown was somewhat anti-climactic, since they were welcomed by a single official in an oyster boat. The conference of the

Henri Bourassa has come down in history as a French Canadian nationalist, but he was perhaps a truer federalist than many who lay claim to the title. Grandson of Louis Joseph Papineau and son of the painter Napoléon Bourassa, he followed an erratic political and journalistic career. In 1896 he was elected to the House of Commons as a Liberal, but soon called himself a Nationalist and in 1910 founded *Le Devoir* to propagate nationalism. But he did not share the xenophobia of many of his political associates, and the vision he really seems to have had was of a Canada that would be no less Canadian because those who spoke English and those who spoke French nurtured and developed their respective heritages. For broken periods he served in the Québec and the federal parliaments, but he fitted easily no political grouping, and was important as a passionate pamphleteer working towards a Canada that would see its destiny arising from the free co-operation of its peoples, liberated from the imperial past.

Maritime ministers had been overshadowed by the arrival of a circus, the first ever to visit Prince Edward Island, to which the islanders flocked. Whatever primitive hotel accommodation existed in Charlottetown was pre-empted, so that the New Brunswick delegation slept on the floor of an oyster bar. There was nothing to rival the hospitality offered on board the *Queen Victoria*, where union was symbolically anticipated by the drinking of champagne from Canada as an accompaniment to feasts of Maritime lobsters and oysters. "The great intercolonial drunk," as a hostile New Brunswick paper called it, continued in Halifax, St. John, and Fredericton, as the rough terms of Confederation were worked out in preparation for the Québec conference a few weeks later. The terms were agreed to in Quebec City to the tune of further celebrations in which the government of Canada ran up a bill for $15,000 in the Quebec City hotels. Confederation, launched on a stream of sparkling wine, became a reality when the British North America Act of 1867 divided the Province of Canada into Ontario and Québec (identical with the former Upper and Lower Canadas) and united them with the colonies of New Brunswick and Nova Scotia to form the Dominion of Canada. The concept of Canadian-ness was thus extended as far as the Atlantic seaboard.

Prince Edward Island and Newfoundland had withdrawn from the negotiations, and at first the New Brunswickers and the Nova Scotians were most unwilling Canadians, having to be politically manoeuvred and bribed to stay within the Dominion. The people of Québec were sharply divided on the issue of Confederation, many fearing they would be submerged by the large English-speaking majority created by the inclusion of the Maritime provinces. Even Rupert's Land, the scantily populated domain of the Hudson's Bay Company between the Pre-Cambrian Shield of Ontario and Québec and the Rockies, entered the new Dominion reluctantly, and then only because the people of the Red River settlements feared that if they were ruled as a territory they would be the victims of Upper Canadians greedy for land. It was only after Louis Riel's provisional government had been established in 1869 and the Dominion had agreed to create the province of Manitoba that Canada was extended to the Rockies. West of Manitoba the lands up to the Continental Divide, which the Hudson's Bay Company had held under license from the British government, were transformed into the Northwest Territories. In 1871 the adherence of the gold-mining colony of British Columbia meant that the Dominion did indeed stretch, as its motto already claimed, "from sea to sea," though even the British Columbians were uneasy Canadians for many years owing to the slowness with which the Dominion government kept its promise to complete the railway that would physically unite the country.

Eventually even the most reluctant colonies found their way into Canada. Prince Edward Island entered the Dominion in 1873, under financial pressure because of the debts it had incurred through rash

Red Lake is typical of the thousands of lakes that were opened to Canadian travellers when the railways began to move into the Canadian Shield country of Ontario in the 1880s.

The completion of the Canadian Pacific Railway in 1885 opened the mountains of western Canada to tourism, and a whole series of national parks were created, among them one which was established in 1914, and centred on Mount Revelstoke.

With **Wilfrid Laurier** began the long period of Liberal political ascendancy in Canada. Born in 1841, he entered politics when Liberalism in Québec was still distrusted by the church, and played a great part in ending direct ecclesiastical interference in Canadian politics. He held office briefly under Alexander Mackenzie in 1877, but he had to wait for high rank until the Liberal victory of 1896. He continued as Prime Minister until 1911, weathering the political storms that gathered over such questions as Canada's participation in imperial defence. In imperial affairs Laurier followed consistently a line of preserving Canada's independence of decision, and in this way played a great part in preparing the British acknowledgment of dominion autonomy in the Statute of Westminster, 1931. He was defeated in 1911 for proposing to conclude a reciprocity treaty with the United States, and again in 1917 because he opposed wartime conscription. Deserted by many English-speaking Liberals, by the time of his death in 1919 he had become a largely isolated figure, but he bore the fading of his influence with an admirable philosophic calm.

When the Canadian Pacific Railway was completed in 1885, it brought many tourists to admire the newly opened scenic splendours of the Rockies, like Sunwapta Falls near Jasper.

railway construction projects. Its people made the best of what some of them regarded as a bad job, and Lord Dufferin, attending the celebrations in his role of Governor General, reported that he "found the Island in a high state of jubilation and quite under the impression that it is the Dominion that has been annexed to Prince Edward. . . ."

In 1905 the new provinces of Saskatchewan and Alberta were carved out of the Northwest Territory, where in previous years the Dominion government's inept handling of settlement problems had provoked Canada's last armed rebellion, that of the Métis and the Indians under such leaders as Riel and Dumont, Poundmaker and Big Bear, whose defeat meant the final triumph of the immigrant white men over the native peoples in the prairies.

It was not until 1949 that Newfoundland gave up a proud but impoverished independence to enter Confederation, and Canada as we know it was complete.

In this chapter we have traced how the concept of Canada, used originally for only a part of the St. Lawrence valley, came to spread over the breadth of a continent and northward into the far Arctic, and to include, as Canadians, people of many origins and traditions living in a country that is the second largest in the world. But this Canada was from the beginning divided inevitably into distinct regions, all of them larger than most of the European nations which have figured so largely in history. These regions were defined geographically by such barriers as the Rockies, the Shield, the northern tree line, the Ottawa River, the Strait of Belle Isle; politically by the co-existence, since Confederation, of a federal government centred in Ottawa, and ten provincial governments steadily pressing for greater shares of power; socially by the varying origins, cultures, and economic interests of the regional peoples.

So Canada came into being; the name and the reality spreading out from the St. Lawrence basin to embrace a land four thousand miles across, yet so thinly populated and so tenuous in so many ways that its stubborn survival has always been a matter of wonder to strangers who see how anomalous it appears as a nation. The Russian poet Andrei Voznesensky remarked with a touch of wonder that "Canada is horizontal . . . a comparatively narrow strip along the American border . . . like a layer of cream on a jug of milk," and the English poet Patrick Anderson, writing almost thirty years ago, described it as:

America's attic, an empty room,
a something possible, a chance, a dance,
that is not danced. A cold kingdom.

As I see Canada, it is a house with many rooms under a single roof that sometimes leaks and is in need of repair. The roof is the Confederation, and the rooms are the regions. They are rooms full of history, inhabited by people of many origins and traditions, the descendants of the settlers.

II A Pattern of Regions

Martin Frobisher made three voyages in search of the North West Passage and in 1576 discovered Frobisher Bay. His encounter with the Inuit was not so pacific as this 1675 print suggests; he fled back to his ship with one of their arrows piercing his buttock.

CHAPTER FOUR

Newfoundland Where the Empire Began

In Newfoundland the British Empire began. St. John's, the capital of the province, is one of the oldest cities founded by Europeans in the Americas. It was burnt so often, by accident and by invaders, that now it seems a Victorian city surrounded by a ring of modern buildings, but John Rut wintered in its harbour as early as 1527 and put up the first dwelling; the Sieur de Roberval found seventeen fishing ships at St. John's in 1542; and by the time Sir Humphrey Gilbert arrived in 1583 there was already a makeshift town to serve the fishing fleets from Devon.

The earliest English settlement of all antedated even the foundation of St. John's. A consortium of Bristol merchants, calling themselves the Company of Adventurers to the New Found Land, obtained in 1502 a royal patent to establish a colony on the island. The Company landed settlers as early as 1503 and provided them with a priest in 1504. The settlement seems to have survived until 1506. The actual site where it was attempted is no longer known, but it preceded by a century the first French settlements on the St. Lawrence, the first English settlements in Virginia, the first Scottish settlements in Nova Scotia; it even preceded the Spanish conquest of Mexico City and Cuzco.

Yet whether the British were even the first to establish themselves on Newfoundland is uncertain. From the beginning, English, French, and Portuguese competed as fishermen on the Grand Banks, where Cabot reported that the sea was "swimming with fish, which can be taken not only with the net but in baskets let down with a stone." The Portuguese never sought to establish themselves territorially, though they have been taking cod off the shores of Newfoundland for almost five centuries, and the arrival of the White Fleet from Portugal is one of the great annual events in St. John's. But the Basques (the memory of them lingers in the southwestern community of Port-aux-Basques) were certainly there very early in the sixteenth century, whaling and fishing; a Basque priest was stationed on the island in 1549. Only in 1713, under the Treaty of Utrecht, did the French, who several times tried to drive the English off the island, acknowledge British sovereignty over Newfoundland, and even then they retained rights to land and cure fish on the French shore

This 1693 Carte des Pecheries, *by "Fitz-Hugh" shows the main fishing areas off the shores of seventeenth-century Newfoundland.*

which extended along the northern and western rims of the island. It was not until 1904 that these rights were finally extinguished — by purchase.

"During the first four centuries of English rule in Newfoundland," says Harold Horwood (*Newfoundland*, 1969), "the colony consisted of a varying strip of the eastern shore, sometimes only a part of the Avalon Peninsula, but never included the west or south-west coasts. Aside from this old 'English shore', Newfoundland was terra incognita, given over to the French and the Indians."

The southeastern Avalon Peninsula (named by Sir George Calvert early in the seventeenth century) contains most of the major sites of Newfoundland history, including St. John's itself — Ferryland where the pirate leaders made their base for expeditions to the Spanish Main;

39 years before it entered Canada, in 1910, Newfoundland was already celebrating with a special issue of stamps the first settlement in 1610 under the leadership of John Guy, the Bristol merchant.

Trepassey and Placentia where the early French fishing fleets gathered; Cupids, originally called Cupars Cove, where in 1610 John Guy of Bristol founded one of the best-documented early settlements; and Harbour Grace, where Robert Hayman wrote the first English poetry in the New World — his *Quodlibets, Lately Come Over from New Britaniola, Old Newfoundland*, published in 1628. Written for Hayman's literary friends in London, who included Ben Jonson, it praised the island in the tones of a lyrical public relations man.

The Aire in Newfound-land is wholesome, good;
The Fire, as Sweet as any made of wood;
The Waters, very rich, both salt and fresh;
The Earth more rich, you know it is no lesse.
Where all are good, *Fire, Water, Earth* and *Aire,*
What man made of these foure would not live there?

The French presence in Newfoundland was certainly no transient one and had left many traces. Norman and Jersey names, deriving from seventeenth-century settlers and sometimes transformed by time, are still common among Newfoundlanders, while in the eighteenth century, when the Acadians were expelled from the Annapolis Valley in Nova Scotia, many of them migrated to Newfoundland, where their descendants still live on the southwestern corner of the island; in this area an antique French was still spoken in living memory. The French seem also to have been more inclined than the English to mingle with the native

Trepassey was one of the gathering places of the French fishing fleet. This sketch was drawn in 1786 by J.S. Meres in the log-book of HMS Pegasus.

The outport of Cupids was the site of John Guy's settlement in 1610. Its curious name is derived by generations of metamorphosis from the original of Cupers Cove.

peoples, and a mixed race, part French and part Indian, with later interminglings of English and Irish, known to other Newfoundlanders as the Jakitars, still inhabits the area of the island's west coast around Port-au-Port.

It is not quite certain what Indians the French mingled with, since the native history of Newfoundland is complex and obsure. As noted, it is no more certain who were the people identified as Skraelings by the Norsemen who settled briefly and smelted their bog iron at L'Anse aux Meadows. Clearly, however, there were Inuit living on Newfoundland in ancient times. Fine bone carvings of seals and fish made by the Dorset Inuit two thousand years ago have been found on Newfoundland sites; the Dorset people were followed by the Thule Inuit, who were still visiting Newfoundland from Labrador when the first Basque whalers arrived in these waters.

When the cod-fishers appeared in the late fifteenth century the most numerous Indian people were the Beothuks, the original "Red Indians." But the Beothuks, who died out by the early nineteenth century from a combination of sickness, starvation, and plain murder at the hands of white settlers, were renowned for their avoidance of white people; as Captain George Cartwright remarked in 1770, "they secret themselves in the woods, keep an unremitting watch, and are seldom seen; a conduct, which their defenceless condition, and the inhuman treatment which

In 1798 R.P. Benton painted this water colour of early St. John's. The key to the numbered sites is as follows: 1. Shed for gun carriages; 2. Fort Townsend, built 1748; 3. Net Factory; 4. Site of Church of England Cathedral; 5. Cathedral Hill; 6. Site of Masonic Temple; 7. Court House; 8. Custom House; 9. W.H. Thomas & Co. fishery; 10. Bulley & Job, fishery.

they have always experienced from strangers, whether Europeans or other tribes of Indians from the Continent, have compelled them to adopt."

The "other tribes of Indians from the Continent" were the Nascopie from Labrador and the Micmac from Nova Scotia; Algonkian peoples who fished and hunted sea mammals on the coast of Newfoundland and who were the allies of the whites in persecuting the Beothuck. Any Indian element in the Newfoundland population is likely to come from one of these two peoples.

The role of the Norsemen in the early history of Newfoundland is still unclear and perhaps incompletely recorded. We know of the late tenth- and early eleventh-century visits through the Sagas, which are now supported by archaeological evidence. But are we to assume that there were no other visits? Are we to assume that, unlike every other race that landed on the shores of Newfoundland, the Norsemen left no trace in the population? Are we to assume that their knowledge of the country died as the settlements of Greenland withered away, without being passed on?

In fact, there is strong reason to believe that accounts of the Norse voyages beyond Greenland were brought back to Europe and that the tradition lingered in the North Sea ports to inspire later voyagers. No more than a century, after all, divided the abandonment of the Norse settlements from the arrival of the first known fishermen on the Grand

Banks and the first Portuguese voyagers off Greenland itself, and we cannot assume that there were no voyages during that blank era of three or four generations. A tenuous continuity between the first European landings on Newfoundland almost a millenium ago and the first actual settlements in the sixteenth and seventeenth centuries seems somewhat more than probable.

Not a great deal is known in detail about the Newfoundland settlements until quite late in the eighteenth century because legally much of the settlement that went on constituted squatting carried out in defiance of official British policy. The era of plantations by chartered companies came virtually to an end when Sir George Calvert departed to Maryland in 1629, though David Kirke managed to extend it a few years longer. The wealthy west-of-England merchants who profited by the cured cod industry had always been opposed to settlement, and they persuaded Charles I to decree that there should be no settlements within six miles of the coast. The British authorities were happy with an anti-settlement policy, since they regarded the sailing of the annual fishing fleet from Devon to the Grand Banks as an excellent school for sailors who could be recruited into the Royal Navy in time of emergency.

In fact settlements continued to grow up, some of them established during the Commonwealth by Royalists who fled from England, and by the mid-seventeenth century there were about forty communities. Attempts to remove them did not succeed, and their inhabitants were augmented by deserting mariners and fishermen who refused to accept the harsh discipline of the fishing fleets. Some of these deserters actually fled into the interior of the island where they set up colonies of outlaws known as the Masterless Men.

Up to 1699 a condition of political chaos prevailed in Newfoundland. The sole form of government was that improvised each season by the fishing fleet, and dominated entirely by the interests of the merchants in England. At each harbour where vessels gathered the captain of the first boat to arrive became "fishing admiral," and the rule of these

During the severe frost of 1838 the seal-fishing vessels had to leave St. John's Harbour by channels through the ice.

This drawing of 1857 shows Cremaillere Harbour on the northern 'French' shore of Newfoundland. By the Treaty of Utrecht (1713), the French had fishing rights from Cape Ray, around the west and north of the island to Cape St. John on the north-east shore. The terms of the Treaty did not allow the erection of permanent dwellings, so the French fishermen built huts and scaffolds for fish drying which they dismantled when they returned to France each autumn.

The Swiss painter Peter Rindisbacher emigrated in 1821 to Lord Selkirk's Red River Colony. He sailed via Hudson's Bay, and on the way he "drew from nature" this Inuit seal hunter off the coast of Labrador.

The Moravian Brethren pioneered in missionary work on the Labrador Coast, and this drawing of ' Esquimaux Indians ', made in 1812, was based on information "communicated by a Moravian missionary".

temporary despots weighed down heavily not only on the fishermen in the fleet but also on the people living along the coast, who in some places became little better than serfs to the merchants, unless they chose to join in the working anarchy of the Masterless Men.

In 1699 the imperial government intervened to bring a semblance of order into the situation — the first direct attempt by Westminster to set up even a rudimentary government in the regions that later became Canada. Ownership of private property was for the first time assured by statute, which gave the settlers a degree of security; they could no longer be treated arbitrarily as squatters. At the same time a right of appeal from the fishing admirals to the commanders of the naval convoys was established, but this was often not a great improvement, since most of the officers sympathized with the merchants and their captains. Only thirty years later, in 1729, was a governor appointed (in these early years he went back annually with the fishing fleet); at the same time local magistrates were appointed. After the middle of the eighteenth century life began to acquire a certain stability, the tyranny of the merchants relaxed, and by 1750 the English shore of Newfoundland had haphazardly acquired about 13,000 inhabitants. A third were Irish and the rest came from the west of England.

They were developing a poor man's culture of considerable vigour which lasted in large parts of Newfoundland into the middle of the present century. It was an extremely decentralized society. St. John's was the only town of any size, a nest of merchants, and most of the people lived in the hundreds of tiny hamlets or "outports," sited on inlets or coves along the island's highly indented shores and each inhabited by a hundred or even a few score people. (The largely mountainous interior was virtually uninhabited, as it remains to this day.) The square wooden houses of the outports, painted dull red with a foul-smelling mixture of ochre and codfish oil, were scattered along the steep rocky paths, for there were usually no roads and most of these places could be reached only by water. On the shore the small boats used for inshore fishing would be moored beside the jetties where lobster pots and cod traps were piled; like shelfs on the rocks above the water jutted out the fishing flakes, wooden platforms where the cod was dried in the long process known as shore-curing.

The people of the outports lived by a precarious subsistence economy, described often in the vivid folk songs.

Now I am intending to sing you a song
About the poor people, how they get along;
They start in the spring and they work to the fall
And when it's all over they have nothing at all,
And it's hard, hard times.

There was not much fertility to the scanty soil of Newfoundland — "This

Sir Edward Parry, the British naval commander, led two expeditions in the sailing ships Hecla *and* Griper, *in search of the North West Passage. On the first — 1819-20 — he proved that Lancaster Sound was not landlocked and discovered Melville Island. On the second — 1821-23 — he discovered Fury and Hecla Strait which was an important link in the Passage. It was to illustrate the* Journal *of the second expedition that this drawing of Thule Eskimos was made.*

poor bald rock," as Joey Smallwood once called it — and the people scraped their livings in a variety of ways. They had fish and seal-meat in season, they hunted for caribou in the interior and netted migrating wildfowl, they gathered seabirds' eggs and wild herbs, they grew potatoes and vegetables in soil laboriously collected in crevices in the rocks, they baked bread, and supplemented it all with cheap rum smuggled from the French islands of St. Pierre and Miguelon. The characteristic Newfoundland dishes are poor men's food, like *brewse* or *brewis*, a kind of stew made of dried salt cod and bread or ship's biscuit, with a bit of salt pork for flavour, simmered on the hob. Everything that could be made by hand was produced in the village, from the locally built fishing boats to the roll-necked and hand-knitted guernseys and the men's trousers made, in many areas, from the wool of sheep that grazed around the hamlet, spun and woven by the women.

Until the early days of the present century, money rarely changed hands in this austere society. In the early eighteenth century the English merchants established a truck system by which goods brought in on the sack ships from Britain — including the salt necessary for curing cod — were bartered for the fish the settlers produced; as in most truck systems, the tallies were manipulated so that the fishermen were perpetually in debt. The worst conditions existed among the "livyers" of Labrador. The livyers, whose name was a Newfoundland dialect word meaning that,

One of the illustrations to Moll's 1712 map of North America was this drawing showing early seventeenth century methods of curing cod in Newfoundland.

unlike other fishermen who migrated seasonally from the island, they actually *lived* all year round on the Labrador coast — existed in a kind of perpetual bondage, complicated by alcoholism encouraged by the merchants who used drink to drive the livyers deeper into debt. Tuberculosis was rampant among them and their children often died from malnutrition.

When the centre of trade shifted to St. John's — which became a busy mercantile city linked to all parts of the world — the same system prevailed, and, outside of the capital with its rich trading families, and a few other smaller towns, cash played a slight role in the island's life. The very concept of a high standard of living was almost unknown outside St. John's during the first four centuries or so of Newfoundland's existence, and as late as 1969 the minimum wage in the province was seventy cents an hour for men and fifty cents for women. It is still the poorest province in Canada, with the lowest average income and the highest rate of unemployment.

In other ways, people in the old Newfoundland led a simple and often

This stage was used in the eighteenth century for throwing the fish ashore before they were prepared for curing.

As a young doctor, **Wilfred Grenfell** became superintendent of the Mission to Deep-Sea Fishermen in 1890, and having heard of the destitution among the livyers — the resident fishermen — in Labrador, he went there and in 1893 established at Battle Harbour a small hospital under the auspices of the Labrador Mission. At the time of Grenfell's death in 1940, the mission operated five hospitals, seven nursing stations and three orphanages, but Grenfell's concern went beyond such institutions. He recognized how much the sickness among the livyers was due to malnutrition and alcoholism and how far these conditions were due to an iniquitous truck system that kept the fishermen in perpetual debt to the merchants. He helped bring this system to an end, and his success was largely due to the tirelessness with which he kept in touch with the people he helped, every year sailing the coasts of Labrador and Newfoundland to survey conditions for himself. Like many capable men, impatient of the shortcomings of others, he tended to seem dictatorial, but his compassion and his understanding of the causes of Labrador poverty were deep and genuine.

deprived existence. Communications were difficult, and many outports had no schools and were unvisited by doctors or nurses. Only in the later nineteenth century, when fishermens' leaders like William Coaker and socially conscious missionaries like Wilfred Grenfell started their work, did conditions begin to change.

Yet, in part at least because of their isolation in the outports, away from the influences of modern mass culture or even Victorian literate culture, Newfoundlanders retained a vital folk culture that had living roots in a distant English past. They spoke dialects that were derived from those of Devon men and Irishmen of the seventeenth century and differed considerably from mainland Canadian ways of speaking. "In Newfoundland," says Harold Horwood, "a gulch is what mainlanders call a gully. A gully is what mainlanders call a pond. A pond is what mainlanders call a lake." Among Newfoundlanders I heard sayings which I have never heard elsewhere in Canada but which I did hear as a child in the west of England, such as "Pigs may fly, but they're rather unlikely birds!"

Cod was cured by drying in the sun and air on 'flakes' — wooden stages constructed in the outports scattered along the six thousand miles of Newfoundland coastline.

An Inuit hunter paddles his kayak beside a herd of sea-lions on the beaches of the Ile de St. Jean. Note the long-peaked hat which was specially designed to save the eyes from excessive glare.

Newfoundland folk songs are famous. Some are old English songs, lost in their place of origin but preserved in the amber of outport isolation. But the tradition was no matter of mere nostalgia, and the most interesting songs are those made by Newfoundlanders themselves about the fisherman's life, about whaling and sealing voyages, about shipwrecks and drowning, about every aspect of the islanders' vigorous pre-mechanical life. "The mystique of the Newfoundland song comes from hardship and hard pleasure," said the poet Paul West, and he quoted as an example "I'se the B'y that Builds the Boat," a song which I find interesting for many reasons — as an example of Newfoundland dialect, with a tune that was accompanied by a stamping dance, and as a view of outport life that combines authentic detail with a kind of wild surrealist fantasy.

I'se the b'y that builds the boat,
And I'se the b'y that sails her!
I'se the b'y that catches the fish
and takes 'em home to Lizer.

Sods and rinds to cover yer flake,
Cake and tea for supper,
Codfish in the spring of the year
Fried in maggotty butter.

I don't want your maggoty fish,
That's no good for winter;
I could buy as good as that
Down in Bonavista.

I took Liza to a dance,
And faith, but she could travel!
And every step that she did take
Was up to her knees in gravel

Susan White, she's out of sight,
Her petticoat wants a border;
Old Sam Oliver, in the dark,
He kissed her in the corner.

And, after every verse, the rollicking nonsense refrain,

Hip yer partner, Sally Tibbo'!
Hip yer partner, Sally Brown!
Fogo, Twinningate, Morton's Harbour,
All around the circle!

Another side of Newfoundland life to the maggoty fish of poverty was shown in the verses of "The Killigrew Soiree," with its authentic rhythms of the Irish reel, so that one can almost hear the strings of the

The English artist, William G.R. Hind, accompanied his brother, Henry Youle Hind, on a government-sponsored exploration of Labrador. This drawing of seal-hunting by Montagnais Indians in the Gulf of St. Lawrence was one of the many illustrations he prepared for his brother's Explorations in Labrador.

outport fiddlers in the background as the Killigrews' strange feast offerings are recited:

> There was birch rine, tar twine, cherry wine and turpentine,
> Jowls and cavalances, ginger beer and tea,
> Pigs' feet, cat's meat, dumplings boiled in a sheet,
> Dandelion and crackies' teeth at the Killigrews' Soiree.

The wayward lyricism of the Newfoundland songs exists also in the strange and haunting names which the Newfoundlanders gave to the places where they lived and the features of the shorescape that were marks for them when they set out, "in oil skins and boots and Cape Anns battened down," as one of the songs had it, for the fishing grounds: names like God Almighty Cove and Famish Gut; Happy Adventure and Ireland's Eye; Harbour Grace and Spanish Room; Witless Bay and Lushes Bight and Seldom Come By. The tradition that created names and songs is not quite dead; Newfoundland events are still liable to be recorded and sung by local folk poets.

The Newfoundlanders developed into an independent people, with the pride of decent poverty. The way they see themselves does not always agree with the way other people see them. "We'll rant and we'll roar like true Newfoundlanders," goes one favourite song, "We'll rant and we'll roar on deck and below . . . ," and this is a self-image many Newfoundlanders treasure. But Paul West saw them rather differently, as "a community of Irish mystics cut adrift in the Atlantic," and A. P. Herbert, the

Joey (Joseph Roberts) Smallwood claims to be the "only living Father of Confederation", and his main reason for recognition by posterity is indeed the fact that in 1949 he led a half-willing Newfoundland into union with Canada, which it had evaded in 1867. A Napoleon-sized energumen, sparkling with Newfoundland humour and braggadocio, Smallwood was born in 1900, and started with a career in journalism and broadcasting that led to association with movements seeking better conditions for the fishermen. He became convinced that the economic base of an independent Newfoundland would be insufficient to create any meaningful improvement in the standard of living, and accordingly, when a national convention was called in 1946 to discuss the colony's future, Smallwood became a leading advocate of integration into Canada, using the media to reinforce his arguments. By a narrow margin Newfoundlanders voted to enter Confederation, and when this took place on the 1st April, 1949, Smallwood, at the head of the local Liberals, became Premier, and remained in office until his defeat in 1971. Newfoundlanders had become tired of his autocratic methods, and his popularity waned so far that his later bids to return to political power were unavailing; he spent his unwilling leisure writing a lively autobiography, *I Chose Canada* (1973).

E.J. (Edwin John) Pratt was one of the finest Canadian poets and certainly the most notable writer to come out of Newfoundland. Born in Western Bay in 1882, Pratt was trained at St. John's Methodist College, and afterwards toured the outpost communities, preaching, teaching and gathering a sense of the tragic aspects of the fisherman's life that inspired many of his lyrics and found its way into longer poems like *The Titanic.* Long before his province, Pratt performed a personal act of Confederation when he enrolled in Victoria College, Toronto, still studying theology in which he took his doctorate in 1917. From this time onward Pratt lived in Canada, changing to the teaching of English in 1920. His first book, *Newfoundland Verse,* reflected his island origins, but after that he moved into the greater scape of the Canadian past, and derived the themes of some of his best poems, like *Brébeuf and his Brethren* and *Towards the Last Spike,* from key points in Canadian history. Writing deliberately in verse forms derived from the seventeenth century, Pratt became in his own way a great mythographer, and often we now see Canadian history through his eyes much as we see Canadian landscape through the eyes of the Group of Seven. If he did not influence younger poets technically (they preferred more modern models) he nevertheless inspired them by raising poetry in Canada to the level of a significant commentary on our history and our views of existence.

English writer who fought hard in the 1940s to save the colony's independence, claimed that the islanders — whom he regarded as completely non-American — were "the best-tempered, best-mannered people walking." He saw them as "gay, good-humoured and generous, God-fearing, sabbath-keeping and law-abiding," and all this I feel to be as true, from what I have known of Newfoundlanders, as the words of the song. The ranting and roaring, after all, usually took place on a Saturday, and in the outports there were few temptations to break the law. Herbert also rightly stressed the self-reliance of the Newfoundlanders. "Every man can build his own house, his own boat."

During the nineteenth century the Newfoundlanders' commercial interests turned towards Europe, where the good salt cod was sold, and the West Indies, where the imperfectly cured fish was sent in barrels to feed slaves and rum was acquired in payment, and they avoided involvement on any side in the colonial politics and conflicts of North America. A kind of democratic politics was finally established, though the Assembly was usually dominated by the merchants of St. John's. Yet the Newfoundlanders seem to have preferred the devils they knew to those they did not. They avoided entering Confederation in 1867, and their reaction to later Canadian overtures was expressed in a song sung with gusto for generations:

> Men, hurrah for our own native isle, Newfoundland,
> Not a stranger shall hold one inch of her strand;
> Her face turns to Britain, her back to the Gulf.
> Come near at your peril, Canadian Wolf!

The Depression broke the back of Newfoundland's independence. Conditions that sorely strained great economies like those of Britain and the United States were fatal to a marginal one like that of Newfoundland. Taxes could not even be raised to meet the country's obligations; the little dominion almost literally went bankrupt, and placed its affairs into the receivership of a commission appointed by the British Colonial Office. The responsible government was suspended until 1949, when the British government, intent on dissolving its imperial obligations, organized a referendum in which the Newfoundlanders were asked to choose between continuing the status quo, becoming independent, or joining Canada. A ranter and roarer named Joey Smallwood, who was popular as a radio commentator, ran a forceful campaign for entry into the Canadian Confederation, but there were still many Newfoundlanders who were unconvinced that the material advantages of joining Canada were worth losing their independence. When the final vote was taken it was by a bare majority of 7,000 that Newfoundland entered Canada and Joey Smallwood was able to boast of being "the only living Father of Confederation." His energy and his plebeian effrontery appealed to his fellow Newfoundlanders, and he ruled as prime minister for twenty-two

The first Transatlantic Cable reached North America at Trinity Bay, Newfoundland, and the first message was carried on the 5th August, 1858, between this terminal and Valentia, Ireland.

The Court House building on Water Street, St. John's, was erected in 1849. The lower portion was used as a market and the court sessions were held in the upper rooms. It was one of the many buildings destroyed in the great fire that swept St. John's in 1892.

Petty Harbour, with its houses clambering up the bleak hillsides of a sheltered cove, was typical of the outports in which, until very recently, most Newfoundlanders lived a largely subsistence existence.

During the fishing season St. John's was always a busy harbour; this scene of the city and its shipping was drawn in 1831.

years. "I am king of my own little island, and that's all I've ever wanted to be," he said, but in the end his crown became tarnished. In 1971 the people finally rejected him and voted him out of office.

Since Newfoundland entered Confederation in 1949, and so completed the pattern of Canada from sea to sea, there have been profound changes in its way of life. The idea of the typical Newfoundlander as an outport fisherman living a mainly subsistence life is long outdated. Even before 1949, industries like papermaking from the island's great forests were beginning to diversify the economy, while mining was becoming important both in Newfoundland and in its dependent territory of Labrador. Now most fishermen are part-time workers and fishing accounts for less than a tenth of the island's industry; even that tenth is threatened by the inroads into traditional fishing grounds made by Russian and Japanese fleets of factory ships. The outports themselves have been vanishing as part of a controversial programme that sought to eliminate more than half of them by moving their inhabitants to larger and more accessible communities where services could be better organized. The programme, which turned five hundred places with sonorous Elizabethan names into ghost hamlets, has been dubiously successful; people in some villages who refused to move are now better off even materially than others who accepted the temptations of an urban existence outside their habits and traditions.

Fishing barrels, tarred ropes and lobster traps, piled together at Hant's Harbour, suggest the basic economic facts of classic Newfoundland life.

There is no doubt the extremes of poverty and hardship that were once the inescapable fate of many Newfoundlanders have been rendered obsolete by a Canadian level of pensions and welfare payments, ensured by federal grants that amount to sixty per cent of the provincial revenue. Thousands of miles of roads, hundreds of schools and many hospitals have been provided since 1949. But still not all of the island's people can find ways to make a living, and thousands leave every year to work or to live on the Canadian mainland; many small places are inhabited most of the year by women, children, and old men, and a high proportion of the graduates from the excellent Memorial University of St. John's depart never to return, as the great Newfoundland poet E. J. Pratt did in an earlier generation.

In spite of his departure, Pratt represented more monumentally than any other writer the basic themes of Newfoundland existence. There have been novelists like Margaret Duley in the 1930s, with *The Eye of the Gull* and *Cold Pastoral,* and more recent fiction writers like Gordon Pinsent in *The Rowdyman,* who have vividly presented the hard realities and the elemental joys of outport life, and in *White Eskimo* Harold Horwood has documented, with perhaps an excess of melodrama, the vicissitudes of existence on the Labrador coast. But it is in Pratt's early lyrics, and in some of his longer poems of heroism and tragedy at sea that the great confrontrations with the impersonal powers of nature, which formed so great a part of Newfoundland life in the past, are most epically recorded. Pratt's earliest published poem, "Rachel", concerned an outport mother waiting for news of a son who has been drowned in a wreck. His first collection of poems was called *Newfoundland* and expressed many aspects of life on his native island, while a poem of the early 1930s, called "Erosion," condensed into two brief verses the whole relationship between natural forces and human sorrows that he had so often witnessed.

It took the sea a thousand years,
A thousand years to trace
The granite features of this cliff,
In crag and scarp and base.

It took the sea an hour one night,
An hour of storm to place
The sculpture of these granite seams
Within a woman's face.

Later, in his sea poems like "The Roosevelt and the Antinoe" and "The Titanic," Pratt distilled into massive epics of conflict with the environment the centuries of endurance that went to make the Newfoundland character, and in the final lines of "The Titanic" his portrayal of the vast indifference of nature to individual human destinies reflects the fatalism that was one aspect of the island view of existence.

And out there in the twilight, with no trace
Upon it of its deed but the last wave
From the *Titanic* fretting at its base,
Silent, composed, ringed by its icy broods,
The grey shape with the palaeolithic face
Was still the master of the longitudes.

Most Newfoundlanders, while they remain proud of their traditions, of the endurance and resourcefulness of their ancestors, have accepted inclusion in Canada as at least a necessary choice. But there are still those who feel that the price of becoming virtually dependent upon the rest of Canada is too high, that Newfoundland might have found her own way of life, as many Third World countries have done, if she had not been tempted with benefits dispensed condescendingly by Ottawa politicians, and who are still ready (with a glass or two of smuggled St. Pierre rum in their veins) to sing loudly about Canadian wolves.

CHAPTER FIVE

Atlantic Canada

Historically and geographically, the three Atlantic provinces of Nova Scotia, New Brunswick, and Prince Edward Island are closely related. They embrace the southern shores of the Gulf of St. Lawrence. They form the double peninsula of New Brunswick and Nova Scotia, linked by the Isthmus of Chignecto, jutting east and south from the Gaspé peninsula, and crowned by the insularities of Prince Edward Island and Cape Breton Island (the Ile St. Jean and Ile-Royale of the days when the St. Lawrence was ruled from France). All three provinces, together with parts of the American state of Maine, were once united in the French colony of Acadia, to which the British also laid claim under the name of Nova Scotia. And to this day, though it is more than two centuries since Prince Edward Island was made a separate colony in 1769, and almost two centuries since New Brunswick was carved out of the fabric of Nova Scotia in 1784, the Atlantic provinces share many traditions and many resentments that distinguish them from the rest of Canada.

Today there are somewhat less than two million people in the 50,000 square miles of this region of populous and intricate coastlines and river valleys and sparsely inhabited forested interiors. When Europeans first touched these shores at the beginning of the sixteenth century, the country was inhabited by two Algonkian peoples; the Micmac who controlled most of the coastlines, and the Malecite who inhabited the inland regions of New Brunswick. They were fishing and hunting peoples, typical nomads of the eastern woodlands with their wigwams and canoes of white birch bark, who built nothing permanent and whose presence is recorded only in the few tools and weapons of stone that they lost or discarded to the benefit of the archaeologist. Both Micmac and Malecite became involved in the post-discovery history of the area, but that was only because they were recruited by the French in the contest with the English that went on for more than a century and a half before the region finally became British in 1758.

It is possible that Leif Ericsson or some other Norse navigator made landfall on the shores of Nova Scotia at the end of the Dark Ages; it is probable that John Cabot did so in 1497. Certainly by this time Bretons and Basques and Devon men were probing into the folds of the coastline in their search for fish and furs, and when the kings of Europe finally turned their minds towards North America as a continent in its own right rather than a mirage of Asia, the nationality of the first man to set foot on

Cape Bona Vista on Cape Breton Island may well have been John Cabot's landfall when, sailing westward in the Matthew, *he sighted land on the 24th June, 1497, and claimed it for King Henry VII of England, imagining he had reached Asia.*

these shores had long been forgotten. All that could be remembered by British and by French was that their ships had been here long before, and each nation felt that it had a prior claim to the land.

Undoubtedly the first actually to settle in Acadia were the French. In 1598 the Marquis de la Roche landed fifty colonists on Sable Island, off the Nova Scotian coast, the first French settlement in the New World. They stayed for a few years, but the supply ships failed to come, and only a few starving survivors were left to be taken off in 1603. The following year the Sieur de Monts, who had been chartered by the French king to conduct the fur trade in both Acadia and the St. Lawrence valley, arrived in the company of Samuel de Champlain at the mouth of the St. Croix River, which now divides New Brunswick from the state of Maine. He made a temporary settlement there, but it was at Port Royal on the Bay of Fundy (now Annapolis) that a more lasting settlement was made in 1605. Here, in the winter of 1606-07, Marc Lescarbot wrote the first French poetry in the New World (*Les Muses de la Nouvelle France,* published in Paris in 1609) and also a masque, "le théâtre de Neptune dans la Nouvelle France," which was acted at Port Royal in 1606 and was certainly the first theatrical performance in Canada. One of Lescarbot's poems, written in August 1606, may be another first — as Lescarbot

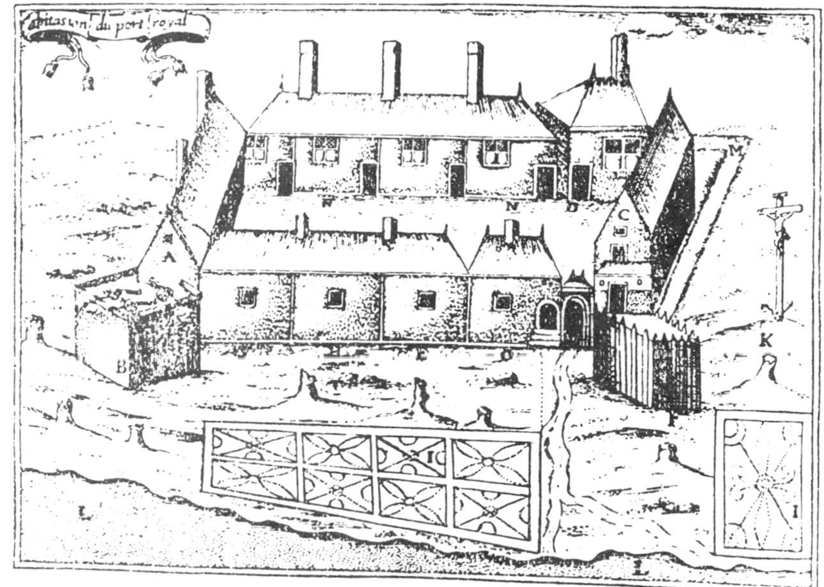

Port Royal, the first permanent white settlement in Canada, was founded in 1605 by the Sieur de Poutrincourt, and in its habitation *both Champlain and the poet Marc Lescarbot lived before it was destroyed by an English raid in 1613. Port Royal was rebuilt, and eventually, when Acadia changed hands at the Treaty of Utrecht in 1713, it was named Annapolis Royal after Queen Anne of England.*

wishes well to a shipload of friends returning to France, he already voices a familiar emigrant's lament.

> 'Tis you who go to see congenial friends
> In language, habits, customs and religion
> And all the lovely scenes of your own nation,
> While we among the savages are lost
> And dwell bewildered on this clammy coast
> Deprived of due content and pleasures bright
> Which you at once enjoy when France you sight.
>
> (translated by F. R. Scott)

From the beginning the English — and after the accession of James I the Scots as well — challenged the rights of the French in Acadia. In 1613 Samuel Argall led a force from Virginia which destroyed the French installations at Port Royal, and in 1621 King James I granted the area, under the name of Nova Scotia, to the Scot, Sir William Alexander who was allowed to establish an order of Baronets of Nova Scotia, most of whom had a financial interest in the colony. Alexander landed his first settlers in 1629, but his venture ended in 1632 when Charles I granted French sovereignty over Acadia. Afterwards it was said in London that "Alexander was a poet who tried to be a king;" he succeeded in neither.

The French settlers, the only people who ever called themselves Acadians, were able to dyke the marshlands in the Annapolis Valley and at various places around the Bay of Fundy and to create a simple peasant society, almost completely detached from the larger French colony centred around Quebec City and Montréal on the St. Lawrence. The Acadians were mostly unlettered and dominated by their priests but they

The New Englanders regarded as a perpetual threat the fortress of Louisbourg which the French began to build in 1713 on Cape Breton Island, and in 1745, with the help of the Royal Navy, they captured it. It was returned to France three years later, but was finally taken by British forces in 1758. This painting by J. Stevens shows the New Englanders landing to begin their assault in 1745.

became so modestly prosperous and contented with their abundant fields and large herds of cattle that they were later embalmed in literary works like Longfellow's *Evangeline* as the embodiments of an idealized pastoral existence.

It was certainly not in reality a very peaceful existence, for there were intermittent raids from New England like that which burnt the settlement of Grand Pré far up the Bay of Fundy early in the eighteenth century, destroying the dykes that protected the rich alluvial farmlands. Eventually, in 1713, at the end of Queen Anne's war, Acadia was ceded to the British. The terms of cession were a subject of further dispute, for the French interpreted Acadia to mean only the peninsula of Nova Scotia, not counting Cape Breton Island. To defend the Island they built the great fortress of Louisbourg, which was captured by the New Englanders in 1745, returned to France in 1748, and finally captured by the British in 1758 and destroyed, to be rebuilt in recent years as a national monument.

This condition of uncertainty militated against the Acadians, who tried to be neutral under British rule, neither resisting the conquerors nor swearing allegiance to the king of England. Eventually, in 1755, the British authorities decided to expel the Acadians from this strategically sensitive area. At this time there were about 15,000 of them. Colonel John Winslow was in charge of the operation, and the entry he made in his journal for October 8, 1755, betrays in the very confusion of his prose

After the Acadians were expelled from Nova Scotia in the 1750s, many of them returned to the region, and they settled especially in what became the northern part of New Brunswick, on the shores of the Gulf of St. Lawrence, in villages like this at the mouth of the Miramichi.

the reluctance with which he supervised the uprooting of these harmless peasants, whose only desire was to live untroubled by men of power.

> October 8th. Began to Embarke the Inhabitants who went of Very Solentarily and unwillingly, the women in Great Distress Carrying off their children in their arms. Others carrying their Decript Parents in their Carts and all their Goods Moving in great Confusion & appeard a Scene of Woe & Diestress.

Winslow had received orders not to parley with the Acadians and to allow no delays, and, though he "Did not Love to use Harsh Means," he had at one point to order his troops "to fix their Bayonets & advance towards the French." It was, he concluded, a "Troublesome Jobb" and a "scheen of Sorrow."

Some of the Acadians joined the French in Louisiana. Others were sent to New England where they pioneered the large French-Canadian community in the State of Maine. A few went to Ile St. Jean or settled in the remote woodlands of New Brunswick. Many of those who went into New England found the English-speaking world they entered uncongenial, and returned as soon as they could, to find their lands at Port Royal appropriated by later settlers. They moved into the northern part of what was eventually New Brunswick, and these were the people of whom Longfellow wrote at the end of *Evangeline:*

After Sir John A. Macdonald's death in 1891, the Conservative party fell into disarrray, and after a series of aged, moribund or incompetent Prime Ministers, it lost power to Laurier's Liberals in 1896. The patient organization of the Nova Scotian lawyer, **Robert Borden,** enabled the party to take advantage of the unpopularity of Laurier's proposals of an agreement with the United States for the reciprocal reduction of tariffs, and the Tories under Borden were returned to power in 1911. Borden continued as Prime Minister through the Great War, leading a National government from 1917 until, in 1920, he retired. His political importance lay in his insistence, at every stage in the war, on Canada's presence as an independent nation, so that eventually Canada participated equally with the other powers in the Versailles conference which determined the peace treaty, and entered the League of Nations as a fully acknowledged member.

Only along the shore of the mournful and misty Atlantic
Linger a few Acadian peasants, whose fathers from exile
Wandered back to their native land to die in its bosom.
In the fisherman's cot the wheel and the loom are still busy;
Maidens still wear their Norman caps and their kirtles of homespun,
And by the evening fire repeat Evangeline's story,
While from its rocky caverns the deep-voiced neighbouring ocean
Speaks and in accents disconsolate answers the wail of the forest.

These returning Acadians lived as farmers and fishermen and loggers, and more recently as industrial workers. They increased from a few thousand until there are now 350,000 people of French descent in the Maritime provinces.

These French-speakers constitute a fifth of the population in the Atlantic region and more than forty-five per cent of the population of New Brunswick. Some are immigrants from Québec, but most are Acadians and regard themselves as a separate people with their own traditions, their own dialect, their own political interests. While in recent years they have become conscious of their strength in numbers and have demanded a far greater share of political power, more educational opportunity in their own language, and more cultural autonomy than in the past, the Acadians of New Brunswick and Prince Edward Island have shown very little interest in joining whatever future the more sophisticated and wealthier people of Québec may make for themselves. The pride that makes them wish to shape their own destiny resists absorption into the more dominant French culture of Canada as much as absorption into the English culture.

Acadia became Nova Scotia in 1713, but it was many years before there was any appreciable English-speaking settlement. The Acadians retained until 1755 the most fertile lands of the region. Raiders from Canada, with their allies among the Abenaki, Micmac, and Malecite Indians, kept the tiny British garrisons close to their posts and discouraged any new settlers. The New Englanders penetrated the region as traders, and most of the commerce of the Acadians was in their hands; they also established in 1720 a precarious fishing post at Canso on the westernmost tip of the Nova Scotian mainland.

But it was only after the first capture of Louisbourg in 1745 that the British government seriously began to consider the settlement of the region. In 1749, mainly for the strategic value of its harbour, Halifax was established, and by 1753 there were 3,000 inhabitants, including about 1,000 Irish. The hostility of the Micmac made settlement in the vicinity difficult, and by 1755 the population of Halifax had shrunk to about 1,500 people, mainly engaged in looking after the needs of the garrison, the naval depot, and the colonial government. The first serious settlement was in fact made by representatives of what is now the third most

The painter William G.R. Hind lived the latter part of his life in the Maritimes; in 1870 he painted a fleet of sailing ships at Pointe du Chêne near Shediac, New Brunswick. Shediac, noted for its oysters, was also, in the eighteenth and nineteenth centuries, a great export centre for New Brunswick lumber.

Executed in 1750, the year after the foundation of Halifax, this map of part of Nova Scotia by T. Jeffrys shows not only the situation of Halifax on its harbour, but also a plan and a view of the new town.

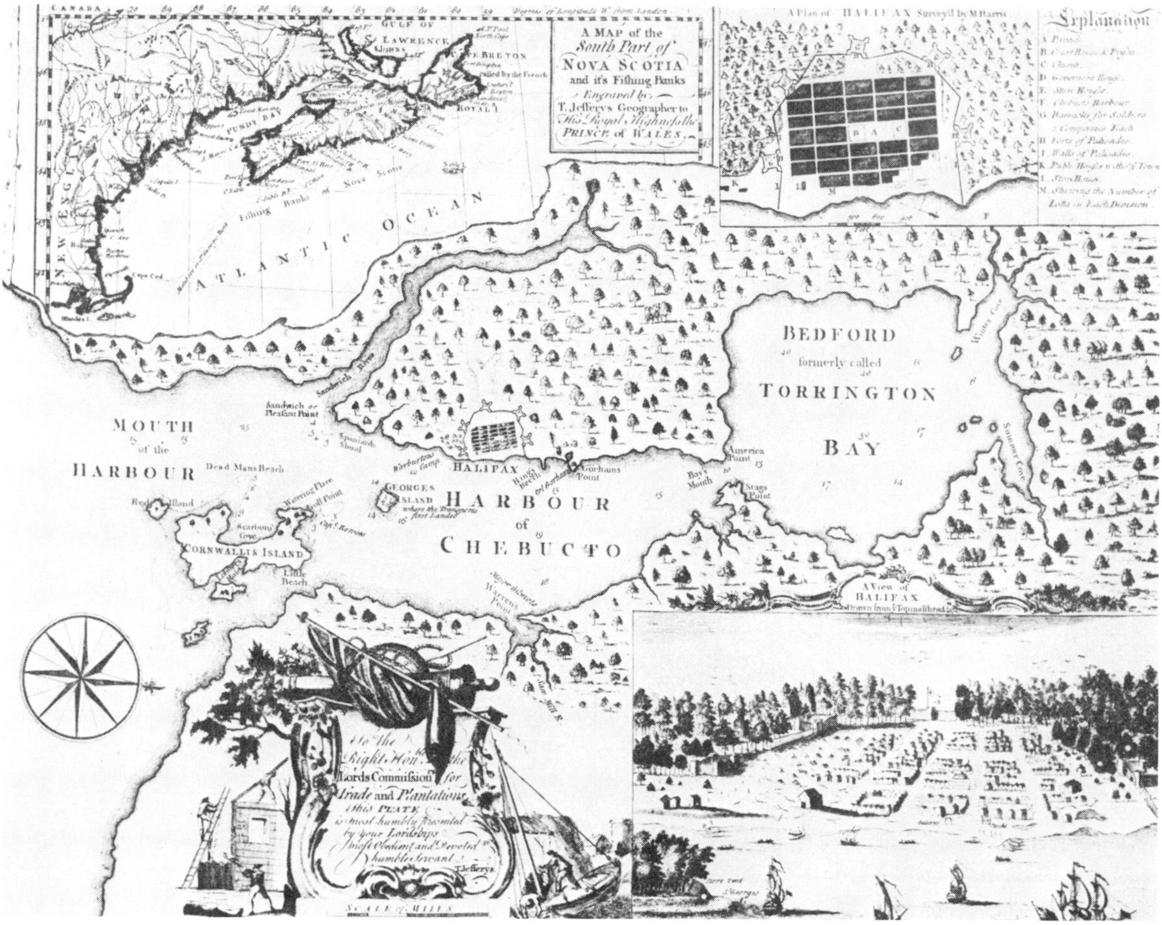

By the time the naval topographer Richard Short made this drawing, probably in 1759, Halifax was already an established town. The drawing shows St. Matthew's Church to the left, St. Paul's to the right, with the Governor's House in the centre and Fort George in the far background.

important ethnic group in Canada, those of Germanic descent. In 1753 some 1,600 Hanoverian immigrants (usually described as "Palatines") established the settlement of Lunenburg, where until very recent years German was spoken and German peasant customs and folk beliefs dominated farming methods (the Lunenbergers sowed their seed according to the phases of the moon) and the curing of sickness. To this day they are among the best builders of wooden ships in the Maritimes.

A few years later, after the expulsion of the Acadians and the destruction of French power in North America between 1758 and 1760, the first major wave of immigration began. It was almost entirely American in origin, consisting of about 7,000 New England farmers who took over the rich lands around the Bay of Fundy vacated by the Acadians; and traders who moved into Halifax to become the dominant mercantile element, balancing the British official element. These migrants who came before 1776 were not Loyalists; their sympathies inclined towards the Americans who wished to separate from Britain, but the stand they took during the revolutionary war resembled that of the Acadians — the watchful neutrality of those who would fight if necessary to keep their lands, but who were not anxious to commit themselves prematurely to the British crown.

From the British point of view, Nova Scotia at this period was a doubtful asset, costly and of not much obvious use now that the French had been driven from Québec. Edmund Burke in 1780, speaking in the

Like refugees in all times and places, the Loyalists who fled from the United States to the part of Nova Scotia which in 1791 became New Brunswick had to live at first in makeshift encampments. On the 6th of June 1784 the English army map-maker James Peachey painted this sketch of such a camp at Johnston on the banks of the St. Lawrence.

By 1869, the city of St. John, here viewed from the Suspension Bridge, was already adding the smoking chimneys of industry to the tall masts of its harbourscape.

House of Commons in Westminster, devoted to the colony some of his characteristically bitter eloquence.

> What sums the nursing of this ill-thriven, hard-visaged and ill-favoured brat, has cost this wittol nation? Sir, this colony has stood us in a sum of not less than seven thousand pounds. To this day it has made no repayment. It does not even support those offices of expenses, which are miscalled its government; the whole of that job still lies upon the patient, callous shoulders of the people of England.

When the American War of Independence ended in 1783, a new wave of immigrants came, American and mainly Anglo-Saxon — though they included some Dutch from New York and some Germans from Pennsylvania — and deeply committed to the imperial allegiance, which made them resentful of the earlier settlers whose loyalty they suspected. They moved into every area of the former Acadia. They doubled the popula-

Among the great shipping lines that plied the St. Lawrence, passing along the northern shores of the Maritime provinces, was the Allan Royal Mail Line, founded by Sir Hugh Allan in 1856, the year after he obtained the government mail contract. Based in Montréal, the Allan Line provided the main competition for the shipping enterprises of Samuel Cunard.

In the winter of 1861 the English and the Newfoundland mail vessels make their way into the harbour of Halifax through a channel in the ice.

tion of the peninsula we now call Nova Scotia, and of Ile St. Jean, which was soon renamed Prince Edward Island in honour of the Duke of Kent, Queen Victoria's father, who was at Halifax in the 1790s as commander-in-chief of the British forces in North America. Fourteen thousand Loyalists settled north of the Bay of Fundy, and their antagonism to the pre-Loyalist merchants who controlled the Assembly in Halifax was so strong that a separate province had to be carved out for them. In 1784 New Brunswick was founded with a population ninety per cent Loyalist. At the same time, Cape Breton Island was made a separate province, though its life was a short one, since it was reunited with Nova Scotia in 1820.

Many of the original Loyalist migrants were officials and even aristocratic landowners, but most of these eventually found their way to Britain. A number of Loyalist regiments were settled on the St. John River, and the remainder of the immigration consisted mainly of tradesmen, artisans, and farmers. The tradesmen became merchants in newly established towns like Saint John and St. Andrews, and the artisans helped to create the shipbuilding industry, utilising local timber, for which the Maritime provinces became celebrated in the early nineteenth century.

This industry was closely linked on the one hand to the logging industry, which received a great impetus during the Napoleonic Wars, when supplies of timber and especially of masts became unobtainable from the Baltic and Britain had to rely on North America for the very materials needed to maintain its navy. On the other hand, it encouraged fishing ("Nova Scotia is a peninsula entirely surrounded by fish,"

quipped an early travel writer) through the local manufacture of boats. Even more important, it created an international shipping industry. The building of ships was carried on in dozens of seacoast towns and even villages and eventually reached such proportions that during 1865 no less than 650 wooden ships were launched from the slipways of Nova Scotia, New Brunswick, and Prince Edward Island. But the Maritimers were shipowners as well as shipbuilders. In the year of Confederation Nova Scotians alone owned 350,000 tons of shipping, and this meant a good many ships when the *Marco Polo* (which went under sail from Britain to Australia in sixty-eight days) was considered a large vessel at 1,625 tons and the famous *Mary Celeste* was only 198 tons.

Samuel Cunard was a successful Halifax merchant and one of the founders of the Halifax Banking Company before he went into shipping on a large scale, and made his fame and fortune. Founding the British and North American Royal Mail Steam Packet Company in 1838, he was the pioneer in regular transatlantic steamship services and changed the character of passenger travel. Under his successors, the Cunard liners carried on their regular crossings of the Atlantic until the classic ocean liner became an extinct species in the 1960s.

The fast clippers constructed in Nova Scotia and New Brunswick, some of the most handsome and most efficient sailing craft ever built, plied to the West Indies and across the Atlantic and around the world, giving Halifax and Saint John and even smaller ports like Liverpool and Yarmouth their periods as active centres of trade with many countries. At least one great oceanic line was built on these foundations, for the Halifax merchant Samuel Cunard founded in 1838 the British and North American Royal Mail Steam Packet Company, which became known as the Cunard Line, sailing originally between Halifax and London.

The coming of the Loyalists and the prosperity created by the Napoleonic Wars established the basic patterns of Maritime life. A few immigrants had come directly from Britain in the 1770s — Scots and Yorkshiremen who settled in the northern part of Nova Scotia. One of the latter, Luke Harrison, wrote home desparingly in 1774:

> We do not like the country, nor never shall. The mosquitoes are a terrible plague in this country. You may think that mosquitos cannot hurt, but if you do you are mistaken, for they will swell your legs and hands so that some persons are both blind and lame for some days. They grow worse every year and they bite the English the worst.

But it was not until 1814, when Highland crofters expelled from their own lands to make way for sheep farming began to arrive on Cape Breton Island, that the movement of people commenced which gave Nova Scotia the Scottish flavour its name demanded. They settled on Cape Breton, where Gaelic (which still survives) was for generations the prevalent language, and along the shores of the Gulf of St. Lawrence. The Highlanders, who came in whole villages and clans, and settled close together, were more noticeable than the thousands of Lowland Scots who came individually and in families and merged into the population. A much smaller but notable migration was that of blacks from the United States, some of whom arrived with the Loyalists, while in later years others were smuggled into Nova Scotia on the legendary Underground Railroad; they have formed ever since a distinct element in the population of Halifax, more economically deprived than almost all of their white

The Maritimes-built Burnt Barnes, *photographed in 1922, was the last Canadian cargo sailing ship to operate on the Great Lakes.*

neighbours. "We came," one of these black pioneers recorded, "like terrapins, all we had on our backs."

By the time of Confederation the Atlantic provinces had reached what Maritimers are now inclined to look back on as their Golden Age, a time of economic self-sufficiency and comparative prosperity. Prince Edward Island, it is true, was only just struggling out of a retarded past. Jacques Cartier had seen it in the sixteenth century as a tiny natural paradise that "needed only the nightingale," but its agricultural potential had been neglected by the French, and under the British it had been given over to a small group of absentee landlords who made no attempt to promote settlement. When settlement did begin, it was often poorly planned, and the people who settled it had inadequate resources. Richard Cobden in the mid-nineteenth century talked of the Glasgow Scots who were emigrating: "Those that are poor, and cannot pay their passage, or can rake together only a trifle, are going to a rascally heap of sand, rock and swamp, called Prince Edward Island, in the horrible Gulf of St. Lawrence." Cobden, of course, had never seen the fertile red earth of Prince Edward Island, which became (and remained) a mainly agricultural province. Good fisheries were also developed along the northern shore where the local Acadians were mainly settled on bays with names like Malpeque and Tracadie.

Nova Scotia was principally dependent on fishing, shipping, and shipbuilding; farming tended, because of the broken nature of the land, to be small-scale, and many Nova Scotians divided the year between occupations like fishing, farming, and seagoing, just as the New Brunswickers were inclined to combine farming or fishing with lumbering in the rich interior forests from which timber was floated down the wide and navigable rivers. The New Brunswick forests attracted men from the other Maritime provinces in search of seasonal work, like Peter Amberley of Prince Edward Island whose sad fate was celebrated in a well-known song of the woods.

> I landed in New Brunswick
> That lumbering countree;
> I hired to work in the lumbering woods
> Down south of the Miramichi.
> I hired to work in the lumbering woods
> To cut the tall spruce down;
> While loading teams with yarded logs
> I received my deathly wound.

There was little industry other than shipbuilding in the region, but coal mining on Cape Breton had already begun by the time of Confederation.

Both the Nova Scotians and the New Brunswickers had been interested originally in the idea of a Maritime federation, to discuss which they had gathered with the representatives of Newfoundland and Prince

The Bluenose, *a 130 feet schooner launched at Lunenburg in 1921, was the last of the great Nova Scotian clippers. After winning many races, the original* Bluenose *was wrecked off Haiti in 1946. A replica,* Bluenose II, *was built by Oland's Brewery in 1963 and presented to the province of* Nova Scotia.

Edward Island at the Charlottetown conference which Sir John A. Macdonald and his associates turned in another direction. The Atlantic region had in fact been ahead of the other parts of what became Canada in terms of political development. Nova Scotia was granted an elected assembly as early as 1759, and achieved responsible government in 1847, as a result of agitations led by the brilliant journalist and poet Joseph Howe. Howe was the centre of the considerable intellectual renaissance in the Maritimes between the late 1820s and the early 1850s, which was represented in learning by the great activity at newly founded educational institutions like Pictou Academy and Dalhousie University, and in literature by works that have become Canadian classics, like Howe's own *Rambles* and his poems, Thomas Chandler Haliburton's *The Clockmaker; or the Sayings and Doings of Sam Slick, of Slickville,* and Thomas McCulloch's *Letters of Mephibosheth Stepsure,* both of which were fictional satire on Nova Scotian life, published first in serial form in lively local newspapers like *The Acadian Recorder* and Howe's own *Nova Scotian.*

If Nova Scotia was a pioneer colony in the achievement of responsible government, which it gained in 1848, the year before Canada, this was largely due to the dedication of **Joseph Howe,** a Halifax printer and poet who moved into publishing. In 1828 Howe founded the *Nova Scotian,* in which he set himself up as a popular tribune, critizing public men and revealing political abuses. He became a popular hero in 1835 when he published an article attacking injustices by Halifax magistrates and was prosecuted for criminal libel. Howe brilliantly carried out his own defence, was acquitted and carried home in triumph. The next year, 1836, he was elected to the Nova Scotian assembly and carried on a running battle with the British-appointed officials until, in 1848, he became Provincial Secretary and shaper of policies in the first Reform government. Having early recognized the need for the union of British North America, Howe opposed Confederation in the form it took in 1867, but in the end he accepted the situation, entered the Dominion cabinet, and died in 1873, three weeks after being appointed Lieutenant-Governor of Nova Scotia.

At the Québec conference of 1865 the New Brunswick and Nova Scotian leaders agreed to Confederation and went home to find that Maritime distrust for the peoples of the two Canadas had flared up. Acadians and Irish Catholics in particular were fearful that their interests would be imperilled, and the Nova Scotians in general felt that their precious ties with Britain might be weakened. Only unwillingly, in the end, did the Maritimes enter Confederation, and the inhabitants have been doubtful ever since of the wisdom of their choice.

The circumstances that led to the stagnation of the Maritimes in comparison with the rest of Canada were not, however, entirely political. The best timber was quickly taken from the forests of New Brunswick and lumbering declined. The growing ascendancy of steam navigation and the use of iron and steel in the construction of ships, killed both the shipbuilding and the shipping industries of Nova Scotia. The completion in 1870 of the Intercolonial Railway to link Nova Scotia with Québec meant that the coal mines of Cape Breton could be developed, and a steel industry established, but this did not compensate for the decline of earlier industries or for the great drain of active young people from the Maritimes that began shortly after Confederation and has not ended. Canada in general benefitted from this youth drain, for Maritimers have been prominent out of all proportion to their numbers in politics and education, in the arts and sciences, in finance and business; and the variety of their achievements, which might be pinpointed by a series of names like Lord Beaverbrook, R. B. Bennett, and Sir Robert Borden among twentieth-century Canadian prime ministers; Bonar Law who became Prime Minister of England; novelists Hugh MacLennan and Lucy Maud Montgomery; painters like Robert Harris and Alex Colville; and poets like Charles G. D. Roberts and — in our own day — Alden Nowlan, and Elizabeth Brewster.

The result of the slower pace of growth and change is that life in the Maritimes is perceptibly different from that in the rest of Canada. Kildare Dobbs has remarked that the Maritime provinces "belong essentially to the Old World. The things that surprise, enchant, and sometimes distress North American travellers in Europe are also to be found here: craftsmanship, tradition, cheerful poverty." Hugh MacLennan remarked that the St. John valley of New Brunswick "makes you think of the growing years of eastern America before the pressures developed." In terms of impression both Dobbs and MacLennan are correct, though I wonder how "cheerful" poverty is any longer in these provinces. Yet in historical terms what one sees in Nova Scotia and New Brunswick and Prince Edward Island is really a glimpse of pre-mechanical Canada, the Canada of beautifully carpentered Victorian houses, of small mixed farms, of fishing with little boats, of covered wooden bridges, and, above all, of a slowness of tempo and a smallness of scale one does not find elsewhere in the country.

As in Upper Canada, much of the settlement in the Maritimes was carried out through land companies which acquired large tracts. The settlement of Stanley, sketched by P. Harry in August 1835, was built on the tract purchased by the New Brunswick and Nova Scotia Land Company in 1833.

Maritimers themselves are conscious of the smallness of the world in which they move, and they see this linked to the poverty which has characterized the region except for its long-past boom period during the great age of sailing ships. But both smallness and poverty, in a strange paradoxical way, are associated in their minds with the power to recognize opportunities, to profit by them, and hence to acquire magnitude. "You don't need a big field to raise a big turnip," said Joseph Howe, thinking of Nova Scotia, and on another occasion he remarked that, "Nova Scotia is an excellent poor man's country, because almost every man, in any walk of industry, by perseverence and economy can secure the comforts of life." Root vegetables — the potato as well as the turnip — play a great part in the metaphorical language with which Maritimers describe themselves and their way of life. A New Brunswick song celebrating hard times included the lines:

> How are your potatoes?
> Very small.
> How do you eat them?
> Skins and all!

And Thomas Chandler Haliburton used the origin of the nickname Blue Nose to say something about potatoes and Nova Scotians alike.

> The Nova Scotian is the gentleman known throughout America as Mr. Blue Nose, a *sobriquet* acquired from a superior potato of that

'New Brunswick Fashionables!!! Fredericton, Jany., 1834.' This print, "drawn on stone by J.W. Giles . . . from the original sketch made on the spot", not merely gives a comic and comprehensive view of winter transport in the Maritimes, it also shows Fredericton fifty years after its foundation, with the main street running down to the river. The Old Market House in the left foreground illustrates the anomalies of contemporary society; the upper half was used as a temperance hall and the lower half as a saloon.

> name, for the good qualities of which he is never tired of talking, being anxious, like most men of small property, to exhibit to the best advantage the little he has.

As all I have just said makes clear, the Maritimer makes a show of modesty, but only to mask a great pride, concealed in the notion that he can always make a great deal out of nothing. This gives him a somewhat superior, ironical view of life, and hence inclines him to acerbic forms of writing. No part of Canada has produced more good satire than Nova Scotia, and it is not merely a matter of English-speaking writers like Haliburton, McCulloch, and their successors; the Maritime viewpoint exists among the French-speaking Acadians as well, and finds lively expression in the vernacular plays of the contemporary writer, Antonine Maillet, whose monologue, *La Sagouine (The Slattern),* consists of a disreputable charlady's wry and scandalous observations of the rich and the powerful.

Maritimers, in general, work longer hours and more years — when they are employed — than other Canadians, but they work and live with less frenzy. They have always been inclined to gather in a multitude of small communities, their area dictated often by the size of a harbour or a river mouth, rather than in large towns, and the only major city in the whole area is Halifax. Charlottetown and Fredericton, the capitals of Prince Edward Island and New Brunswick respectively, are more like English market towns than central or western Canadian cities, though Fredericton has a long history of literary creativity and intellectual

Mercenaries recruited by Howe in the United States in 1855, to support the exhausted British troops at Sebastopol in the Crimea, were quartered in these barracks on Melville Island. Although condemned later, by both the United States Attorney-General and by Gladstone, Howe's action was born of a passionate conviction that the mother country should be able to rely on colonial support in any emergency.

fervour, associated especially with the first truly indigenous Canadian literary movement, that centred around the Confederation poets, including Charles G. D. Roberts and Bliss Carman, who were Maritimers drawing their inspiration largely from their native landscape, interpreted in celebrated poems like Robert's "Tantramar Revisited" and Carman's "Low Tide at Grand Pré." Roberts, and the best Maritime poets who have followed him, like Alfred Bailey and Alden Nowlan, succeed in conveying the contrasting starkness and brilliance of the Maritime world, and the sweep of grandeur that often combines — in Canadian terms at least — with the smallness of scale I have talked of.

Literature had, of course, existed earlier in the Maritimes, and it tended from the beginning to express the intellectual life of the developing regional societies and their growing individualization. Oliver Goldsmith's poem, "The Rising Village," celebrated the efforts of the Loyalists to build a new life for themselves in the woods of New Brunswick. In such satirical sketches as Thomas Chandler Haliburton's *The Clockmaker* and Thomas McCulloch's *The Letters of Mephibosheth Stepsure,* pre-Confederation Nova Scotian writers portrayed the faults of colonial societies, and sketched out the degrees of hypocrisy that emerged among people who cultivated religious enthusiasms without having the moral fortitude to apply them consistently or even charitably. The heavy hand of Calvinism in certain parts of the Maritimes, and particularly in Nova Scotia, was a prominent theme in the early novels of Hugh MacLennan, perhaps the most important prose writer to emerge from the region. In *Each Man's Son,* the story of a Cape Breton miner

When the Canadian delegates arrived at Charlottetown to persuade the Maritimers that there were virtues in the idea of a Confederation of all the North American colonies, they found no welcoming delegation awaiting them. A single official, the Prince Edward Island Colonial Secretary Edward Pope, was concerned enough to commandeer an oyster boat which he himself rowed out to their vessel to take them ashore. The modern painter Rex Woods has imaginatively envisaged the scene.

who turns prize fighter and returns from his wanderings to murder his wife and her lover, MacLennan shows in mordant terms the stultifying operation of the Presbyterian conscience among the miners and fishermen of Highland descent. In *Barometer Rising* he paints a remarkable portrait of Halifax as a working urban society at the flash point of the great explosion of 1917, a portrait somewhat less romantic than the picture of an earlier Halifax which the historical novelist Thomas H. Raddall had presented in books like *The Governor's Lady*.

More than any poet before him Charles G. D. Roberts saw the landscape of New Brunswick with an extraordinary clarity of vision, and wrote the first Canadian rural poetry that was based on true perception rather than romantic convention. "Tantramar Revisited" is doubtless his best work, and one of the great Canadian poems, but it is in some of his shorter pieces, like the sonnets in *Songs of a Common Day,* that one finds the landscape of New Brunswick treated with the same powerful directness as Hardy treated the landscape of England.

Winds here, and sleet, and frost that bites like steel.
    The low bleak hill rounds under the low sky.
    Naked of flock and fold the fallows lie,
Thin streaked with meagre drift. The gusts reveal

The House of Assembly Library in Province House, Halifax. During his years as Premier, Howe's undiminished energy carried him through many a "laborious session" in the House, when, as he records in his diary he "often sat to 8 or 9 with no food but a few figs and crackers and a glass of water".

By fits the dim grey snakes of fence, that steal
Through the white dusk. The hill-top poplars sigh,
While storm and death with winter trample by,
And the iron fields ring sharp, and blind lights reel.
("The Winter Fields")

It is not only a smallness of scale that I am writing of. It is also a different style of living from the conspicuous affluence of some other Canadian regions. Large cars are rare, people do not worry greatly about this year's or even last year's fashions, houses are small, and even the farms often too modest and rocky for modern equipment to be feasible. Incomes are commensurate in scale with everything else. They average about two-thirds of the incomes of the rest of Canada, and even much of that reaches the region through equalization payments from the federal government: handouts which the Maritimers resent even when they have to accept them, since they believe almost without a dissenting voice that if they had not entrusted so much of their future to Canada they might have been more able than a distant and uncaring government in Ottawa to avert the decline of their economy.

At the same time, there are richnesses in Maritime life that are not evident from a distance or even to the unperceptive visitor. A great deal of

William Maxwell Aitken, who eventually achieved his own kind of fame as **Lord Beaverbrook,** was an outstanding example of the young men who found the post-Confederation Maritimes too small for their abilities and departed to make their careers elsewhere. At the age of 31 he retired from business, and went to England to become private secretary to another Maritimer, Andrew Bonar Law. Playing at politics in Britain, and becoming Minister of Information in 1918, Aitken was given a peerage when he was 37. He chose his title from the Acadian hamlet of Beaver Brook Station. Then he went on to a career as one of the leading newspaper magnates in Britain, and wielded immense power in Britain, particularly during World War II.

the heritage of the Old World has indeed survived, as it did in Newfoundland, in the form of archaic English and French dialects, and of folk songs and stories in English, Gaelic, Acadian French, and even, at Lunenburg, in German, that have lingered from the eighteenth century. Education is respected in the Maritimes, rather as it is in Scotland, there are good schools and colleges, many remarkable writers and painters have remained to work there, and in recent years an active local theatrical movement has developed in Halifax.

But perhaps what strike one most about the Maritimes as a visitor, apart from the sheer visual charm of the riverside towns along the St. John and Miramichi rivers, and the old coastal communities of the Nova Scotian peninsula with their dreaming memories of the vanished fleets of white-sailed clippers, are the individualisms of lifestyle and life view that are expressed in many ways and most noticeably in the intricate religious divisions between Maritimers, often based on abstruse theological divergences. Even a small Nova Scotian village will often have four wooden churches of as many denominations, raising their miniature spires above the modest houses. The local, the individual, the intimate: communities small enough for everyone to know or at least recognize everyone else: communities as small as those of ancient Greece in a country that often, with its rocks and sea, looks remarkably like parts of Hellas. And perhaps there is not only a touch of Athenian austerity about the daily life of the Maritimers, but also a measure of Attic astringency in the realism that has emerged from it and inspired the many remarkable Canadians who were born beside these sparkling waters or in the inland hills that in the autumn blaze with translucent colour, and about which Lady Dufferin, that indefatigable traveller and describer, enthused to a stay-at-home English peeress:

> . . . our *trees* are quite as brilliant as your best flowers, and if you can imagine your conservatory magnified a million times, and spread over miles and miles of hill and dale, you will begin to understand how we do things in this Canada of ours.

Winter Sun, A.J. Casson

Behind Bonsecours Market, Montreal, William Raphael

Heina, Emily Carr

CHAPTER SIX

Québec
Remembrance of Time Past

For generations and centuries the first land that travellers and immigrants saw, coming to Canada by sea, was Québec — the wide expanse of the Gulf of St. Lawrence, and then the great river slowly narrowing inwards, until they could see on the two shores between which they sailed the farms running down to the river; long, and so narrow that the houses stood quite close together on their road frontages, and, as visitors remarked as early as the eighteenth century, the settlements seemed like a single village, many miles long. Every few miles the monotonous succession of farmhouses would be broken by the glittering spires and steep eaves of a tin-roofed church around which a few houses clustered to form the village nucleus; and the church would always seem gigantic in proportion to any other building in the vicinity.

Such an entry into Canada was a way of plunging deep into the country's past, for it was along the St. Lawrence that the first complete society — even if a miniature one in terms of population — appeared in Canada. Acadia had provided a simple peasant life; Newfoundland remained until the nineteenth century a haunt of transient fishermen and primitive settlers with the most rudimentary political organization. But Québec in the late seventeenth century, with its government modelled on those of the provinces of Old France, with its powerful established church, with its merchants and industries centred around the growing little towns of Quebec City and Trois Rivières and Montréal, was a complete small world of its own whose people were highly conscious of their special character. From a very early period they called themselves "Canadians", as distinct from Frenchmen, and the Baron de Lahontan, who visited the colony in 1683, remarked on the sturdiness, vigour, bravery, and illiteracy of the *habitants* he encountered. He added, "they are presumptuous and full of themselves, putting themselves ahead of all the nations of the earth."

Undoubtedly the independence of these original Canadians was largely due to the fact that the kind of feudal oppressions which peasants suffered in Old France, and which helped to produce the furies of the French Revolution, did not survive transplantation. It is true that early in the seventeenth century a seignurial system was created in Québec which in a rather attenuated form lasted until the mid-nineteenth century. The

The first Jesuits arrived in New France in 1633, and under the patronage of Bishop Laval they grew powerful so that they not only carried out arduous mission duties that often ended in martyrdom, but also owned considerable properties, like the Jesuit College and Church in Québec City, of which this is an early eighteenth century view.

seigneurs, often men of quite humble origin, were ranked as belonging to the *petit noblesse;* apart from being able to exact quit rents from the settlers or *habitants* on their estates and being allowed a monopoly of flour milling, they could exact a few days of work a year, while the state itself could impose *corvées* for public duties such as road building, as well as obligatory service in the militia. But these demands rarely became oppressive and attempts to keep the *habitants* tied to their land in the European feudal manner were unsuccessful because a man could always escape to the great wild hinterland of the *pays d'en haut* and share in the free life of the *coureurs de bois.*

The close settlement of the St. Lawrence valley did not begin for some time after the establishment of Quebec City by Champlain in 1608. The officials and soldiers and fur traders established themselves first, and then, borne on the wave of enthusiasm created by the Counter Reformation, came the priests seeking converts. First, in 1615, came the *Recollets* — a reformed order of Franciscan friars; and then in 1625 the Jesuits. Finally in 1659 arrived the formidable Bishop Laval, who established himself as equal in power and prestige to the great state officers of the colony — the governor and the *intendant* — and who gave a powerful institutional status to the Church in Québec, a status that survived the British conquest and continued to influence public events in Québec until the "Quiet Revolution" of the 1960s removed the Church as the dominant influence it had been in the life of the province for three centuries. During the seventeenth century priests and monks, friars and nuns flocked to New France, and formed such an important part of its early population that in 1665 no less than 150 out of 500 people in Quebec City were members of religious communities.

At first, conversion of the Indians was the main task of this numerous priesthood. The Jesuits showed great enterprise in establishing communities of converted Indians, like those among the Hurons, and great courage when, like Jean de Brébeuf, they were tortured and killed by the Iroquois. It was not until 1627 that settlement was seriously begun, over the protests of the fur-trading interests, and even then there was an interruption when Quebec City was captured in 1629 by British privateers led by David Kirke. The year 1633, the date of Champlain's return, can be taken as the real beginning of the peasant society so deeply associated in Canadian minds with the people of Québec.

It was then that towns first began to appear along the river — Trois Rivières in 1634 and Montréal in 1642. The estates granted to the *seigneurs* began to fill out as the slow trickle of settlers crossed the Atlantic. When the first census was taken in 1666 there were still only 3,215 people who could be numbered in the whole colony (though there must have been many *coureurs de bois* who escaped the count), and there was a notable disproportion between the sexes until 1,100 peasant girls, called *les filles du roi,* were recruited and sent over to marry the early *habitants.* During the whole century and a half between the foundation of Quebec City and its surrender to the British, it is estimated that no more than 10,000 people actually emigrated from New France, in comparison with the much larger number of immigrants to the British colonies on the Atlantic coast; it was a healthy rate of reproduction that was the main reason why the population of Québec had reached about 65,000 by 1760.

Ethnically and in religious terms it was a very homogenous population. Richelieu had decreed the exclusion of Protestants in 1628, and Europeans other than the French were not allowed to enter New France, so that the greater part of the population were Bretons or Normans with a small amount of Indian blood in some of the families. Small industries sprang up in the towns (the most important were iron-founding and shipbuilding), and in the villages there were artisans who had brought with them peasant styles in woodwork, weaving, and pottery that gave rise to a very distinctive folk art which lasted long into the nineteenth century. Many of the early Canadians were also involved at some time or another of their lives in the fur trade; it has been estimated that during the seventeenth and eighteenth centuries no less than 15,000 men set out from Montréal into the *pays d'en haut.* Some stayed to be lifelong *voyageurs,* but most came back to take up the *habitant* life which in the early days was not greatly superior in terms of comfort or security to that of Indian peoples like the Iroquois who had developed a fairly productive type of agriculture and who lived in settled villages for large parts of the year. The early *habitant,* like the Indian, was mainly a subsistence

In 1659 **Francois-Xavier Laval-Montmorency** arrived in New France as Bishop of Québec. In 1708 he died in the Québec seminary, though ill-health had forced him to give up his see twenty years before. During the three decades of his incumbency, **Bishop Laval** established the dominant role that the Church was to play in Québec until the Quiet Revolution of the 1960s. He was a member of the Sovereign Council of New France, where he wielded an influence equal to that of the Governor and the Intendant. His power was largely due to the strong connections he maintained with the French Court. Governors who followed policies of which he disapproved were liable to be recalled; this even happened to the formidable Frontenac. He was autocratic and aggressive where the political interests of the church were concerned, but he was also pious and compassionate to individuals, and he fought hard to end the iniquities of the liquor trade among the Indians. His faults and virtues were those of the feudal aristocrat. He was ready to grant that *noblesse oblige,* but first he expected his *noblesse* to be recognized.

The most famous of the Jesuit martyrs were Jean de Brébeuf and Gabriel Lalemant, tortured and killed by the Iroquois at St. Ignace in Huronia in 1649.

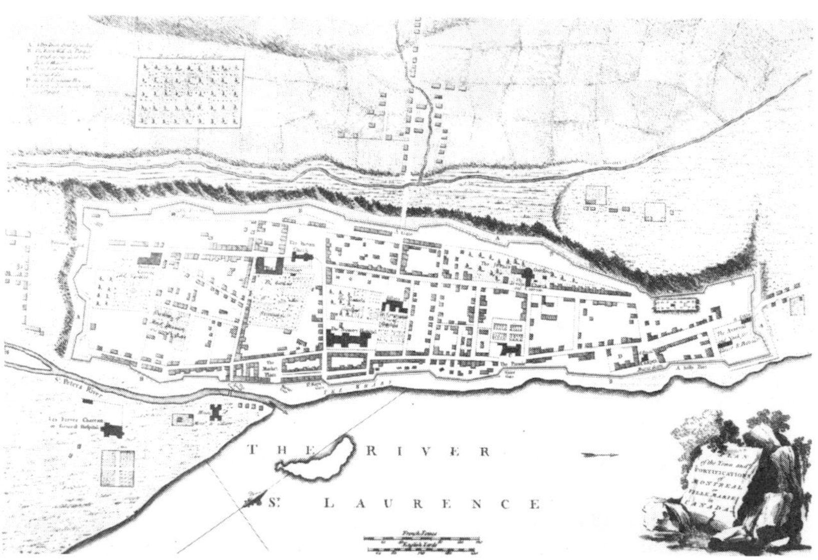

Prepared in 1758, on the eve of the British conquest of Québec, this map shows Montréal in the last days of New France, a city almost completely contained within its fortifications.

farmer; it was only towards the middle of the eighteenth century that wheat-growing was productive enough to provide a surplus for commerce. And, again like the Indian, he depended on hunting and fishing to supplement the produce of his fields, and also on wild vegetable products, of which the syrup and sugar of the maple tree are probably the best known.

Even as late as 1784 only one French Canadian out of five could read, and in general they were a people of simple beliefs and simple life, tenacious of tradition, doggedly Catholic, and, in spite of the good opinion they held of themselves, inclined to defer to the prestige of the parish priest, who became even more powerful as the authority of the *seigneurs* was weakened after the British conquest.

A nineteenth century artist, after consulting early manuscripts, drew this conjectural picture of the kind of French merchant who would be trading out of Breton ports to the New World in the sixteenth century.

It was a closed little society, with the wilderness pressing on it from all sides, and enemies on the frontiers; even links with Old France were tenuous, and all through the long winter Canadians, rather like traders in the Arctic before the days of air transport, had to wait for the spring thaw that brought the first ships sailing up the St. Lawrence with news and supplies and fresh faces. There was a touch of Jansenist puritanism about Québec Catholicism right from the beginning, as there was about English Canadian Protestantism with its strong Calvinist overtones, but this did not prevent the people of New France from living with an appearance of fecklessness that impressed visiting Europeans. French Canadians of all classes seemed willing to put down their work at any moment if pleasure offered itself: canoeing or *calèche*-riding in the summer, sleighing or skating in the winter, hunting and fishing and card-playing in all weathers. There were times, during the spring sugaring of the maple trees, when even work took on the aspect of a festival. The *canadien* responded to the call of enjoyment more easily than to any appeal to his industriousness; he was, as one early eighteenth-century visitor remarked, "naturally indocile."

The restrictions on immigration which made the population of French Canada homogenous also made it militarily vulnerable. In the long eighteenth-century struggle in North America between French and English, with Indians drawn in on either side, mere demographic facts ensured that those of English descent, of whom there were well over a million, should in the end — supported as they were by England's naval power which perpetually threatened communications between Québec and France — prevail over the French Canadians who never, up till 1760, numbered more than 65,000. It is true that the *canadiens* became very adept at the warfare of ambush and terror which the Indians had developed even before the white men came, but tactics that spread fear in the villages of New England were not sufficient to defy the regular troops and the ships of line that came in overpowering numbers from England.

Yet the very homogeneity that had made the *canadiens* so weak in a military sense made them strong in the fortitude that brings survival to

The 'Friendly Game of Cards', a typical mid-Victorian genre painting of habitant *life by one of the many imitators of Cornelius Krieghoff.*

individuals and to communities alike. It is true that at the moment of conquest the Québecois were completely at the mercy of the British; they might have been uprooted like the Acadians and their lands given to others. But once the conquerors had decided to leave them in occupation of their lands, and under General James Murray and the later military governors had framed a policy of non-interference in local affairs (retaining French civil law and seigneurial customs), the survival of the French culture in Québec was assured. Out of the sixty-odd thousand inhabitants of the St. Lawrence colony in 1760, only about one per cent decided to return to France, and these were either high officials who could expect to continue their careers in Europe or landless members of the *petit noblesse* who realized that there would no longer be the opportunities of adventure combined with profit which the endemic forest wars between the French and the British had offered. Most of the *seigneurs*, as well as all the *habitants* and the *voyageurs* occupied in the fur trade, remained. So did the small professional class of doctors and notaries and almost all the priests, whose role became even more important than in the past, since the Church was the only large institution that survived from the old regime.

In the early days of the colony, relations between the French and their British conquerors were reasonably open. The *seigneurs* and the more influential members of the priesthood gave their support to successive British governors, and formed part of the so-called Château Clique of English officials and wealthy French who ruled the province for many years. Many of the Highlanders of Murray's regiments married Québecois girls, and their descendants became submerged — all but their Scottish names — in the French-speaking population.

Henri Julien was a well-known cartoonist for the Montréal francophone press, but he also painted many studies of habitant *life which lacked Krieghoff's besetting sentimentality. 'Au Marché' is typical of this aspect of his work.*

Between 1757 and 1790 the British officer Thomas Davies performed four turns of duty in North America, and during this time he painted many vibrant water-colours of the Canadian landscape. 'View of the Bridge on Rivière La Puce' was painted in 1790.

This peasant house in Beaupré shows the solid construction and harmonious design of traditional rural buildings in Québec.

Bishop Ignace Bourget was one of the most controversial of Québec ecclesiastics. As Bishop of Montréal from 1840 to 1876 he established many charitable and educational institutions, but he also belonged to the ultramontanist right wing of the church, which he sought to purge of the radical liberalism represented by the Rouges.

It was with the arrival of merchants from New England and New York, as well as Britain, anxious to take over the trade of the St. Lawrence, that ethnic differences, compounded by religious ones, became acute. Accustomed to the democratic manners of the Atlantic colonies, the New Englanders demanded an elected assembly, but at the same time they wanted to retain the laws which then in Britain prevented Roman Catholics from holding office. This would have meant a tiny minority of English-speaking new residents governing the affairs of the French community, and the British government decided to avoid such a situation by creating no assembly until in 1791 the influx of Loyalists into the region around the Great Lakes made it necessary to divide the old province of Québec into the two Canadas — Upper and Lower. Each province was given an assembly. This merely emphasized ethnic differences, since it divided the colony into a predominantly English province and a predominantly French one, initiating the historic rivalry between Québec and Ontario. At the same time, within Lower Canada, it created an aggrieved English-speaking minority led by the wealthy merchants in the towns, and also, until the advent of responsible government in 1849, it pitted a mainly French-speaking assembly against a governor and council appointed from Britain and inclined to protect the English-dominated mercantile interests.

I have already sketched lightly in an earlier chapter some of the political history of Lower Canada, leading up to the tragic *Patriote* rebellion of 1837-38, and a more detailed account has no part in this essay, which is about people rather than politics. Even before these events took place there had been on the popular level a kind of instinctive gathering of forces among the French Canadians that resulted in the celebrated "victory of the cradle;" the extraordinary rate of population increase — encouraged by the Church — which led to the traditionally immense Québec families and the unparalleled growth in the French-speaking population of Canada. From about seventy thousand (including the Acadians) in 1760, it has grown to six million today, not counting the two million people of French Canadian descent now living in the United States, which means that in just over two centuries the French in Canada have multiplied their numbers more than a hundred times, a unique demographic phenomenon. Only in very recent years has the rate of natural increase in Québec fallen to a level similar to that of the rest of Canada.

Yet a mere increase in population would not have guaranteed the survival of the French culture if more conscious forces had not been at work. The Catholic priesthood regarded the preservation of the language and traditions of Québec as essential to the survival of their Church, and for this reason the Catholic hierarchy in Québec became intensely nationalist, even to the extent of keeping its distance from Irish Catholics in Canada whose interests were politically different from those of the Québecois. And to the positive encouragement of the Church was added the negative challenge provided by the contempt which even liberal Englishmen were inclined to show towards *canadien* traditions. Lord Durham was typical when he said in his famous Report:

> There can hardly be conceived a nationality more destitute of all that can invigorate and elevate a people, than that which is exhibited by the descendants of the French in Lower Canada, owing to their retaining their peculiar language and manners. They are a people with no history and no literature.

Such judgments rankled in the minds of young French Canadians and drove them to the opposite extreme of a glorification of La Nouvelle France, expressed most eloquently by the historian François-Xavier Garneau in his great work, *Histoire du Canada depuis sa découverte jusqu'à nos jours*, published between 1845 and 1848. Garneau's history really united past and future; it gave mythical power to the vision of a lost world and at the same time it gave a shape to the new culture that was just emerging in Québec, a culture that at first was largely based on a psychological retreat from the modern world, reflected in the motto adopted by the province of Québec in 1867: *Je me souviens* — I remember.

When Lower Canada was created in 1791, it had about 156,000 people, of whom the 10,000 of English descent, or at least English speech, lived mostly in the towns of Montréal, Quebec City, and Trois Rivières. The provincial boundaries did not then stretch very far beyond

Engraved from studies by the German-born genre painter Cornelius Krieghoff, who worked in Canada between 1849 and 1867, these two engravings represent Québecois trappers in winter and in summer garb.

In 1758 Hervey Smyth, General Wolfe's aide-de-camp in the siege of Louisbourg, sketched the village of Gaspé Bay on the St. Lawrence. This settlement used to provide Québec City with its supply of fish, but Wolfe destroyed it after the surrender of Louisburg.

the St. Lawrence valley, whereas now Québec extends to Hudson Strait and, with its 523,000 square miles, is Canada's largest province. But most of this area is barren land, useful only as a source of minerals and timber and water. Of the small proportion of Québec that is arable (much less than ten per cent) most lies in the southern part of the province, the traditional heartland of New France, where the greater part of the population still lives along the St. Lawrence and its main tributaries, the Saguenay and the Richelieu.

From the beginning the *canadiens* retained most of the land. There were settlements of English and Americans in the south shore Eastern Townships, founded at the time of the Loyalist emigration and shortly afterwards, but basically farming was carried on by those who spoke French. Already before the conquest they had begun to press inland from the St. Lawrence as the first networks of roads were built into the bush. By the time the Québecois entered Confederation in 1867, on the understanding that their traditional culture would be respected and protected within their province, there were already a million inhabitants, and a ratio between linguistic groups had been established that has remained surprisingly constant over the years. Almost eighty per cent spoke French, and these were mostly to be found in the rural areas and small towns where eighty-five per cent of the total population still lived. The cities — Montréal, Quebec City, Trois Rivières, Sorel — had developed

Hervey Smyth was present during the assault on Québec and drew this "View of the Fall of Montmorenci and attack by Gen. Wolfe on French Intrenchments near Beauport, with the Grenadiers of the Army." The vessel in the foreground is HMS Centurion, *which Admiral George Anson used as flagship on his voyage round the world, 1740-44.*

since 1760 into enclaves virtually controlled by the English, meaning a mixture of English and Scots, Irish (both Catholic and Orangemen), and Jews, who dominated trade and manufacture and inhabited the good residential districts. Partly from choice, because they despised commerce and were encouraged to do so by the Church, and partly from lack of opportunity, the *canadiens* in general avoided involvement in finance or trade or manufacturing, preferring either agriculture, journalism, or the professions. They also competed with the Irish in performing the labouring tasks in the towns, and there is no doubt that in fact if not in theory a language-dominated caste system developed in towns like Montréal and Quebec City, with divisions between communities becoming so sharp that by the early years of the present century social intercourse between the English and French, who inhabited different parts of the city and did not even work together, was quite unusual. Westmount, the rich English-speaking suburb of Montréal, was more than a symbol of racial division; it was an abrasive reality in the social and political life of Québec.

Yet it was a reality whose meaning changed over the years. At the time of Confederation Montréal, with its 115,000 people, was the largest city in the new country of Canada, and in 1871 the balance of population was only just beginning to tip towards a French majority. Montréal had moved ahead of Quebec City decades before. It had experienced a

Louis-Joseph, Marquis de Montcalm, a native of Provence, was the commander-in-chief of the French forces in Canada during the Seven Years' War. Disputes with the Governor-General, the Marquis de Vaudreuil, and a failure to understand that European military tactics were not necessarily fitted to North American circumstances, hampered Montcalm in his defence of Québec when it was assaulted by the British forces under Wolfe in 1759. He did not survive the defeat that was brought about partly by his poor generalship, for, like Wolfe, he died from wounds received on the Plains of Abraham on the 13th September, 1759.

setback in 1821, when the union of the fur companies meant that the centre of the trade shifted from Montréal to Hudson's Bay. During this same period Quebec City had been the centre of a timber trade which sometimes loaded 350 British-bound ships in a single season, and of a shipbuilding industry equal to that of the Maritimes. But by the 1850s the accessible supplies of timber had run out in the lower St. Lawrence region and the development of iron and steel ships had — as in the Atlantic colonies — ruined shipbuilding.

The final blow came when steamships appeared which could travel up the St. Lawrence as far as Montréal, while the sailing ships had found it difficult to proceed beyond Quebec City. Quebec City ceased to be a busy seaport, and declined into a centre of small industries and local government. It remained intensely traditionalist because it was Québec's little Rome as well as being the most historically handsome town of Canada; here, with its seminaries and convents the Catholic Church maintained its main citadel in Canada.

Montréal, on the other hand, developed into the major Canadian seaport even though it operated only during the season when the St. Lawrence was free of ice; when the railways developed, it was the centre of the web they traced across Canada; most of Canada's growing export and import trade was centred in Montréal, and the city became and remained until very recently the banking capital of Canada. St. James Street, Montréal — which nobody ever thought of as the *Rue St-Jacques* — became the business capital of Canada for many decades.

Now inhabited by well over two million people, Montréal was for long the largest city of Canada, until recently a little ahead of its main rival, Toronto, and a great deal ahead of Canada's third city, the western metropolis of Vancouver. As it grew, Montréal developed into the most cosmopolitan city of the Americas. More French-speaking people live there than in any city in the world except Paris, but there are more than half a million people of British descent, living in areas where still little but English is spoken. Montréal also contains the largest Jewish community in Canada, descendants of those who came from Russia and Poland to escape the great pogroms that began in the 1880s. The Montréal Jewish community has fostered a number of leading Canadian writers and academics remarkable in proportion to its own numbers, yet it is only one of several large and self-conscious ethnic groups established in the city, including Italians and Germans and the more recently arrived communities of Greeks and Portuguese. This mixture of peoples has made Montréal a livelier and far more graceful and entertaining city in a European sense than other Canadian communities, and until the late 1950s it was an active centre of literature, painting and film-making, not only for French-speaking but also for English-speaking Canada. It was a city where two traditions met and fertilized each other. Yet below the intellectual level those communities did not meet in equality, and the very

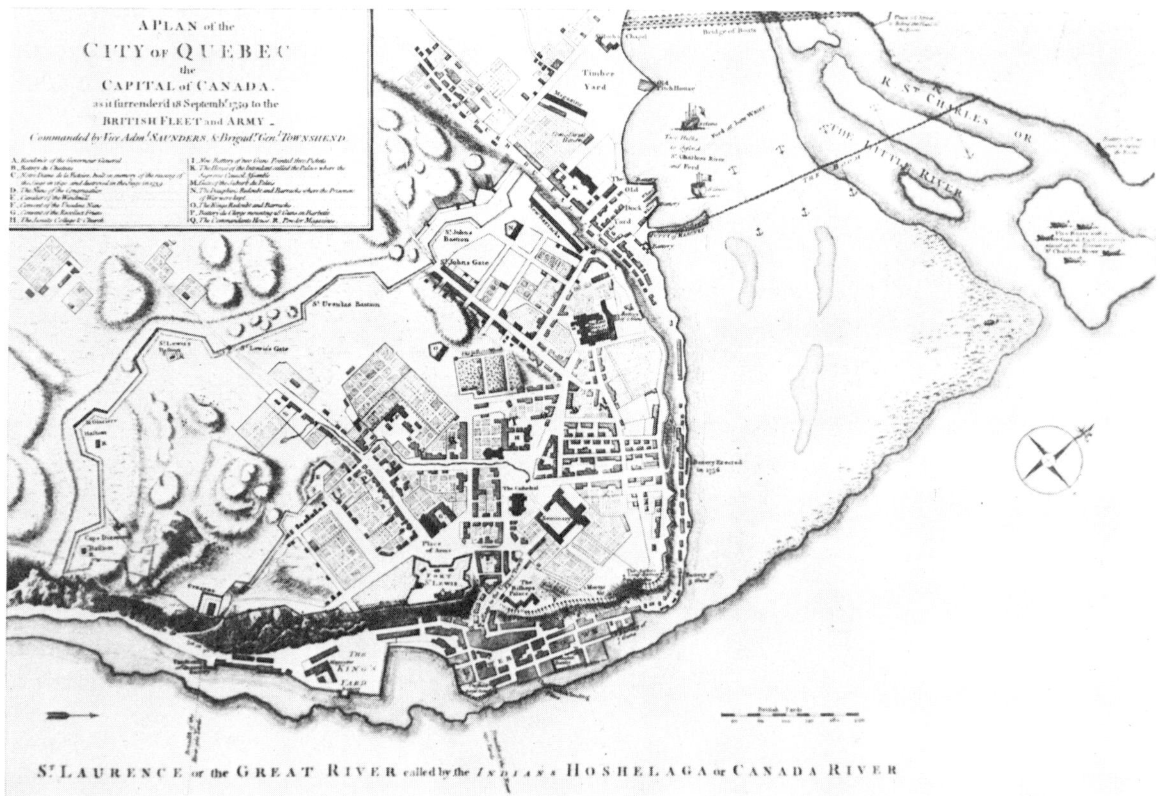

Five days after the battle on the Plains of Abraham, on the 18th September, the city of Québec surrendered to the British forces, now commanded by Vice-Admiral Saunders and Brigadier-General Townsend, at whose orders this map of the city and its fortifications were prepared.

forces that made Montréal into a populous metropolis were those that in the last two decades have changed almost unrecognizably the cities of Québec.

The transformation of Québec from a highly rural to a mainly urban society had already begun at the turn of the century, when the number of people living in a rural setting had fallen from eighty-five per cent to fifty per cent. Québec has long suffered a shortage of farm land, and, unlike the people of Upper Canada, the French Canadians were rarely tempted to try their luck in the Prairies; the largest emigration outside the province was to New England, and the next largest to the northern parts of Ontario. But neither movement was sufficient to stem the flow of landless people into the cities that began in the late nineteenth century and has continued ever since. Even a decade ago only twenty per cent of the province's population was left in the rural areas, and the myth of Québec as a peasant land could no longer be sustained.

While they remained in the countryside, the Québecois were hardly aware of the hold outsiders had on the economy of their province. But once they came into the towns they usually found themselves working at inferior jobs in plants or operations which were run by English Canadians and in which English was the language of communication with superiors. The pay and the living standards of the French-speakers of Québec were not only lower than those in Ontario and the west, but also lower than those of English-speakers in Québec itself. It was rather like the situation of the people of India under British rule, except that the Québecois were theoretically Canadians equal to all others and not a subject race.

Sir Guy Carleton was Governor of Québec from 1768-78, and it was on his recommendation that the Québec Act was passed in 1774. He directed the successful defence of Québec against the American invaders in 1775-6, and later, as Lord Dorchester, he was Governor-in-Chief of British North America from 1786 to 1798.

Ever since the days of Papineau and the *Patriotes,* nationalism has been a force in Québec, but in those early generations nationalism did not usually imply separatism. It aimed rather at the recognition of Québec as a nation within a true federation in which all the component parts would be equal members of a Canada free from imperial bonds of any kind. Henri Bourassa, one of the most idealistic of all Canadian political leaders, gave expression to that early aim of the French Canadian nationalists in a notable speech he made in 1904:

> The fatherland, for us, is the whole of Canada, that is to say, a federation of distinct races and autonomous provinces. The nation that we wish to see developed is the Canadian nation, composed of French Canadians and English Canadians, that is to say, two elements separated by language and religion, and by the legal arrangements necessary for the conservation of their respective traditions, but united in an attachment of brotherhood in a common attachment to a common fatherland.

This kind of nationalist feeling, with its reluctance to become involved in the quarrels of imperial powers, was the reason why the people of Québec so staunchly resisted conscription in both world wars.

This older nationalism tended to be intensely traditional; it allied itself to the Church which, even when it retreated at the end of the nineteenth century from the kind of open political interference rep-

The 'French Cathedral and Market Square' of Québec, portrayed in a lithograph by Sarony and Major.

A distant view of eighteenth century Québec from Point Levi, with an Indian encampment in the foreground.

Notre-Dame-des-Victoires is one of the historic churches of Québec City. It was built in 1688 in the Place Royal near the site of Champlain's habitation, *and was named to celebrate a series of victories over English invaders. Note the model of a ship-of-war which hangs from the ceiling as a votive offering.*

Amusements on the ice were a feature of Québec winters, provided they were hard enough for the St. Lawrence to freeze over, and in 1831 Colonel James Cockburn sketched this scene of soldiers and civilians promenading among the booths erected where ships plied in summer.

Saint-Anne-de-Beaupré is one of the great pilgrimage sites of Québec; it has been called "the Lourdes of North America". The first shrine was erected in 1658 by three Breton sailors washed ashore at Beaupré; they attributed their deliverance to the intervention of St. Anne. Since then many miraculous cures have been claimed, and the shrine still attracts many thousands of visitors every year.

resented by the priest giving voting instructions from the pulpit, still kept a close control over education in Québec. The transformation to a socially radical type of nationalism was delayed by the long rule of the conservative nationalist premier, Maurice Duplessis, who died in office in 1959. His death brought in an era of rapid change in Québec society, beginning with the election in 1960 of a Liberal government under Jean Lesage that was dedicated to ushering the province into the modern age. Perhaps the most significant early manifestation of the "Quiet Revolution" was the rapid decline in the Church's power. Most Québecois remain practicing Catholics, but they have expelled the clergy from many of their former seats of authority. Education has been secularized; the Québecois trade unions, founded originally to sustain ecclesiastical influence, have broken away into radical independence; the vocation of priesthood had lost much of its attractiveness and the seminaries are no longer full.

At the same time, since 1960 there has been an intensification of nationalism in the direction of an independent Québec. Founded in 1968, the Parti Québecois unexpectedly won the provincial elections of 1976 and took power under the leadership of René Lévesque, a political leader in his own way as charismatic as Pierre Trudeau. The effects of this avowedly separatist administration on the relations of the Québecois with other Canadians belong to another chapter. Its effects on the Québecois themselves have already been notable. There has been a move towards a new homogenization of the Québec community, manifested most strikingly in laws making the use of French mandatory in education and work relationships.

Some of the effects of such measures have been indirect yet important. Firms dominated by English-Canadians have begun to move out of the province, in anticipation of more discriminatory legislation, while multi-national corporations have engaged greater numbers of French-speaking employees at higher levels. The minority communities feel imperilled, and already there has been some migration, even of long-established English-speaking families. Montréal itself has been undergoing a physical transformation through a massive rebuilding that accompanies a psychological transformation. It is losing gaiety and grace as the political voices become more strident. It is ceasing to be a great cosmopolitan city. During the 1930s and 1940s Montréal was one of the main centres of English Canadian literature. Apart from the Jewish novelists like Mordecai Richler and Leonard Cohen, Hugh MacLennan wrote his best novels there, and *Two Solitudes* is essentially a Québec novel. Two of Morley Callaghan's later novels, *The Loved and the Lost* and *The Many Coloured Coat,* were set in Montréal, as were many of the stories of Mavis Gallant, a native of the city. In the modern poetry movement of English-speaking Canada, Montréal played a key role, for it was here, in the *McGill Fortnightly Reivew,* that A. J. M. Smith,

Louis-Joseph Papineau was the leader of the French-Canadian resistance to autocratic government in Lower Canada during the early part of the nineteenth century. As a young man he supported the British rulers and in 1812 took part, under General Brock, in the capture of Detroit. It was after he became Speaker of the Lower Canadian assembly in 1815 that Papineau began to move in a democratic direction, at first to defend the rights of the elected representatives. The Parti Canadian, of which he became leader, moved leftward with him, and in 1826 became the Patriote Party. The *patriotes* fought for responsible government, but they were also attracted by American republicanism, and when they could not win reforms by open means, turned to conspiracy. Eventually, in October 1837, they rose in rebellion. Papineau's role on this occasion remains obscure. Having appeared as leader of the *patriotes* up to the moment of insurrection, he fled south and left others to fight and suffer. He spent years in exile, and when he did return to Canada in 1845, he was a spent force. Yet, on the strength of his active years, he remains one of the fathers of Québec nationalism.

This view of Montréal from St. Helen's Island, was painted by Thomas Davies in 1762.

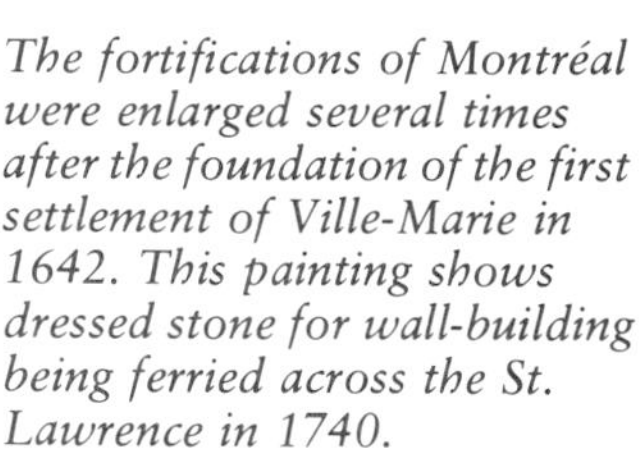

The fortifications of Montréal were enlarged several times after the foundation of the first settlement of Ville-Marie in 1642. This painting shows dressed stone for wall-building being ferried across the St. Lawrence in 1740.

The first steamboat in Canada, The Accommodation, *was built at Montréal by John Molson in 1809, to ply between Montréal and Québec, and by the 1830s, when this drawing was made there were many vessels leaving downriver from the Steamboat Wharf.*

F. R. Scott and A. M. Klein laid the theoretical foundations of the movement as early as 1925. In later decades two of the pioneer Canadian poetry magazines — *Preview* and *First Statement* — were published here and a brilliant galaxy of poets, including P. K. Page, Patrick Anderson, Irving Layton and Louis Dudek, gathered around them. Today all that ferment has died away, and the polarised pattern of English-Canadian literary and artistic culture has moved westward and now rests between Toronto and Vancouver rather than between Montréal and Toronto.

But for the French-speaking people of Québec, descendants of the original *canadiens,* there is undoubtedly a sense of being in control of their own destinies such as they have not known since the conquest, and probably did not know even before it if one remembers the kind of authoritarian rule by officials sent from France that existed under the *ancien régime* of New France. There is a new kind of Québecois pride that is no longer based on remembrance of the past alone, but just as much on expectations for the future.

Something of that new pride can be traced in the development of Québec writing seen in relation to the changing consciousness of regional identity. There have always been three ways in which the French writing of Québec has differed from that of English Canada as a whole. To begin, there is the fact that the French tradition is present as a touchstone,

Camillien Houde, mayor of Montréal in the 1930s, was a man of elephantine proportions and nimble wit, with a nose so large that he once played Cyrano de Bergerac without an artificial nasal appendage. He was popular in Québec as a reform mayor, but he also liked to run an open city, and once he remarked, "As long as we keep a good balance between praying and sinning, I know my city is not going to fall into wickedness." Houde was a dedicated enemy of all kinds of imperialism, and one of the first Canadians to perceive that American cultural influence could become a kind of colonialism. As war grew near in 1939 he warned Mackenzie King against imposing conscription, and when the National Registration Act was introduced, Houde publicly called on Montréalers to refuse to register. For this he was interned in 1940, and the Canadian government unjustly tried to smear him as a fascist, which he was not. He was released in 1944, and went home to a hero's welcome. When Houde died in 1958, 150,000 Montréalers attended his funeral; he was buried in a tomb modelled, at his request, on Napoleon's tomb in Paris.

positive or negative as the times dictate. However nationalist the French Canadian poets of the nineteenth century may have been, one is aware of the kinship with their French counterparts, of the fact that Victor Hugo and Lamartine stood in the background to the writings of Louis Fréchette and Octave Crémazie, and the fact that the symbolist poetry of Baudelaire and Verlaine and Rimbaud helped to shape the tempestuous lyrics of Emile Nelligan. The fact that some recent poets and dramatists, like Michel Tremblay in his play, *Les Belles-Soeurs,* should have turned to using *joual,* the patois of working-class Montréal, may seem a reaction against the French influence, but the very vehemence of the gesture is in fact a compliment to the strength of the tradition.

At the same time, there was a more local tradition at work, that of *habitant* folklore, with its extravagant tales of good spirits and demons and supernatural happenings which has given a strong vein of fantasy to French Canadian writing from the mid-nineteenth century days of Aubert de Gaspé with his masterpiece, *Les Anciens Canadiens,* down to contemporary novels, steeped in symbolism and merging fantasy with realism of various kinds, like Anne Hébert's *Le Torrent,* Marie-Claire Blais's *La Belle Bête* and, more recently, with a new touch of satire, Roch Carrier's sardonically amusing novels, such as *La Guerre, Yes Sir!* and *Floralie, où es-tu?*

The third crucial link between French Canadian literature and the special situation in Québec can be seen in the extreme sensitivity among recent writers in French to the shifts in the collective consciousness which they themselves sometimes help to create. It was in novels like Ringuet's *Trente arpentes* and Gabriel Roy's *Bonheur d'occasion* that the consequences of the decay of the *habitant* way of life and the rapid urbanization of Québec were first imaginatively considered. The malaise of French-speaking intellectuals who felt they had no roots in France yet saw themselves as isolated in an English-speaking continent found expression in the deep alienation of the poetry of Anne Hébert and Hector de Saint Denys Garneau. And the alternations of optimism and pessimism that the separatist movement created have resulted in a series of exceptional novels of which the most remarkable include Hubert Aquin's *Prochain episode,* Jacques Godbout's *Le Couteau sur le table* and Claude Jasmin's *L'Outaragasipi.* Whether in pessimism or in optimism, these writers express the new pride of Québec, and most of them are separatists, seeking to establish a completely sovereign culture along the St. Lawrence. Perhaps the most urgent question in Canada now is whether this pride of the poets will carry out of Canada the people of the province that, more than any other, has been the true Canadian heartland, the province that was the first of all the Canadas of history.

Montréal in 1978; the small city drawn by Thomas Davies more than two centuries ago has long been submerged under the great towers of modern commerce.

Joseph Brant, here shown in the well-known National Gallery portrait by William Berczy, was the principal chief of the Six Nations of the Iroquois. In his teens he fought among his people on the side of the British in the Seven Years' War, and later led the Iroquois against the rebel forces during the War of the American Revolution. Like other Loyalists, he came northward in 1783 and supervised the settlement of his people on a reserve granted to them on the Grand River in Upper Canada. He built himself a large cedar house at Burlington Bay, and encouraged his people to become farmers using European methods. He became something of a celebrity in Britain as well as Canada, and apart from the Berczy portrait, he was painted by George Romney on a visit to England. For his time and place he was a well-educated man, and translated parts of the Gospels and of the Book of Common Prayer from English into Mohawk.

CHAPTER SEVEN

Ontario

John Graves Simcoe, who had commanded the Queen's Rangers in the American Revolutionary war, was named the first lieutenant-governor of Upper Canada in 1791 and arrived in 1792 at Newark (now Niagara-on-the-Lake), which he used as his capital until he transferred the centre of administration to York (now Toronto) which he founded in 1793. He encouraged immigration and built roads to open up the new province before, in 1796, he left to become Governor of San Domingo. His wife, Elizabeth Posthuma Simcoe, kept a diary of their years in Canada (published in 1911 as The Diary of Mrs. John Graves Simcoe *with 90 of her own sketches) which has become an early Canadian classic.*

Upper Canada, which became Ontario, was as much a child of the American Revolution as the United States itself, for it was settled first by the Loyalists. Ten thousand arrived in 1783, and, as we have seen already, it was because of their presence along the northern shores of Lake Ontario and, later, Lake Erie that the province was carved out of Québec in 1791.

Until the Loyalists arrived the land that became Canada was part of the great wilderness hinterland where the French *coureurs de bois*, and after them the Scottish traders who formed the North West Company, moved at will. The fur-bearing animals had by now declined in numbers, but the waterways of the region still provided the highways by which the traders reached the Saskatchewan and Athabaska countries. The Indians lived in the region nomadically, and the traders and *voyageurs* passed through, but nobody settled there, and the earliest place inhabited by Europeans was a French military post called Fort Frontenac, which was first built in 1673. Later, in 1764, the British built a similar post at Fort Erie on the west bank of the Niagara River.

Both of these places played their part in the early settlement of Upper Canada, for Kingston was built by the early Loyalists around the site of Fort Frontenac, and Newark, which was the first capital of Upper Canada and became Niagara-on-the-Lake, was built near Fort Erie. There was also a small French fur-trading post, called Fort Rouillé, and here, in 1793, Governor Simcoe of Upper Canada supervised the building of a small village named York which had been selected as the new capital, and which, after being destroyed by the Americans in the War of 1812, eventually grew into the city of Toronto.

The first settlers in the Canadas who were of neither French nor British descent, came with the Loyalists. They were Germans, Mennonites by religion, whose ancestors had been offered asylum in Pennsylvania by William Penn. During the American Revolution they had been pro-British, but because of their pacifist convictions had taken no part in the fighting. They settled in the Kitchener-Waterloo area; Kitchener in fact was called Berlin until the Great War, and this part of Ontario still remains surprisingly German in its domestic customs, largely because of the traditionalism of the Mennonites, some of whom still resist the use of machinery on their farms.

Otherwise, the early immigration into Upper Canada was composed

Susanna Strickland, member of a famous literary family, married in 1831 a half-pay officer named J.W.D. Moodie, and in 1832 emigrated with him to Canada. For seven years she endured the rigours of pioneer life, first near Cobourg and then north of Peterborough. Out of this experience she wrote two classic accounts of early Upper Canadian life, Roughing it in the Bush *and* Life in the Clearings.

almost entirely of peoples of British stock. The first, after the Loyalists, were American farmers who were not actual Loyalists but were willing to accept the rule of King George provided they could acquire good free land. Thousands of them found their way by river and lake and portage from New York, Pennsylvania, and Vermont. After the War of 1812, American immigrants were discouraged, and efforts were made to populate Upper Canada with people from England, Scotland, and Ireland whose loyalties would be less problematical in a future conflict.

Some of the immigration from Britain was encouraged by generous land grants, particularly to former army officers, who, it was hoped, would form a kind of aristocracy in a social system modelled on the English. Such hopes foundered in the physical realities of frontier existence and in the democratic views that even Loyalists had brought with them, and the minor English gentry who did venture into the backwoods of Upper Canada had to adapt themselves, like their neighbours, to the harsh and often squalid conditions of pioneer life, vividly described by one of the most talented of these immigrants, Mrs. Susanna Moodie, in *Roughing It in the Bush*.

Speculative companies also gained title to large stretches of land such as the 1,100,000 acres acquired and settled by the Canada Company in the later 1820s on the shores of Lake Huron. This was an enterprise associated with one of the earliest and most colourful of Canadian writers, William "Tiger" Dunlop, whose nickname came from his exploits as a hunter in Bengal.

During the 1820s and 1830s a series of crises in Britain, including crop failures and unemployment in England and the dispossession of crofters in Scotland, led to the assisted immigration schemes which so angered William Cobbett, who believed that if agriculture had been properly organized there would be no need to send people to the New World, of which he had no great opinion, having once served as a soldier in New Brunswick.

There was a great deal of justification for Cobbett's indignation, since many people were sent from England by the Poor Law guardians merely to save expense for the parish, and landed in Canada with no money and with none of the abilities that might be useful to them in a pioneer society. Even for those who came with the advantages of health, skills, and modicum of cash, the process of transfer must have been a traumatic one.

To begin, there was the journey across the Atlantic, which in the early days of the nineteenth century was usually by sail and could take weeks or even months, depending on the weather. The better-off sailed by reasonably well-appointed passenger ships, but the poor were often packed into roughly converted timber ships making the return voyage. There were many shipwrecks with all passengers lost, and many people died from sickness at sea without even seeing the shores of Canada.

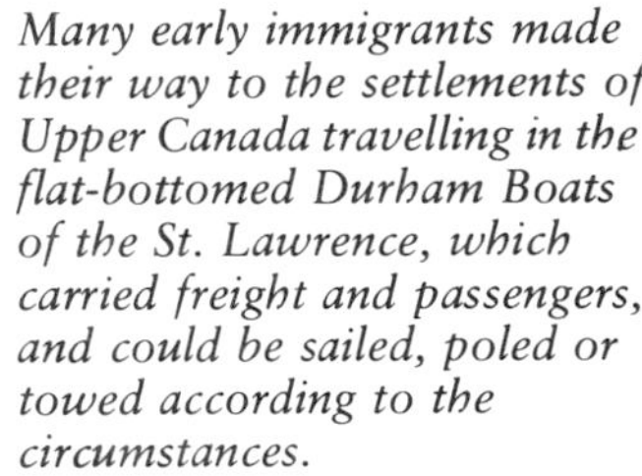

Many early immigrants made their way to the settlements of Upper Canada travelling in the flat-bottomed Durham Boats of the St. Lawrence, which carried freight and passengers, and could be sailed, poled or towed according to the circumstances.

THE

Canadian Settler's Guide:

BY

MRS. C. P. TRAILL,

AUTHORESS OF

THE "BACKWOODS OF CANADA," &c., &c., &c.

FIFTH EDITION.

CHRISTMAS DAY IN THE BACKWOODS.

TORONTO, C.W.:

PRINTED AT THE OLD COUNTRYMAN OFFICE.

1855.

Catharine Parr Traill was Susanna Moodie's sister. She also married a half-pay officer and emigrated in 1832, settling near Rice Lake. Her view of the emigrant life was less acerbic than that of her sister, and the books she wrote were designed to encourage rather than discourage the prospective immigrant. Her Backwoods of Canada *was published in 1835; her* Canadian Settler's Guide *(also published under the title of* The Female Emigrant's Guide*), went through many editions.*

William Dunlop was called "Tiger" because of his frequent reminiscences of the period he spent in India after having served as an army surgeon in the War of 1812. He came a second time to Upper Canada as employee of the Canada Company, started the clearing of land for Guelph and founded Goderich. After a few years in the legislative assembly (1841-46) he became superintendent of the Lachine Canal. All the time he was writing witty essays in Blackwood's *and other magazines, and, under the* nom-de-plume *of 'A Backwoodsman', wrote* Statistical Sketches of Upper Canada *(1832).*

Epidemic diseases bred quickly in the crowded holds of the ships, and cholera spread to Canada with the emigrants, so that from 1832 onwards there was a series of alarming outbreaks in York (to become Toronto) and in Montréal.

Some of the immigrants never proceeded beyond Montréal, where many found work as skilled craftsmen, and others sank into the pool of casual labour, inhabiting the slums that now began to appear in Canada as the towns became more populous. Those who continued to Upper Canada faced a hard journey once they left Montréal, for there were no roads or railways.

The journey had to be made by water, and this meant negotiating first the rapids-strewn stretch of the St. Lawrence which extended from Montréal to Prescott in Upper Canada. For this part of the journey Durham boats and *bâteaux* were used; the difference between them was mainly of size, for both were flat-bottomed craft, which were worked up the river by oar and pole, sometimes by sail, but very often by towing. The *bâteau* was a short sturdy boat usually about forty feet long, but the Durham boat, whose design was introduced by Americans, was often a hundred feet long or more. At some parts of the journey there would be horses to do the towing, but very often the passengers were obliged to man the ropes, and at the worst rapids there could be delays while the freight was portaged and reshipped at the next stretch of relatively quiet water. This hundred and twenty miles of bad water often took twelve days to travel, and when it was over the passengers had to transfer to a sailing ship for the rest of the journey up Lake Ontario to the port nearest their destinations. Here again there was the risk of shipwreck, for the winds and weather of the Great Lakes are very uncertain.

Even within Upper Canada, water was the favoured means of transport, and the fortunate settlers were those who had land on a lake or a river shore that was accessible by boat. Soon, however, there was no alternative but to take up land away from the shore, and then the problems of transport became even greater, for during the earlier years there were very few and very short stretches of real road in Upper Canada. Even the streets of early Toronto were notorious for their mud, and what passed for roads beyond the towns were tracks where trees had been felled and the wagons jolted over the ground that had been cleared, sometimes not too efficiently, since often stumps would remain in the middle of the road and the cart wheels had to be carefully led between them. Metalling was unknown, and the only kind of surfacing in use for a long period (known as "corduroy" after the material it vaguely resembled), consisted of logs laid edge to edge across the track in muddy stretches. With or without corduroy, many of the roads were almost impassable bogs for long periods of the year. They were probably at their best during winter when a firm snow surface would build up over which sleighs could pass without great difficulty.

Named after York Factory, the York boats were built to sail in shallow water and were used in the fur trade, particularly in the rivers flowing into Hudson's Bay.

To overcome the 326 feet difference in level between Lakes Erie and Ontario the Welland Canal had eight locks, like this one near Thorold through which one of the last sailing ships on the Great Lakes is passing.

The Welland Canal was built between Lake Erie and Lake Ontario to avoid Niagara Falls. The first canal, built between 1824 and 1829, ran for 28 miles between Port Weller and Port Colborne, where this sketch was made.

On many Ontario rivers transport was still by canoes that could be manoeuvred with poles through the rapids, like these on the Abitibi River.

Provincial Exhibitions reflected the rural concerns of mid-Victorian Ontario. In 1852 the three main halls were dedicated to agriculture, to flower-growing and to the mechanical arts.

The settler's problems did not end when he reached his land, which was likely to be a forest that had to be felled before any crop could be sown (and which incidentally provided material for houses, barns, and fencing, as well as ash for lye), and often marshy into the bargain. Settlements were few and scattered, often consisting of little more than a store, a grist mill, a smithy, and a tavern, and early farm life in Upper Canada was of necessity largely self-subsistent, with almost all the food grown on the holding, much of the furniture home-carpentered, and even items like soap and candles made on the farm. Though there are some accounts by early gentleman farmers of planting potatoes during the day and dancing the same evening at balls in York, many early settlers were lost in the great brooding woods and suffered acutely from loneliness.

Yet, as the country began to fill, a great communal spirit arose among the farmers, and though life was always rough, and people often rough-mannered, mutual aid was widely practiced. Neighbours would gather at "bees" to co-operate in harvesting or in building each others' houses or barns. Such occasions were often very festive, and locally-distilled whiskey, which was cheap, would be dispensed by the bucket. But even such neighbourliness could not compensate for the unrelenting toil and the difficulty of communications, and Susanna Moodie spoke with the bitterness of experience when she warned other prospective immigrants:

In most instances, emigration is a matter of necessity, not of choice.

Mutual aid was an essential element in Upper Canadian pioneer farm life. Neighbours would gather in bees for such occasions as raising a barn.

> Few educated persons accustomed to the refinement and luxuries of European society ever willingly relinquish those advantages. Emigration may generally be regarded as a severe duty performed at the expense of personal enjoyment.

Susanna Moodie, who had come to the backwoods area of Douro Township in 1832, wrote those words twenty years later, and by this time conditions had in reality changed very much for the better. Canals had been built to avoid the St. Lawrence rapids; steamers had appeared on the lakes; the first railways had started to run. The Rebellion of 1837 had ended with a whimper, and the two Canadas had been united in 1840 into the province of Canada. In 1849 responsible government had been granted by the Governor General, Lord Elgin, and the attempt to create an aristocratic society ruled by the Family Compact of pro-British magnates had failed.

Already, in 1840, the population of Upper Canada had reached 400,000. By 1851 it had leapt ahead and there were 950,000 Upper Canadians. About half this population still consisted of people born elsewhere. There were over 93,000 English and Welsh, 90,000 Scots, and no less than 227,000 Irish, divided very sharply between the Catholics and the Protestants from Ulster. By now, though the Loyalist tradition was still strong, the American element in the population had declined, and in 1851 there were only 56,000 Upper Canadians who had been born in the United States.

Many of the immigrants tended to settle in groups shaped by their origins. Among the Scots the clan traditions were still strong, and in the

On the small farms of Ontario most of the work, like harvesting, was done by hand far into the nineteenth century.

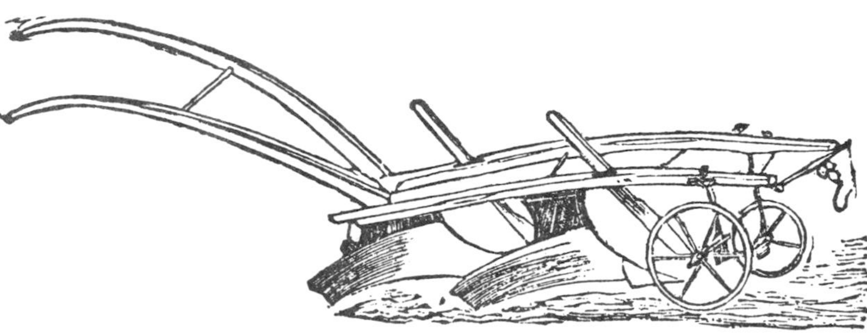

The double plough, originally designed in England, was the predecessor of the multiple ploughs that came later with the invention of the tractor.

Glengarry settlement on the Ottawa river Gaelic was spoken for generations in a very cohesive community. The Ulstermen settled in towns like London, Kingston, and Toronto, where their influence was so great that most mayors of Toronto during the nineteenth century were members of the Orange Order. The Catholic Irish settled largely in the country, particularly along the shores of Lake Erie.

Ontario did not attain its present area of 344,000 square miles until 1912, when its northern boundary was extended to Hudson's Bay, but by 1852 settlement had already reached up the Ottawa River, where the farmers often spent part of their year working in the great forests of the region. These were largely denuded of usable timber in the mid-nineteenth century. Immense rafts of timber were floated down to Montréal, and a tough and daring race of raftmen, mainly French Canadians, dominated the river for decades. In 1855 the lumbering and canal settlement of Bytown, celebrated for the fighting rowdiness of its Irish labourers, would be renamed Ottawa, and two years later this raw city in

Barns made of prefabricated units and precut lumber to be erected by the farmer and his friends were already being advertised by the mail order houses before the end of the nineteenth century.

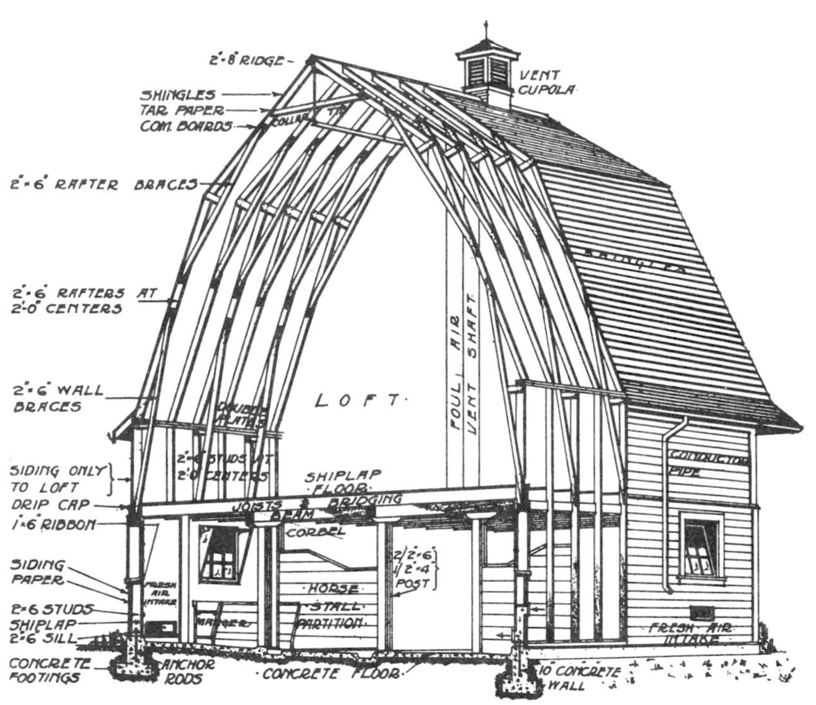

the northern forests would become the capital of Canada, dedicated to a new industry that would burgeon over the decades, that of bureaucracy. It would not be until 1903, after the discovery of silver in Cobalt, that the rich mineral deposits farther north in the province would first be developed and the miners, many from Poland and other areas of eastern Europe, would rival the numbers of the loggers in Ontario.

By 1861 there were almost 300,000 more people in Upper Canada (or Canada West) than in Lower Canada (or Canada East), and this was certainly one of the main reasons for terminating the union of the provinces established in 1840. The two parts became Ontario and Québec at the time of Confederation in 1867; only in this way, the Upper Canadians believed, could their interests be properly represented since under the law of 1840 the two Canadas had been given equal representation without regard to the difference in the sizes of their populations.

But there were other reasons, also related to population, why Lord Durham's solution of placing the two Canadas under a single government could not work. Lower Canada was predominantly French and Catholic; Upper Canada became predominantly British and Protestant. The attachment to Britain which had brought the Loyalists northward developed into a loyalty to the Empire which was hard to reconcile with the Québecois desire to be free of imperial obligations. Even the patriotic Canada First movement, which developed in Ontario during the 1870s, accepted the idea of an imperial federation of autonomous dominions.

Born in Aberdeen in 1778, **John Strachan** came to Upper Canada in 1799 to take charge of a college projected by Lieutenant-Governor Simcoe which did not in fact materialize, and for twelve years he taught at schools in Kingston and Cornwall. In 1803 he was ordained in the Church of England, becoming rector of Cornwall. In 1812 he became rector of York, and at the time of the American occupation of that settlement in 1813 Strachan was virtually the only person capable of negotiating with the invaders. From this time onward he became a power in Upper Canada, influential not only in religious but also in political and educational affairs. In 1818 he was appointed to the Executive Council of the province, and in 1820 to the Legislative Council; until 1841, when he ceased to sit on either of these councils, he remained a leading member of the Tory Family Compact which autocratically ruled the province and resisted attempts at reform. When King's College was founded in 1827, Strachan became its first principal, and when Toronto was made a diocese in 1839 he became its first bishop. He was also the founder and first chancellor of Trinity College in 1851. The men he taught in school and in college were — as much as Strachan himself — responsible for the maintenance of his influence as they rose to high positions in Upper Canada. He died, perhaps appropriately, in 1867, when Confederation started a new age in the political life of Canada and his world began to fade away.

Timothy Eaton revolutionized retail trade in Canada. The son of an Ulster farmer, he was brought up according to strict Calvinist principles, so that he always condemned smoking, drinking and dancing, but had no objection to the amassing of wealth. Indeed, Eaton set out to prove that, so far as money-making is concerned, honesty is in fact the best policy; if your customers trust you, they will buy more readily. Eaton had already worked for fourteen years as partner with his brothers in a general store in St. Mary's, Upper Canada, when in 1868 he opened his own store in Toronto. A year later he founded the firm of T. Eaton and Company and announced that he was going to do business on new principles. In his stores everything would be sold for cash; there would be fixed prices, with none of the bargaining then customary in the retail trade, and a customer not satisfied with his purchase would have his money returned. By eliminating bad credit risks, and working on the basis of cost plus a reasonable profit, Eaton was able to keep his prices low. Soon his example was followed, and, even if the system did not entirely guarantee customers from exploitation, it at least was better than the non-system it replaced, by which storekeepers haggled over prices and did not guarantee their wares. For Eaton it meant the building of one of the largest department store empires in North America, and one of the few businesses of such size that has remained in the hands of a family dynasty.

A typical Upper Canadian pioneer farm in its earlier stages, in which the felled timbers have been used for construction and fencing, and a log cabin precedes the frame-construction farmhouse that will come with prosperity. The illustration is from The British Farmer's Guide to Ontario.

There was a brief flaring of the embers of rebellion in 1838, when American sympathizers of the rebels of 1837 crossed the St. Lawrence on the 12th November and seized a stone windmill on Windmill Point near Prescott. They surrendered on the 16th, and their leader, Nils von Schoultz, was executed. This view of the battle was drawn from the American shore.

In 1855, when William S. Hunter drew this view from Barrack Hill, the settlement of Bytown had just been renamed Ottawa. Two years ahead, in 1857, it would be chosen as the capital of the Province of Canada.

Since the Irish Catholics of Ontario were disregarded by the French hierarchy of Québec, they became a relatively powerless group among the Protestant majority in the province. Protestant influence, strongly Calvinist in its nature, was responsible for the rigorous sabbatarianism that gave Toronto its epithet of "Toronto the Good" and created sombre Sundays throughout the province until very recent years. The Protestant majority found its most extreme expression in the Orange Order, which interfered in politics where religion and education were mingled, objecting to special arrangements in this area for French-speakers and Catholics. Orange pressure on Sir John A. Macdonald and his Conservative government in 1885 was largely responsible for the execution of Louis Riel and the lasting antagonism between Québec and Ontario which that incident created.

Ontario's lead in population over the other provinces of Canada has been maintained ever since Confederation. Today, with more than 8,000,000 people, it is the home of over a third of Canadians. They live mainly in a fairly thickly populated triangle bounded by the Ottawa and St. Lawrence Rivers, by Lakes Ontario, Erie, and Huron; here all the larger towns of the province are situated except for the northern mining

Fort Cataraqui was built on Lake Ontario by the Comte de Frontenac in 1673. Later it became Fort Frontenac, but the settlement around it was still called Cataraqui until the year of 1783 when James Peachey made this sketch. Shortly afterwards a party of Loyalists from New York settled here and named the place Kingston.

centre of Sudbury. The north of Ontario is as sparsely populated as is the north anywhere else in Canada.

This great expansion of population has been accompanied by profound changes in the character and the lifestyles of Ontarians. For generations after the coming of the Loyalists, the typical Ontarian was a farmer. By the time of Confederation the forested Upper Canada known to the *coureurs de bois* had almost vanished as the arable land in southern Ontario was cleared and brought under the plough, so that there was actually a land hunger which led some Canadians to migrate to the Prairies beside the Red River. The farmers were long the most numerous group in the province, and as late as 1919 the United Farmers of Ontario, who had formed themselves into an agrarian political party, were able to win enough seats in the provincial legislature to form a government. Even today there are large areas of Ontario where the well-tended, prosperous farms and the small rural towns with their colonial-style buildings speak for a tradition that makes farming, after manufacturing and construction, the most important industry in Ontario.

But before the end of the nineteenth century the process that turned Ontario into Canada's most important manufacturing region, with fifty per cent of the country's industry, had begun. The farms, the mines, and the forests all provided raw materials for the new factories; American iron ore and coal could easily be imported across the Great Lakes to establish a Canadian iron and steel industry; there were ample hydro power resources; Ontario's central situation in the Dominion made distribution of its products relatively easy; and the province's federal

Kingston, sketched by J. Gray (and aquatinted by J. Gleadah), from Fort Henry in 1828.

voting power made politicians inclined to impose tariffs that favoured Ontario industries. Between the two world wars, despite the effects of the Depression, the balance between manufacturing and primary industries like farming, mining, and forestry was tipped irrevocably. In 1938, farming accounted for only thirteen per cent of the value of production, as against sixty per cent for manufacturing, and now the ratio has fallen to five per cent as against seventy-two per cent. The modern Ontarian is much more likely to be employed in a factory or on a construction job or in a service industry than he is to be working on a farm.

Partly because of the growth of manufacturing in Ontario, the early preponderance of people of British origin has been greatly weakened. The great influx of immigrants from countries outside the English-speaking and French-speaking worlds began after the Second World War, and it has turned Toronto into the kind of cosmopolitan city that Montréal is ceasing to be. Germans, Italians, Portuguese, Greeks, East Indians, and people from the Caribbean form considerable enclaves of population in Toronto and the other large Ontario towns, and, while they accept English as the general language of communication, they retain a great deal of their own culture in the sense of traditions, customs, festivals, and eating habits. Slowly they have changed the habits and broadened the tastes of other Ontarians, particularly by establishing a multitude of restaurants offering something different from the solid but somewhat limited traditional Canadian menu. Ottawa has been affected by the special influence of the many foreign missions established there since the Second World War and also by a considerable influx of Québecois as a result of the government's policy of fostering bilingualism

This drawing of Toronto Harbour in 1793 is one of the many sketches of Upper Canada made by Elizabeth Simcoe when she lived there as the Governor's wife.

In 1836, when the architect Thomas Young made this drawing of King Street East, the settlement of York had only two years before been incorporated as the city of Toronto, with William Lyon Mackenzie as its first mayor.

Brockville was founded in 1785 by the Loyalist William Buell and by the time this drawing was made in 1828 by James Gray from Umbrella Island, it was already a flourishing town.

in the civil service. Most Ontarians, of course, are still of English, Scottish, or Irish descent, but the solidly and almost stolidly British character of the province is now a thing of the past.

All these changes — from a rural to an urban way of existence, from an agrarian to a manufacturing ecomony, from a unicultural to a multicultural society — have relaxed the pressures to social and moral conformity that were once so characteristic of Ontario life. A large proportion of Ontarians are still sincerely religious Protestants, but Protestant puritanism no longer shapes the mores of society and influences its politics any more than Roman Catholicism does in Québec.

One result has been a great upsurge in artistic creativity, and — a more dubious development — in the apparatus that exploits creativity. Most Canadian books written in English are published in Toronto, and the national magazines are situated there, as is the headquarters of the English-speaking network of the Canadian Broadcasting Corporation. The Canada Council is situated in Ottawa.

Many Ontarians, in other words, belong to bureaucracies of the arts as others do to the political bureaucracies of Ottawa and the province of Ontario, and Canadians in other regions are inclined to credit the Ontarian, and especially the Torontonian, with a centralizing arrogance that ignores the regional nature of Canada as a country. Toronto and Ottawa have never been popular in the rest of Canada; their myths have become even more negative since Toronto took over from Montréal the business power of the country and Ottawa became the centre of a paternalistic state. But most Ontarians, like most other Canadians, are far from the sources of power, and in their farms and mines and factories follow occupations that are essential to the country's life on its most basic levels.

Like other parts of Canada, Ontario has reflected in its literature its

Bytown began in 1827 as a camp for Colonel By's Royal Engineers building the Rideau Canal, but it soon became a lumbering centre to which the rafts of squared timbers were floated down the Ottawa River from the camps in the forest.

special regional experiences. The best early writing was informational prose, and the most interesting of it was written by women: Susanna Moodie and her sister Catherine Parr Traill, with their immigrant narratives of life in early Upper Canada (*Roughing It in the Bush* and *The Backwoods of Canada* respectively) and Anna Jameson, a more temporary visitor, whose *Winter Studies and Sunny Rambles in Canada* is a remarkably acute and perceptive account of travel in a pioneer country. A somewhat different flavour from the prose of these genteel and cultured women is provided in the poems of the immigrant tailor Alexander McLachlan, who published *The Emigrant and Other Poems* in 1861, and whose "We Live in a Rickety House," for all its doggerel, gives a bitterly eloquent picture of the underside of early Ontario life.

We live in a rickety house,
    In a dirty dismal street,
Where the naked hide from day
    And thieves and drunkards meet.

And pious folks with their tracts,
    When our dens they enter in,
They point to our shirtless backs,
    As the fruits of beer and gin.

And they quote us texts to prove
    That our hearts are hard as stone,
And they feed us with the fact
    That the fault is all our own.

The last raft of squared timber was assembled at Ottawa in 1901 for transport to Quebec and England. One of the piers of the Interprovincial Bridge, then under construction, can be seen in the middle of the river.

Rideau Street, Ottawa, in the early 1900s.

Industry reaches Toronto in the nineteenth century:

The Toronto Rolling Mills on Mill Street, drawn by William Armstrong in 1864.

Freeland's Soap and Candle Factory, drawn in 1888.

Jex & Sons' Broom Factory.

JEX & SONS
BROOM FACTORY

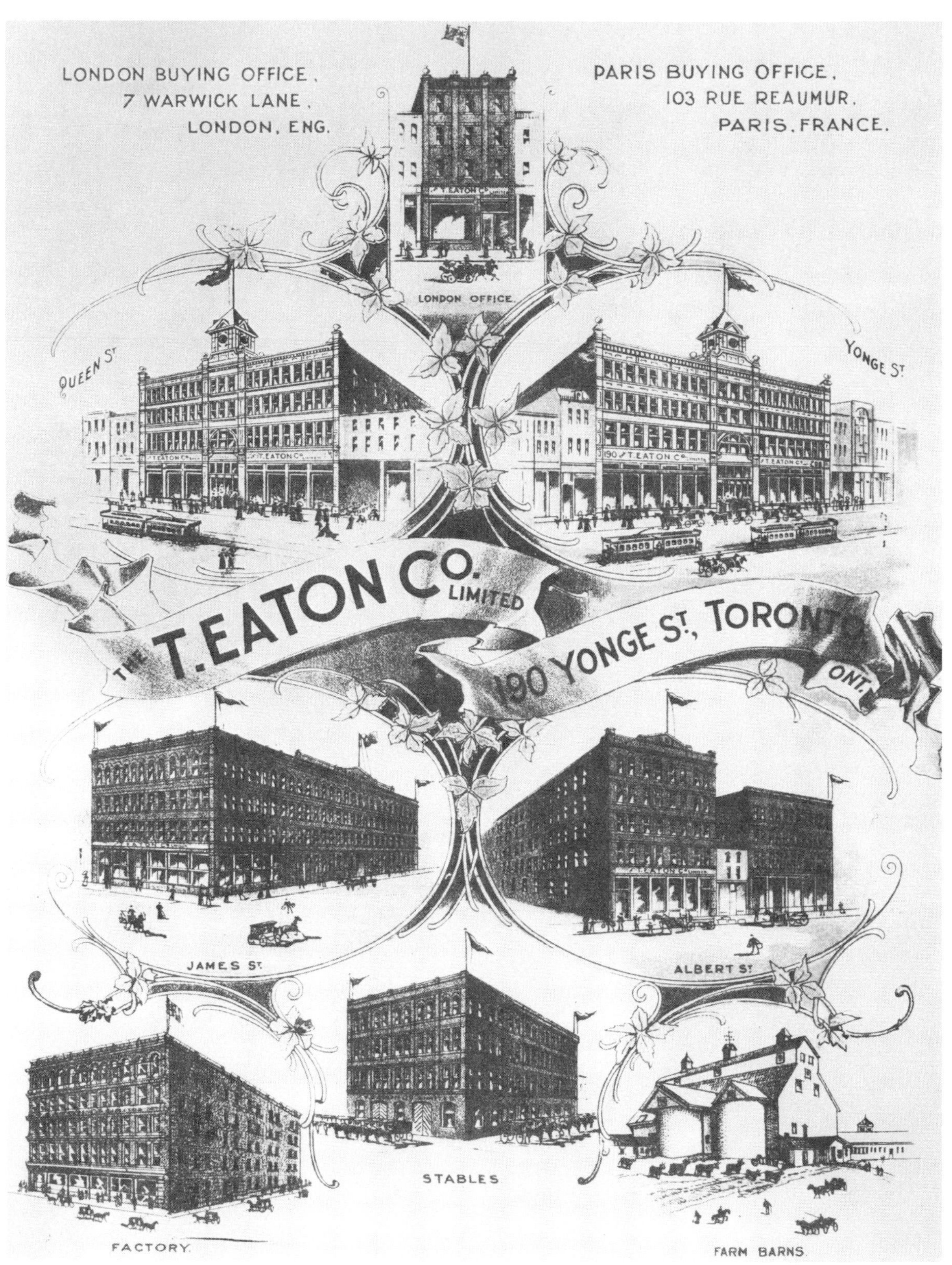

LONDON BUYING OFFICE,
7 WARWICK LANE,
LONDON, ENG.
PARIS BUYING OFFICE,
103 RUE REAUMUR,
PARIS, FRANCE.
LONDON OFFICE
QUEEN ST
YONGE ST
THE T. EATON CO. LIMITED
190 YONGE ST, TORONTO
ONT.
JAMES ST
ALBERT ST
STABLES
FACTORY
FARM BARNS

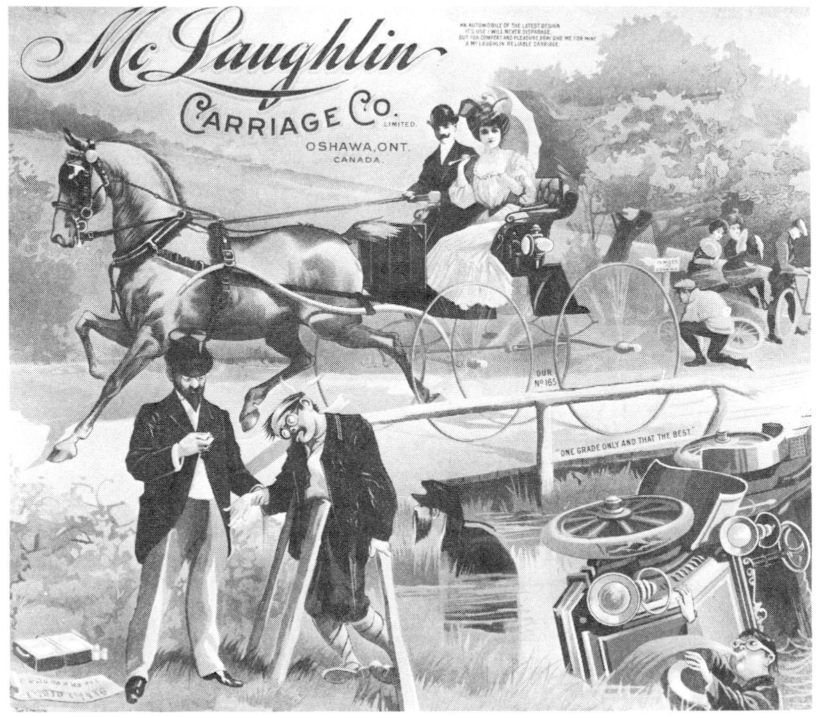

The carriage companies fought a hard rearguard action against rival modern forms of transport; this advertisement by the McLaughlin Carriage Company stressed the perils of motor cars and the inconveniences of bicycle riding as against the comfort and safety of a horse-drawn buggy.

It will be long ere the poor
    Will learn their grog to shun
While it's raiment, food and fire,
    And religion all in one.

I wonder some pious folks
    Can look us straight in the face,
For our ignorance and crime
    Are the Church's shame and disgrace.

We live in a rickety house,
    In a dirty dismal street,
Where the naked hide from day,
    And thieves and drunkards meet.

Imaginative literature of real originality did not appear on any scale in Ontario until after Confederation, when it was no longer pioneer country. It is true that Isabella Valancy Crawford, the first important poet in the region, liked to evoke both the individualist ethos of a superseded backwoods society and the flavour of an earlier Indian past, but she wrote as a town dweller foreseeing, in her verses about the Axe in "Malcolm's Katie", how

For every silver ringing blow
Cities and palaces shall grow.

OPPOSITE:
In 1868 Timothy Eaton started his first dry goods store in Toronto. Thirty years later, by 1899 it had already proliferated into an empire of department stores.

When a clear Ontarian poetic tradition did begin to develop, at the same time as that of the Maritimes, it was represented by poets like Archibald Lampman, who wrote of the settled agricultural landscapes of the lower Ottawa valley, or like Duncan Campbell Scott whose work was so largely dominated by his experiences among Indians far out from the settled centres in the north country. It is perhaps significant that the most typical of contemporary Ontario poets, Al Purdy, should be so much a poet of nostalgia, evoking again and again the Loyalist past in the decaying small towns he had known since childhood.

The varying ways in which fiction presents Ontario life can be well charted by considering four of the better known writers of the region. In Stephen Leacock there is a transference of the satirical tradition which Haliburton and McCulloch had already established in the Maritimes. But while they were attempting to shape by criticism a society still in the process of formation, Leacock is revealing the contradictions and pretensions of already established societies. There is nothing of the pioneer past in the small town of *Sunshine Sketches of a Little Town* or the plutocratic city of *Arcadian Adventures with the Idle Rich*. Economic orders, codes of behaviour, patterns of polite deception are already in operation, and Leacock engages himself in revealing the discrepancy between the way the people see themselves and the way they are, in the process emphasizing the Philistine smugness that was characteristic of the classes which dominated Ontario life in the Edwardian era.

Mazo de la Roche romanticizes what Leacock satirizes. Her Jalna novels provide a vivid but highly over-coloured panorama of the WASP establishment in its more rural manifestations. But if Mazo de la Roche portrayed the Ontario patricians as they liked to see themselves, Morley Callaghan, in books like *They Shall Inherit the Earth* and *Such is My Beloved*, created an essentially plebeian world in his mainly urban novels, which portray the vulgar, narrow, and hypocritical life of Ontario cities a generation ago, of sabbatarian Toronto and its satellites. In contrast to the British-oriented world of Jalna, Callaghan's Ontario is very American in flavour, and in prose Callaghan represents a reaction against British models that at the same period was being expressed among Toronto poets such as Raymond Souster, who were turning towards American poetic styles.

Modern Ontario, changed by the great post-Second-World-War immigration from Europe and the Americas and by the social ferment of the 1960s, is shown with all its tensions in the novels of Margaret Atwood — *The Edible Woman, Surfacing*, and *Lady Oracle*. One of the most interesting aspects of these novels is the way they reflect the development of a real intelligentsia of writers, artists, and academics in Ontario which is inclined to use its own mental and emotional life as a mirror of the world in general, and this in turn is a sign of the growing sophistication and mental autonomy of Ontario as a regional society.

CHAPTER EIGHT

The Prairie Provinces Canada's Third World

It is for historical rather than geographical reasons that one talks of the three Prairie provinces as a single region. Topographically they are much more varied than the stereotyped image of flat land receding to a far horizon leads one to believe. In fact only the southern plains along the American border fit this description, and there is little of such pool-table land in Alberta. Manitoba's northeastern triangle is typical Shield country of lakes, rock outcrops, lodgepole forest, and muskeg, reaching up to the Arctic waters of Hudson's Bay at Churchill; one does not emerge on to the flat open plain until one is very close to Winnipeg. Central and northern Saskatchewan is rolling parkland with lush natural grass and many small woods and lakes. Even in southern Saskatchewan the plains are broken by the Great Sand Hills near Swift Current and the strange and beautiful enclave of the Cypress Hills, exempt from the last Ice Age and so the home of exotic creatures such as the horned toad and the kangaroo rat. By the time one reaches Alberta on the long day and night that it takes to traverse these provinces by rail, the land has risen in a series of steppes from near sea level at Winnipeg to more than two thousand feet in most of Alberta (Calgary's elevation, in fact, is more than three thousand feet), and the western edge of the province rises through wooded foothill country to the eastern slopes of the Rockies, many of whose highest peaks are within Alberta.

This topographical variation has meant that many ways of life other than the wheat farming for which they are best known have been fostered in the Prairie provinces. The metal miners and trappers of northern Manitoba, the ranchers and oilmen and coal miners of Alberta, are as typical of the region as are the farmers who till the flat fields, surveyed on the American quadrilateral system almost a century ago when Canada began to offer free homestead land. Yet the typical Prairie farms, with their great regular squares of golden wheat or black ploughed earth, a red barn and a farmhouse tucked behind a windbreak of trees in the corner of each square, creates one of the two most enduring images of this region of Canada. The other is also connected with wheat farming: it is the image of the grain elevators which, miles ahead, as one travels a straight and monotonous road, herald the approach of the next small Prairie town, with its railroad station, its decrepit hotel, its false-fronted store, and its

The horses step like Arab racers rather than Prairie mustangs in this painting of Assiniboine Indians shooting the buffalo from horseback.

Chinese restaurant, set among a few dozen houses with grass plots for gardens and hardy lilac blooming by the door. More than any other kind of building the grain elevator, usually coloured in bright, arresting tints, and as solid against the sky as a building in a painting by Cézanne, is the architectural symbol of Canada.

The physical characteristic which the Prairie provinces share in all their variability is the enormous sense of openness in every direction, including upward, that one experiences in them. "I think of western skies as one of the most beautiful things about the West, and the western horizons," said Marshall McLuhan, who was born in Alberta. "The Westerner doesn't have a point of view. He has a vast panorama; he has such tremendous space around him." It is a spaciousness that awes and often inspires. In 1906 the English poet T. E. Hulme worked for a while on a Manitoba farm, and afterwards he recorded that "the first time I ever felt the necessity or inevitableness of verse, was in the desire to reproduce the peculiar quality of feeling which is induced by the flat spaces and wide horizons of the virgin prairie of western Canada." Hulme was the founder of Imagism, and so one of the great movements of modern poetry grew out of a poet's personal contact with the vastnesses of the great Canadian plains.

OPPOSITE:
At the end of the nineteenth century, after the classic Indian cultures of the plains had died away, the photographer E.S. Curtis took many posed studies of Indians who retained the old costumes and remembered the old ways, like this of a Piegan with his medicine pipe.

In social terms the features which the Prairie provinces most strikingly share are their rapid and relatively recent settlement, and the unique mixture of races that has resulted. The population of Manitoba was 62,000 in 1881; by 1901 it had quadrupled to 255,000; and ten years

To settlers, travellers and Indians, and also to the animals of the Prairies, the fires that in summer ran through the dry grass were a perpetual danger.

On his way north to the Arctic with Sir John Franklin in 1820, Lieutenant George Back of the Royal Navy drew this sketch of Indians chasing buffalos into a pound fenced with hurdles, a method widely used before rifles were common in the west.

After serving in Garibaldi's Redshirts, Frederick Verner returned to Canada in the 1860s and spent many seasons painting among the Indians of the Prairies and the northern woodlands. These are the wigwams of a band living on the edge of the plains, near enough to the forest to have a good supply of birchbark for their shelters and their canoes.

When Peter Rindisbacher drew this sketch of the fur trading posts at Pembina, they were still operated by the Hudson's Bay Company and Pembina was regarded as within the Red River Settlement. When the international boundary was agreed, it was found to be south of the border; the present town of Pembina is in North Dakota.

later it had almost doubled again to 461,000; The populations of Alberta and Saskatchewan multiplied almost five-fold in the great immigration decade between 1901 and 1911. As a result of this flood of people to the Prairie grainlands, the "founding" races were dislodged from their majority situation as they were nowhere else in Canada. British Columbia, Ontario, the Maritime provinces, all have majorities of people whose ancestors came from the British Isles (as high as ninety-three per cent in Newfoundland and eighty-two per cent in Prince Edward Island), while Québec has its enduring French majority. But in every Prairie province those of British descent are a minority (as low as forty-two per cent in Saskatchewan) and those of French descent, including the Métis, average only about six per cent. On the other hand, twelve per cent of Albertans and sixteen per cent of the people of Saskatchewan are German by descent; thirteen per cent of Manitobans and nine per cent of the people of Alberta and Saskatchewan are Ukrainians. In addition there are fair numbers of Scandinavians (eight per cent in Alberta), and Dutch and Poles (five per cent of each in Manitoba). Even the religious patterns show the strength of this third force in Canadian life; the onion-domed steeples of Greek Orthodox and Ukrainian Uniate churches are almost as familiar interruptions of the Prairie horizon as are the grain elevators.

This great mingling of the peoples in the Canadian Prairies really began in the 1880s, and it was an extraordinarily quick process, virtually ending with the outbreak of the Great War in 1914, by which time all the good land (except that in the remote Peace River region) had been settled. Deep as their loyalties to their old fatherlands may be — and in the case of Ukrainians especially they are very deep indeed — almost all the Prairie farmers with central or eastern European ancestry were in fact born in Canada, and the chances are that their fathers also were born here.

Before 1870 Rupert's Land had been a peculiar kind of colony held under a charter granted by Charles II in 1670 to The Governor and Company of Adventurers of England Trading into Hudson's Bay. The

Lord Selkirk's philanthropic concern for dispossessed Scottish crofters led him into the heart of the conflict between the rival fur companies at the beginning of the nineteenth century. After establishing settlements at Orwell Bay, Prince Edward Island, and Baldoon, Upper Canada, he acquired a substantial interest in the Hudson's Bay Company which granted him the land for his Red River Settlement. Opposed by the Northwest Company, which used violence to try and destroy his venture (which Selkirk countered by attacking Fort William), the Settlement involved Selkirk in a maze of litigation and undoubtedly hastened his early death in 1820.

Commanded by Captain J.S. Falbister, the English sailing ship Wellington *left Dortrecht in 1821 to carry colonists via Hudson's Bay, bound for the Red River. The artist Peter Rindisbacher was among the passengers.*

Company held monopolistic trading rights over the whole area whose rivers drained into Hudson's Bay, and also rather vague "rights of government", which amounted to suzerainty rather than sovereignty. In practice — and in the interests of trade — the Company interfered as little as possible with the lives of the Indians on whom it depended for furs, and occupied the vast terrain with a thin scattering of forts and trading posts that were linked by canoe routes followed by the fur trades. The Company was ill prepared to defend the territory named in its charter, and interloping merchants from Montréal, of whom the best organized were the North West Company, operated in the territory for decades until the rival companies were united in 1821 in the enlarged Hudson's Bay Company.

Some of the forts created by the fur traders, such as Edmonton and Brandon, became the nuclei of important Prairie towns, but that was far from the intention of the Hudson's Bay Company, whose interests did not coincide with populating the country. For at least two centuries the fur traders shared this vast country with their Métis *voyageurs* and hunters and with the Indians; no British official came here, and the independent travellers who arrived, like the artist Paul Kane, who wandered through in 1844, or Viscount Milton and Dr. Cheadle, the first authentic tourists, who arrived in 1866, were so rare that we know about all of them. It was not until 1857, when Captain John Palliser and Henry Youle Hind made their independent expeditions into the North West, that even a scientific survey of the region and its economic potential was attempted.

The missionaries, in fact, arrived before the scientists and long before the settlers. There had been itinerant Jesuits in the region during the

The Selkirk settlement survived the difficulties of its early years, and many of its residents remained to form a lasting element in the population of the Red River region.

French period, and in 1818 fathers Provencher and Dumoulin arrived on the Red River. By the 1840s Father Thibault had crossed the plains and established his mission , which later became a considerable Métis settlement, at Lac St. Anne near Fort Edmonton. The Anglicans appeared at Red River in 1820 and in later decades sent lay catechists into northern Manitoba. The Methodists operated from Norway House on Lake Winnipeg from the 1840s onwards, and one of their ministers, the Reverend George McDougall, became as influential among the Indians during the period of readjustment that followed Canadian penetration into the area as did the celebrated Roman Catholic Father Lacombe, who prevented the Blackfoot from stopping the building of the CPR and from joining the Northwest Rebellion of 1885. The missionaries were more concerned with conversion than colonization, but occasionally they would embark on settlement, and one locality that was pioneered by a religious group is Prince Albert in Saskatchewan, which was founded by a group of Presbyterians from the Red River in 1866. They were not very successful in gaining Indian adherents, but they provided the nucleus around which the first white settlement in the Saskatchewan region developed.

The one area in which settlement did begin in the early nineteenth century — and existed alone in the west for many decades — was the Red River valley. In 1811 Lord Selkirk, a philanthropic Scottish nobleman concerned over the plight of the Sutherland crofters driven from their lands to make grazing for sheep, gained control of the Hudson's Bay Company. The Company granted Selkirk a large area of Prairie land around the junction of the Red and Assiniboine rivers, for the purpose of colonization, and, late in 1811, the first settlers set off from Scotland on their difficult and discouraging enterprise. They arrived at York Factory,

Father Albert Lacombe was the best known of the Catholic missionaries who worked in the Prairies, and certainly the most trusted by the Indians. He had a touch of Ojibway in his veins, and in 1849 when he was ordained and sent out to the Northwest, he fitted in well with the roving Métis society; when the Métis were forced by the extinction of the buffalo to abandon their nomad existence, he founded for them the settlement of St. Albert, near Edmonton. He was also greatly loved by the Blackfoot, and on at least two occasions he prevented their becoming involved in conflict with the Canadian authorities — once when they talked of stopping work on the Canadian Pacific Railway, and again when Gabriel Dumont called on them to join the Northwest Rebellion of 1885.

Hudson's Bay, and had to winter there before proceeding in spring up the Red River. The first seasons were hard because of the climate and the difficulty of getting food, but even more so because of the hostility of the North West Company and the Métis, which came to a head in the Seven Oaks massacre of 1816. Tenuously, the settlement survived, and it gave rise to a series of villages along the river inhabited by retired Hudson's Bay Company officials, by Métis and by Scots half-breeds, and by the survivors of the original Selkirk settlers. By 1870 these small beginnings had grown into a population of almost 12,000, of whom more than 10,000 were half-breeds or Métis or Indians. There were about l,500 whites, including 290 migrants from Upper Canada. Many of the Métis lived in a semi-nomadic settlement at White Horse Plains, but most of the Red River people cultivated long and narrow farms stretching back from the river in the Québec style.

The Hudson's Bay Company's Fort Garry dominated the settlement, and housed the ruling Council of Assiniboia, a company-appointed body which had almost no real power in a community that carried on surprisingly harmoniously with very little formal government. In the shadow of the fort arose the Red River's only semblance of a town, the traders' village of Winnipeg, described variously by visitors as "unsightly" and "a sorry scene," and consisting of about fifty log houses along a mud street, and "a few small stores with poor goods and high prices;" Colonel Wolseley, who led the military expedition there in 1870, remarked that "grog shops are the principal feature of the place."

The Métis of the Red River had already shown their spirit of independence in 1848 when, under the threat of armed rebellion, they had forced the Hudson's Bay Company to allow free trade in furs over the border to the United States. The idea that their fate had been decided between the Hudson's Bay Company and the British and Canadian governments, without their being consulted, aroused the ire of most of the Red River people, and that ire was increased when the Canadian authorities, with tactless arrogance, sent in surveyors in 1869 before the territory had even been transferred to them.

The Métis decided to resist a Canadian takeover until satisfactory terms were offered to them. They set up an insurrectionary committee, stopped the Lieutenant Governor, who had been despatched from Ottawa, at the border, and established a provisional government of the Red River led by Louis Riel. It was not exactly a rebellion, since Canada's sovereignty over Rupert's Land had not been proclaimed, and the leading Hudson's Bay Company official, representing the departing authority, regarded the provisional government as better than no government at all. Métis rule claimed a single victim — the Orangeman Thomas Scott who had been active in inciting an armed uprising against Riel; otherwise the whole affair was surprisingly bloodless. But it was less successful than it seemed, for though Riel obtained provincial (rather than territorial)

Fort Garry was built by the Hudson's Bay Company between 1817 and 1822 at the junction of the Red and Assiniboine Rivers. For many years it was the administrative centre of Assiniboia and of the Red River fur trade. This sketch was made in 1869, just before Louis Riel siezed the Fort as the headquarters for his provisional government during the Red River Rising.

status for the Red River settlements as the new province of Manitoba (named after the great Indian spirit Manitou) he could not keep the province intact for its original inhabitants. Almost immediately Canadian and other migrants began to flow into Manitoba and the North West Territory; the Métis, unable to compete with these aggressive intruders, moved out towards the South Saskatchewan region, where, in 1885, they would make their last stand for independence under Riel and Gabriel Dumont in the tragic Northwest Rebellion. The defeat of this uprising after the siege of Batoche broke the pride and the cohesion of these people who had once regarded themselves as a nation, the Horse Lords of the Prairies.

It was in 1885, at the trial for his life which followed the defeat at Batoche, that Riel laid down the principle on which the Métis defended themselves, and made a wound on the Canadian conscience that has festered ever since. The fact that the Métis needed to rebel, and the fact that Riel was hanged for the rebellion, point to the imperfections of our notions of democracy.

> I suppose — said Riel — the Half-breeds in Manitoba, in 1870, did not fight for two hundred and forty acres of land, but it is to be understood that there were two societies who treated together. One was small, but in its smallness it had its rights. The other was great, but in its greatness it had no greater rights than the rights of the small, because the right is the same for everyone, and when they began by treating the leaders of that small community as bandits, as outlaws, leaving them without protection, they disorganized that community.

Winnipeg in 1871, just after the foundation of the province of Manitoba.

It was the kind of plea that would be echoed time and again, for fairness and understanding, by minority groups such as the Doukhobors and the Hutterites and various native groups, and which in each case would emphasise the complexity of Canada's variety of peoples and the injustice and impracticality of any attempt to create a homogenous culture.

According to Stephen Leacock, "the Lord said, 'Let there be Wheat,' and Saskatchewan was born." The same might be said of all the Prairie provinces, for the lure of vast areas of unoccupied land, whose fertility had been vouched for by Palliser and Hind's expeditions in 1857, was what made both the people of Ontario and the government of the new Dominion of Canada anxious to acquire the west before the Americans annexed it. When British Columbia came into Confederation in 1871, it was thought that the railway promised under the terms of entry would hasten the peopling of the great open plains that lay between the Pacific province and the rest of Canada. But the railway was long in building, and two earlier measures had more immediate effect. One was the passing of the Dominion Land Act of 1872, which offered free homesteads to settlers who would break, cultivate, and live on the land, and the other was the creation of a para-military force, the North West Mounted Police, intended to save the advance of the Canadian frontier from the violence that had characterized its American counterpart. The Mounted Police established generally good relations with the Indians, and their preparatory work was largely responsible for the successful conclusion of the two important treaties of 1876 and 1877 by which the Cree, the Assiniboine, and the great Blackfoot Confederacy agreed to accept the land designated for them as reservations and left the greater

Louis Riel's Council on the Red River in 1870. In the top row are Charles Larocque, Pierre Delorme, Thomas Bunn, Xavier Pagée, Ambroise Lépine, Baptiste Tournond, Thomas Spence; in the centre row, Pierre Poitras, John Bruce, Louis Riel, W.B. O'Donoghue, Francois Dauphinois; and seated in front, H.F. O'Lone and Paul Proulx.

part of the plains free for settlement. Faced with the disappearance of the great buffalo herds, on which their whole social economy had been based, the Indians had little alternative to accepting a situation that made them wards of the state, second-class citizens of the plains they had once ruled, unchallenged except by each other.

In spite of the absence of the railway, the settlers came, singly and in groups, bringing their belongings in convoys of creaking Red River carts over the historic Carlton trail as far as the North Saskatchewan, where, in 1875, they founded Battleford, for a time the capital of the North West Territory. American ranchers pushed up during the 1870s from Montana into the Alberta foothills country. In 1874 the first of the great collective settlements began, when 7,500 German-speaking Mennonites, leaving Russia, where they had been allowed to settle in the eighteenth-century by Catherine the Great because of religious persecution, arrived in Manitoba. In Russia the Mennonites had farmed the open steppes, and they made a great contribution to the settlement of the Canadian plains by showing that it was possible to farm successfully without being close to a river as the Red River settlers had believed was necessary. The next year, in 1875, 1,250 Icelanders founded their settlement of Gimli ("the great hall of Heaven") on Lake Winnipeg, where they combined farming with commercial fishing. A few Swedes and some Swiss mercenaries had arrived on the Red River as early as 1812-14, but few of them stayed; in the 1870s larger numbers of Swedes began to arrive in the Canadian west by way of the United States. By the early 1880s English gentlemen farmers were attempting to establish themselves in southern Saskatchewan, and at the same period 300 Jewish refugees arrived in Winnipeg

Gabriel Dumont was the most important Métis of the Saskatchewan country, leader of the buffalo hunt and president in the early 1870s of the commune of St. Laurent. In 1884 he was one of the delegates who fetched Louis Riel from Montana to lead the agitation for land rights on the South Saskatchewan, and when frustration led the Métis to rebel, Dumont became the general in charge of their small army. When Batoche fell to General Middleton's Canadians in 1885, Dumont fled south, and this photograph was taken just after he had crossed the border to safety in the United States.

from Russia. While the majority of these remained in the city becoming artisans and shopkeepers and sweatshop workers, there were some who decided to homestead, and a few Jewish settlements were actually attempted, with little of the agricultural success that has attended the *kibbutzim* in Israel.

Once all the political difficulties had been solved and all the surveys had been made, the Canadian Pacific Railway advanced quickly over the Prairies. There were times in the summer of 1882 when three miles of line would be laid in a day over the plains of southern Saskatchewan. As the railway probed forward it spawned villages and towns. Regina and Calgary were born in those years, railway towns populated by merchants and land speculators and lawyers, with local daily papers burgeoning where once it had been necessary to wait for the annual fur brigades to bring in the news from outside. Winnipeg emerged from its dependence on Fort Garry to become an important railway depot and eventually the major industrial centre of the Prairies.

With all the Prairie railways, the Canadian Pacific and its successors, there was a necessary symbiosis between settlement and transportation. Entering an unpopulated land, the railways had to create their own traffic, and this they did largely by selling the choicer areas of the land they had been granted as partial subsidy. But neither the government's offers of free homesteads nor the railway's salesmanship populated the Prairies as quickly as had been anticipated. It was not until Clifford Sifton became Minister of the Interior in 1896 that the greatest flood of immigrants began.

Sifton recognized that if the west were to be filled quickly, Canada must persuade Europeans that it had something better to offer than the closed societies of the old world. Up to now immigration policy had been racially directed. Anglo-Saxons were most desirable, and then Scandinavians and Germans. The Slavs of eastern Europe were regarded with prejudiced distrust until Sifton began to direct his efforts to persuading the subject peoples of the Austrian and Russian empires that Canada offered them not only land but freedom. He was particularly fortunate with the Ukrainians (in those days generally called Galicians); they were a people used to farming the steppes and therefore not inclined to be troubled by the climatic extremes of the Prairies. When he was attacked for bringing them in, Sifton made a classic reply: "I think a stalwart peasant in a sheep-skin coat, born on the soil, whose forefathers have been farmers for ten generations, with a stout wife and half-a-dozen children, is good quality."

By 1910 some 75,000 Ukrainians had arrived, the founders of a community now more than half a million strong and still largely located in the Prairies. Czechs and Slovaks, Poles and Hungarians, Serbs and Croats also arrived in considerable numbers, and all of them preserved something of their native culture, retaining their languages, publishing

This drawing of a Métis home appeared in the Canadian Illustrated *in October, 1874.*

Crowfoot was born a Blood Indian but brought up among the Blackfoot. He became a famous warrior in the wars between the Blackfoot and the Cree, fought in nineteen battles, was wounded six times and killed several of his adversaries in the days before the North-West Mounted Police arrived in 1874 to pacify the Prairies. Crowfoot recognized the plight of the Indians, who, faced with the extinction of the buffalo, had to make the best terms they could with the white men, and so, having become one of the leading chiefs of the Blackfoot, he signed Treaty 7 on their behalf in 1877. After that he kept the peace, even ignoring the appeals of Louis Riel in 1885 to join the Northwest Rebellion. He died in 1890, asking "What is life?" and answering, "It is as the little shadow that runs across the grass and loses itself in the sunset."

Before roads reached the Prairie, the usual means of transport was the Red River cart, whose high wheels were suited for the rough ground pitted with gopher holes. The carts were made entirely of wood, even down to the axles, and could be easily dismantled for ferrying across rivers. William G.R. Hind, who accompanied the Overlanders travelling across the plains to Cariboo in 1862, made this drawing of his companions crossing the Battle River in this way.

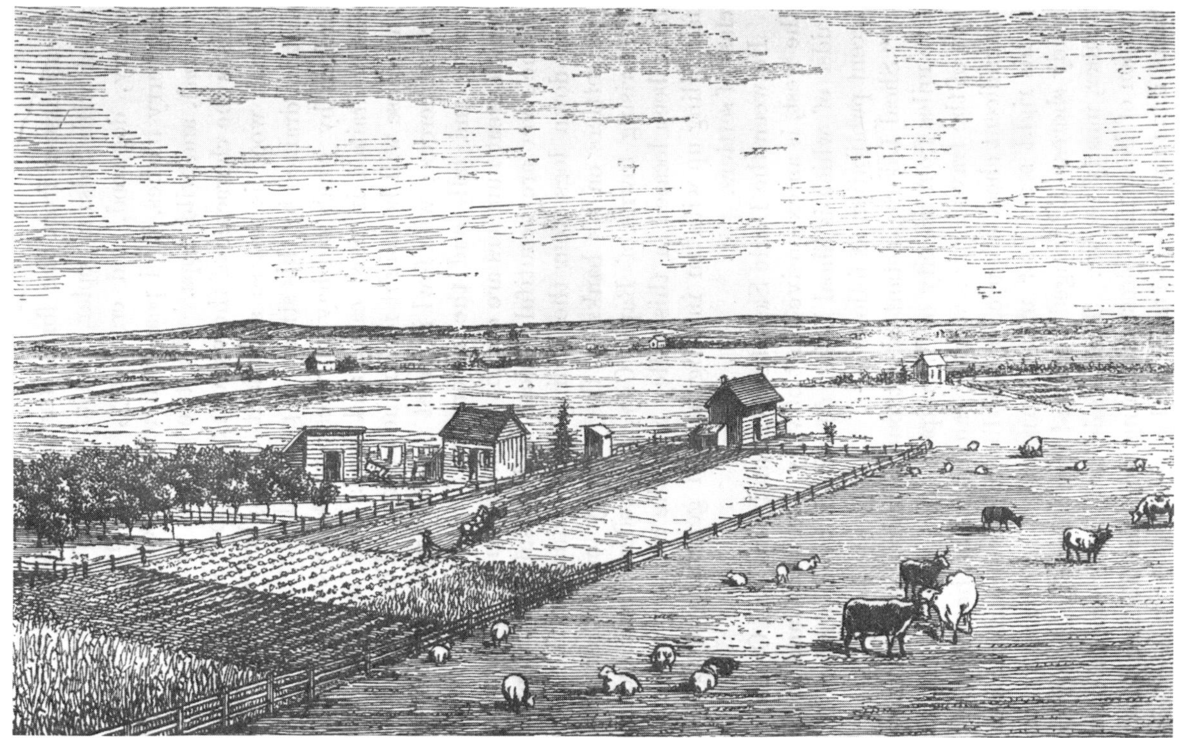

After the creation of the province of Manitoba in 1870, settlement began to spread on the Prairies, and settlers who obtained free homesteads of 160 acres often made rapid progress. In this drawing of 'Settlement 219', made in 1883, two years of work have already tamed the wildness of the virgin Prairie.

their own newspapers, and even maintaining literary traditions, so that to this day there are good Canadian poets whose languages of expression are Ukrainian or Hungarian or German.

Some of the immigrants came for religious reasons, as the Mennonites had done, and notable among these were the pacifist Doukhobors. The Doukhobors were persecuted by the Tsarist authorities of Russia for their refusal to bear arms, and, thanks to Tolstoy's intervention, 8,000 of them were allowed to leave for Canada in 1898. They were given homestead land by Clifford Sifton on the understanding that they would be exempt from military service and would be allowed to hold their land communally. But when they refused to take the oath of allegiance under the homestead regulations because they feared it might lead to demands for military service, their land in the Prairies was taken away from them, and most of them followed their leader, Peter (the Lordly) Verigin, to British Columbia. The unimaginative attitude of the Canadian government on this occasion led to generations of conflict during which the more zealous of the Doukhobors, called the Sons of Freedom, indulged in spectacular forms of protest such as public nudity and arson.

These later groups of migrants tended to spread into the parklands of northern Manitoba and Saskatchewan, and here there was an even closer relationship between railway building and settlement. The Canadian Pacific was too far south to serve this area, and two competing railroads finally moved into it. The Canadian Northern, running through

One of the first tasks of the North West Mounted Police after it was founded in 1873 was to suppress the illegal liquor traffic to the Indians of the plains. In this drawing they are shown inspecting the Red River carts of traders for contraband whisky.

Edmonton over the Yellowhead Pass to Vancouver, was started in 1899. The Grand Trunk Pacific, also using the Yellowhead Pass and reaching salt water at Prince Rupert in British Columbia, was started in 1906. Most of the labouring work on these lines was done by East European homesteaders for whom it provided a basic income until their farms began to produce, and the railways, in their turn, brought about the final occupation of all the areas of the Prairie provinces that could be settled. Even the arid southwestern corner of Saskatchewan, the so-called Palliser Triangle, was eventually occupied by Americans accustomed to the dry-soil farming methods of the midwest.

Anyone who takes the Trans-Canada Highway through the Prairies today has the impression of a landscape more tamed and humanised than any other in Canada. The roads run onward without a curve; the land is divided into its regular squares of grain and stubble, fallow and ploughland. Only in the occasional stretches of smooth-curved hill country where the antelope linger, or in the deep wooded coulees cut by the rivers, does one any longer have a sense of surviving wilderness. Yet for the first settlers this was a wild land indeed. Before the railways came they had to set out over the open plains on trails deep-rutted from the high wooden wheels of the Red River carts, and even the railways only brought them part of the way; there might still be many miles to be travelled by wagon over roadless country, with livestock following behind and nightly bivouacs until one reached the designated section — 160 acres of home-

OPPOSITE:
Under Frank Oliver, Clifford Sifton's successor as Minister of the Interior from 1905-11, immigration propaganda was turned towards American farmers, who were encouraged by slogans like "The Last Best West."

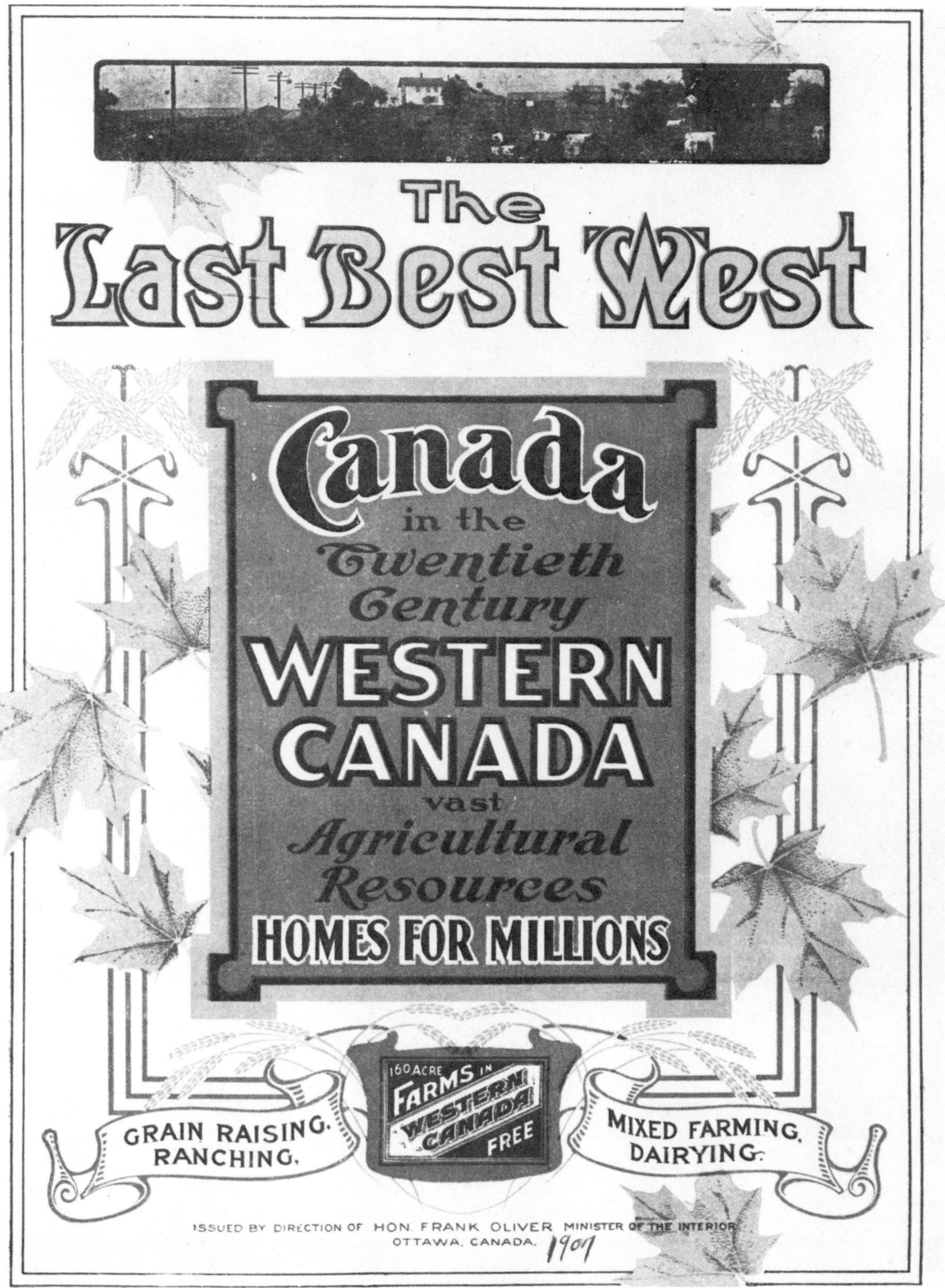
The
Last Best West
Canada
in the
Twentieth
Century
WESTERN
CANADA
vast
Agricultural
Resources
HOMES FOR MILLIONS
160 ACRE FARMS IN WESTERN CANADA FREE
GRAIN RAISING.
RANCHING.
MIXED FARMING.
DAIRYING.
ISSUED BY DIRECTION OF HON. FRANK OLIVER MINISTER OF THE INTERIOR
OTTAWA, CANADA. 1907

Almost eight thousand Doukhobors, persecuted for their pacifist beliefs by the Tsarist government of Russia, emigrated to Canada in 1899, the first of them on board the Lake Huron. *They founded communal villages in Saskatchewan, but a lasting bitterness was created between them and the Canadian authorities when they were driven off their land in 1907 for refusing to accept an oath of allegiance, which they regarded as repugnant to their religious beliefs.*

As Minister of the Interior from 1896 to 1905, Clifford Sifton made it his task to populate the empty prairies, and when he could not get enough Anglo-Saxon immigrants he encouraged Slavs with farming experience to emigrate from the Russian and the Austro-Hungarian Empires. Among those he brought were the first Ukrainians (then known as 'Galicians') and the Doukhobors, and he defended to the end of his time in office his choice of the "Men in sheepskin coats."

stead which, as Douglas Hill remarked in *The Opening of the West*, was likely to be "a patch of nothingness in a flat immensity of the same — an artificial island of wild prairie, in no way different from the vast sweeping ocean of grass around it."

The "wild prairie" had its own beauty, which was often at its height when the settlers reached their land in spring or early summer, but it was a beauty that was soon to be changed utterly, and a vivid image of that change was given by Mary Hiemstra in her Prairie autobiography, *Gully Farm*.

> "Just smell that breeze," Dad said as we rounded a little grove. The warm air was both sweet and sharp; a delightful mixture of wild honeysuckle, roses, wild sweet peas, green grass, sap, tall slough plants, rich brown earth and the yeasty odour of the silver wolf-willows. We came to the top of a little rise and Dad let Nelly stop.
>
> "Take a good look at it, Mary," Dad said quietly. "You'll never see it this way again."
>
> How could the prairie change? I wondered. I did not realise then what an instrument of change a plough is.
>
> The trees and willows are gone now, grubbed out and burned, and the roses and wild mint have been ploughed under. Wheat now grows where the chokecherries and the violets bloomed. The wind is still sweet but there is no wildness in it and it no longer seems to have wandered a great way over grass and trees and flowers. It now smells of dry straw and bread. The wild keen fragrance the wind knew in those days has gone for ever.

The grass had to be broken, and very often the first result of its breaking was the building of the homesteader's first house. Since there

Le Chant de la Pierre, Paul Emile Borduas

Trans-Canada, Jean-Paul Lemieux

JEAN PAUL LEMIEUX

Homage, William Ronald

With his furniture and the lumber for his shack, a settler sets out from railhead at Kindersley, Saskatchewan, driving over the open Prairie to his homestead.

were few trees, turf was the only available building material, and the sod house, or "soddy", had at least the virtues of being warm in winter and cool in summer, though it was never impervious to sustained rainfall. Like the early *habitant* in Québec, the homesteader had to be largely self-sufficient, at least until his fields were ploughed and producing one of the hardy wheats that had been specially bred to suit the Prairie climate. His first task of all would be to establish a garden, and a good part of his food would still be what the Prairie gratuitously provided — wild berries, wild birds who gathered on the Prairie ponds or sloughs — fish from those sloughs, rabbits, and even, when rabbits were scarce, gophers.

Even if he had some experience of ordinary farming, the settler might find breaking the tough tangle of Prairie grasses a difficult task. Yet break it he must, with oxen or horses or even women (as happened with the Doukhobors) dragging the plough, for this could be a matter literally of life and death, not only because of the crops that must be grown, but also because the best precaution from the lethal Prairie grass fires was to plough a good stretch of land on every side of one's house. Water — one way or another — was a frequent problem. Either the settler found that his homestead was mostly marshland or he had the greatest difficulty sinking an adequate well. Summers were a time of agony from the heat and the mosquitoes; winters were a time of peril because of the blizzards that could obliterate roads, fences, any kind of landmark, and because of the danger of frostbite and snowblindness. In bad weather horses and cattle, and sometimes men, might freeze solid only a short way from the farmhouse.

"All around me, when I was a child," said Fredelle Maynard in her recollections, "men broke the land under the fierce promise of the

A train load of settlers with their effects arrives in Winnipeg from North Dakota, 1891.

Many settlers built their first sod homes out of turf cut from the virgin Prairie, for some regions were virtually treeless.

While their men went to earn money working on the railway grades, the Doukhobor women stayed in their Prairie villages to carry on the farm work, including the winnowing of grain in the traditional Russian manner, by hand.

Homestead Act — a quarter section free if within three years you could plough the prairie, raise house and barn, and survive. It can never come again, that free wild perilous world. No one who has known it would willingly return. No one who has left it can forget." But there were those who left without proving the titles to their land and so, in a sense, without proving themselves, like the "Alberta Homesteader" of a traditional Prairie song.

> So Farewell to Alberta, farewell to the west,
> It's backward I'll go to the girl I love best.
> I'll go back to the east and get me a wife
> And never eat cornbread the rest of my life.

It was a life whose harshnesses women and men shared in equally, for the women who settled as pioneers on the Prairies had to do everything that their predecessors in Ontario had done, in addition to enduring greater remotenesses (for Prairie towns were fewer and farther between than eastern towns) and a far harsher climate, in which it was possible to grow less on the farm than had been the case in eastern Canada; as a result many of the necessities of life had to be bought with money raised from grain crops, and, until the first crops came in, or when they failed, such necessities were in short supply. During the summers, particularly in the decades before manual work had been displaced by machines, the women — and the children as well — had to help in the harvest, first reaped with scythes and sickles and only in later decades with Massey-Harris combines, and when the itinerant threshing crews came through, the women also had to cook for them. But all this toil on their holdings did not prevent the Prairie women from creating, as soon as there were enough settlers to form local communities, mutual aid systems, largely operating through the churches, by which they maintained contact and helped each other in the crises of childbirth and sickness and death.

Yet despite all these dangers and discomforts, and largely because of a survival code of co-operation and mutual support, the settlers converted the Prairie provinces in a surprisingly short time from a harsh frontier to a more-or-less stable agricultural economy that already existed in 1905 when Saskatchewan and Alberta were separated from the North West Territory and turned into provinces. A unique Prairie society had come into being, with its quarter-section farms and its simple one-crop economy whose high point came each autumn when the wheat was cut and the threshing teams wandered over the golden plains. The farmers would take their grain in to the clusters of elevators in the villages scattered every twelve miles or so along the railways, villages with names derived — like Many Berries and Seven Persons — from old Indian place names, or — like Balzac or Bassano — from the cultural predilections of the surveyor.

It was a life whose simplicity and harshness profoundly influenced

The first great machines to appear on the Prairies were the steam traction engines operating the threshing machines which went from farm to farm with their itinerant teams of workers.

human attitudes. The extremities of the natural world, the torrid summers and bitter winters which the utmost cultivation of the land could not avert, produced a breed of men who tended towards radical extremes in their attitude to this world and the next.

It is deceptively easy to draw distinctions between the ways the Prairie economy developed in the three provinces and affected the local human types. The ranching tradition, reinforced by the oil-rich decades, has produced among Albertans the stereotype of a loud, large, breezy man, with a broad-brimmed Stetson, high-heeled half-boots and a hard eye for business; the stereotype Saskatchewanian, citizen of the most rural and wheat-centred province of the west, tends to be a serious, practical man, tied to his geometrical farm, over which, in cap and dungarees, he drives his crimson tractors and science-fiction combines; the Manitoban, as likely as not, will be an urban man, for Winnipeg contains more than half the province's population. If he is not from Winnipeg the Manitoban may well be a miner from Flin Flon or a pulpmill worker from the northern forests.

But whatever he is, the Prairie dweller tends to have more than his due share of outrightness and individuality. Wallace Stegner, who spent his childhood on a Saskatchewan farm, expressed well the relationship between man and terrain.

> It is a country to breed mystical people, egocentric people, perhaps poetic people. But not humble ones. At noon the total sun pours on your single head; at sunrise or sunset you throw a shadow a hundred yards long. It was not prairie dwellers who invented the indifferent universe or impotent man. Puny you may feel there, and vulnerable, but not unnoticed. This is a land to mark the sparrow's fall.

The mechanical combines that harvest grain today were preceded by horse-drawn reapers and binders; this one harvests 'Red Fife' wheat in Manitoba before World War I.

There is likely to be more than a touch of spiritual and political dissent in the Prairie dweller's make-up. The gospel billboards that line the highways are signs that revivalist religion is strong. In fact, its manifestations tend to run parallel with the activities of the established churches. Belonging to the United Church, or the Presbyterian, or the Anglican Church of Canada or even the Greek Orthodox Church, does not make a Prairie dweller immune from the appeal of a good camp-meeting-style preacher, and such a preacher's influence can go far beyond his tiny sect or small congregation, as was shown when William Aberhart, who ran a radio gospel programme from a modest Calgary church, embraced Social Credit and found himself at the head of a province-wide populist movement that swept him to political victory. Aberhart ruled Alberta from 1935 to his death in 1943, and the impetus which he gave to the Social Credit movement was so strong that it remained in power under his successor, Ernest Manning, until 1968.

In politics the Prairies have been the home of radical trends ever since a characteristic local society began to develop with special interests and special grievances against the central government in Ottawa. All the important English Canadian minority parties that have challenged the dual role of Liberals and Conservatives in controlling politics have originated in these provinces. They were bred out of the discontent of town workers, many of whom were trade unionists before they migrated from Britain, and out of the despair of the farmers, particularly during the Depression years when a slump in the world wheat market coincided with a period of drought that literally blew away in clouds of dust the top soil from thousands of south Saskatchewan and Alberta farms.

Prairie radicalism did not in fact begin with the Depression. Its first manifestation was the historic Winnipeg General Strike of 1919, co-

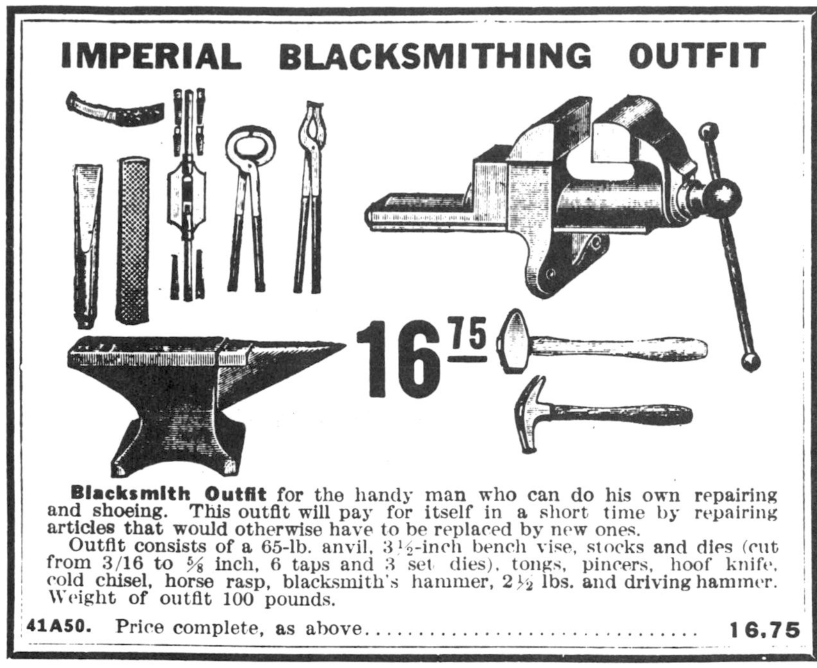

On a distant homestead, far from the nearest town, the early Prairie farmer was often of necessity a jack-of-all-trades, and the mail order houses stocked the equipment that enabled him to become his own blacksmith and general mechanic.

inciding with a farmer revolt against high tariffs and freight rates that in the same year turned the United Farmers of Alberta and the United Farmers of Manitoba into provincial parties and in 1920 created the populist Progressive Party to fight in federal elections. The farmer parties won power in Alberta in 1921 and in Manitoba in 1922. In 1921 the Progressives, with sixty-four seats, formed the second most powerful party in the federal House of Commons, but they refused to form the official opposition and allowed Mackenzie King to manipulate them into insignificance.

One area in which Prairie radicalism was especially strong was the emancipation of women. The Prairie outrightness and individuality I have mentioned were not the prerogatives of men alone. They produced a series of pioneer women doctors and lawyers and of remarkable fighters for women's rights, of whom the most notable were probably Nellie McClung and Emily Gowan Murphy. As a novelist, Nellie McClung was sentimental and even sanctimonious, but as a crusader against the worst evils of drinking she earned the epithet of "the Holy Terror." She carried her uncompromising vigour into the agitation for equal franchise, and was largely responsible for the vote being given to women in Alberta in 1916, before it was gained by women federally. In the same year the Alberta government appointed Emily Gowan Murphy, who had long campaigned for married women's property rights, as the first woman magistrate in the British Empire. Nellie McClung and Emily Murphy, with three other Prairie women, were later involved in the famous "Persons Case," relating to the clause in the British North America Act

But work was not everything, and elegance was available at reasonable prices for skating and other distractions of the long and leisurely winter months.

John Diefenbaker imported into the House of Commons the histrionic gestures and resonant eloquence of a successful criminal lawyer, as this photograph from thirty years ago (1948) suggests. Born in Ontario, Diefenbaker was reared in Saskatchewan, and the Conservatism he adopted was of the Prairie populist kind, tinged with moral fervour. He served a long political apprenticeship before he became leader of the Tories in 1956 (at the age of 61) and in 1957 the first Conservative prime minister for 22 years. At the next election (1958) he won, with 208 seats out of 265, the largest majority ever gained by a Canadian prime minister. Diefenbaker was also the first prime minister to come from Canada's third nation (the quarter of the population of neither English nor French descent,) and his interest in minorities led him to appoint the first Indian senator. Diefenbaker's concern for the underdog was broad and sincere, but he proved an inept leader and after his defeat in 1963 never returned to power, though he had remained a powerful spokesman for political decency. He represented the riding of Prince Albert, Saskatchewan, until his death in August, 1979, a month before his 84th birthday, at his home in Ottawa.

about appointments to the Senate, which used the word "persons." Up to 1927, when the group petitioned the Supreme Court, "persons" had been interpreted to mean only men. The Supreme Court turned down the women's petition, but the Judicial Committee of the Privy Council in London, then the supreme arbiter of matters arising out of the BNA Act, ruled in their favour, and in 1929 the senate was eventually opened to both sexes, a victory gained for all the women of Canada.

Women also were in the forefront of the literary movement in the Prairies. Adele Wiseman's vivid novels of Winnipeg Jewish life (especially *The Sacrifice*), Martha Ostenso's realistic *Wild Geese* (concerning Norwegian immigrants) and Laura Salverson's fictional accounts of Icelandic settlers in northern Manitoba (of which *The Viking Heart* is probably the best) added notably to Canadian writing in past decades, but all of them were surpassed by Margaret Laurence, whose Manawaka novels about Manitoba life (dealt with more extensively elsewhere) are among the first achievements of our national literature.

The Depression produced a surprisingly positive reaction among Prairie people. For several reasons, this was the hardest-hit region of Canada. Disruptions of world markets brought the grain prices down to an unprecedentedly low level, but even worse off than the producing farmers were those in the dry regions of Saskatchewan where dust-bowl conditions were created. The wind blew away the topsoil from fields which eventually grew crops of Russian thistle and nothing more. In the long run world markets recovered and new methods of dry-soil farming reclaimed many of the lost holdings. In the meantime, the situation resurrected pioneer virtues that belonged to the recent past. Cashless farmers reverted to barter. Destitute people shared with those more destitute. A characteristic sight of the period on Prairie roads was the Bennett Buggy (nicknamed after the incumbent Prime Minister, R. B. Bennett) which consisted of an old Model T Ford, for which the farmer could no longer afford repairs or gasoline, drawn by a team of skeletal horses. People co-operated in a way that ensured both individual survival and the survival of the Prairie society of large farms and small towns. Many people who lived through those years look back on them with nostalgia, despite the hardships they endured, because of the human warmth and mutual aid they encountered and found themselves projecting in a world where the welfare state was still far in the future.

If the Prairie people had felt even before the Depression that they were discriminated against by eastern politicians, now they felt they were wholly neglected, and having seen how earlier farmers' movements had been manipulated by experienced politicians, they decided to create independent radical parties. The discontented farmers, particularly from hard-hit Saskatchewan, came together with labour groups from Winnipeg, British Columbia, and Ontario in 1932 to found the C.C.F., the Co-operative Commonwealth Federation, a democratic socialist party led by the former Methodist preacher J. S. Woodsworth. In 1944 the C.C.F. formed the government of Saskatchewan, and even today that province has the only Socialist government in Canada, although both Manitoba and British Columbia have had their periods of government by the C.C.F.'s successor, the New Democratic Pary (N.D.P.). The other political movement to emerge from the rebellious minds of the Prairie people, was the Social Credit Party, which William Aberhart led to power in a wave of populist enthusiasm in 1935, and which governed the province until 1971, spreading its influence to British Columbia, which even today is still Social Credit.

The end of the Depression did not terminate the political intransigence of the Prairies, whose voters have maintained a principled opposition to any party in power in Ottawa, with the sole exception of the period of Conservative rule under John Diefenbaker, who in his own way had been as intransigent a Prairie radical as any claiming allegiance to the N.D.P. or Social Credit.

At the same time, there have been great changes of other kinds in Prairie society. The phenomenal strike of oil near Leduc in 1947 changed both the society and the economy of Alberta. Just as Texans arriving with cattle herds during the 1880s had helped to establish the ranching industry, so Texan oil riggers helped to establish the oil industry, and many of them stayed on in the province. Oil made Alberta's economy no longer dependent on wheat sales, as did, in Manitoba, the growth of industry in Winnipeg and of mining in northern centres like Flin Flon and Thompson, in what had, in the past, been merely trappers' country. Even in Saskatchewan the discovery of oil and of large deposits of potash have lessened the province's dependence on the single crop of the grain farms. But perhaps more important in transforming Prairie society outside the large cities have been the changes in farming methods and transport patterns. These have rendered largely obsolete a way of life which came into being little more than two generations ago, so that the railway-side communities which were founded in 1880s and 1890s, and which, in their day, were vital centres of economic and social life, have now become little more than ghost towns. The mechanization of farming had made the old quarter-section farm unprofitable. The average contemporary Prairie farm now runs around 600 acres in size, and it is growing as large agribusiness corporations buy up and consolidate individual holdings. Partly because of the disappearance of so many small farmers, and partly because the Trans-Canada Highway and its subsidiary roads have made travel so much more rapid and easy, the small Prairie communities have shrunk into tiny vestiges as the people trade in the larger towns that are scattered at roughly fifty-mile intervals over the plains. Thus the microcosmic small place with which we are familiar from so many Prairie novels is virtually obsolete.

The Prairie provinces have in fact undergone their own process of

Margaret Laurence is one of the best Canadian novelists and certainly the finest writer to emerge from the Prairies, where she was born in 1926 in the little Manitoba town of Neepawa. Though she began to write in childhood, it was a period in Somaliland and Ghana, from 1949 to 1957, that shaped Laurence as a writer, and produced her first novel, *This Side Jordan,* and a splendid book on Somali life, *The Prophet's Camel Bell.* But these books on exotic places, perceptive and limpidly written, merely prepared for the series of four novels *(The Stone Angel, A Jest of God, The Fire-Dwellers* and *The Diviners)* that together represent the greatest collective achievement of any Canadian novelist. Laurence cannot be classed merely as a regional writer, though she presents a rich and memorable view of smalltown Prairie life. Her novels open to broader implications when she considers the inner lives and outer roles of women, the nature and uses of memory, the discordances between body and mind in growing old, the nature of artistic creation: major themes that have always concerned major novelists and in Laurence's works are discussed with sensitivity, courage and a fine verbal accuracy.

During the Depression the Prairie farmers were hard hit by the decline in world wheat markets. But there were other troubles in the dreadful Thirties. Drought parched the fields.

And with drought the precious top soil blew away and drifted like snow around houses and other obstacles.

Depression-poor Prairie farmers who could not afford gasoline hitched their cars to teams of horses. The hybrid vehicle that resulted was called a Bennett-buggy after Prime Minister R.B. Bennett. This Bennett-buggy was driven in 1933 by Mackenzie King, Bennett's great political rival.

urbanization, and the cities have become far more dominant than in the days when they existed as transit centres for immigrants and service centres for the settlers. Saskatchewan is the only province in the region whose population remains more rural than urban; it is also the only province whose population fell steadily for years on end because it had no dynamic centres to attract its departing farm boys. Winnipeg alone contains about fifty-five per cent of the population of Manitoba, and the rival cities of Edmonton and Calgary between them contain more than half the population of Alberta.

Thus the typical Prairie dweller is no longer the wheat farmer diligently working the fields. He or she is much more likely to live in a town and to earn money in other ways than from the land. Only in Saskatchewan does wheat still account for roughly half the province's income; in Alberta and Manitoba it accounts for no more than a fifth, and even those small proportions are produced by methods which have turned farming into a mechanized and rationalized industry. No longer is it the way of life and freedom which, harsh as it was known to be, drew people from the ends of the earth to populate the Prairies and established there a multicultural society, the Canadian "third world" of those whose past is neither British nor French.

Perhaps more than in any other part of Canada, literature in the Prairies has reflected the rapidity of social change. The archetypal form of Prairie writing is realistic fiction, a fiction based on an attempt to unlock the riches of a hostile world. Frederick Philip Grove — a German writer named Felix Paul Greve who abandoned his European career, his friendships with Gide and Stefan George, and even his name to bury himself in a Manitoba rural school — became eventually the most ambitious chronicler of the pioneer life, in books such as *Settlers of the*

The angular outlines and luminous complexities of refineries like that in Edmonton manifest the shift from poverty to prosperity that came to the western Prairies after the great oil strike at Leduc in 1947.

Marsh and *Fruits of the Earth*. The very clumsiness of Grove's handling of human relationships seemed almost in keeping with the harshness of the life he portrayed. At the same time, he was extremely sensitive to the Prairie environment, and his volumes of descriptive essays, *Over Prairie Trails* and *The Turn of the Year*, have been unexcelled in their evocation of the landscape and its moods. His most important novel, *The Master of the Mill*, was a powerful work which took as its theme the dehumanization of a society that becomes steadily more dominated by the machine; it anticipated later Prairie fiction in veering from strict realism towards a more symbolic treatment of his subject.

Robert Stead's *Grain* and Martha Ostenso's *Wild Geese* were other ralistic novels about farming life on the prairies, while Adele Wiseman's *The Sacrifice,* set in the Winnipeg Jewish community, is one of the few notable urban novels written in the Canadian west. Ostenso and Wiseman, like the Icelander Laura Goodman Salverson in her novel, *The Viking Heart*, wrote mainly of the immigrants, neither British nor French in origin, who form such a large proportion of the Prairie population.

A later generation of Prairie novelists was concerned less with the hardships endured by the pioneer than with the narrowness of the life that developed in the small wheat-growing communities, isolated from major centres of culture. Books like Sinclair Ross's *As for Me and My House* and W. O. Mitchell's *Who Has Seen the Wind?* explore the struggle of sensitive people in such an environment against both inner stultification and external prejudice.

In Margaret Laurence's splendid cycle of novels set in part in the Prairies and stretching from *The Stone Angel* to *The Diviners,* the realism becomes historical. In creating her Prairie town of Manawaka out of experience and imagination she gave the history of the Prairie culture that extension into the quality of myth that mature art creates. This was because of a sense of complete rooting in the local cultures. On the last page of her book of essays, *Heart of a Stranger*, she says:

> This is where my world began. A world which includes the ancestors — both my own and other people's ancestors who become mine. A world which formed me, and continues to do so, even while I fought it in some of its aspects, and continue to do so. A world which gave me my own lifework to do, because it was here that I learned the sight of my own particular eyes.

Perhaps, indeed, the importance of the Prairies in the development of Canadian literature, and Canadian culture in general, was that the great mingling of peoples which took place there meant that no past existed elsewhere, no common Old Country, to which everyone looked back as they did in Québec and Upper Canada, in British Columbia and the Maritimes, where the cultures were fairly homogenous and oriented towards either France or Britain. In the Prairies the pasts were all different, but the present was the same, and so Prairie literature started not somewhere far away, but on the spot, in the realistic fiction that eventually, in Margaret Laurence and later writers like Robert Kroetsch, acquired historical depths and the power of myth.

The men of Cook's expedition collected sea otter skins from the Indians of the Pacific Coast, which they later sold for high prices to Chinese merchants in Canton. The news of their profits brought many sea traders to the Coast, among whom was Captain John Meares, who in 1788 launched into Nootka Sound the Northwest America, *the first vessel other than Indian canoes built on the shores of what is now British Columbia.*

CHAPTER NINE

British Columbia Beyond the Great Divide

The Continental Divide, for many British Columbians, is a mental as well as a geographical barrier which makes them feel isolated from the rest of Canada. There is a legendary British Columbian, whom I have never met but who tends to figure anonymously in the reports of Toronto newspaper correspondents visiting the province with the remark: "I couldn't care if the rest of Canada were submerged and the Atlantic were breaking on the western foothills of the Rockies." Such a character may — and probably does — exist only in the journalistic imagination, like the proverbial New York taxi driver, yet there is the customary fragment of truth in the story. British Columbia's history began apart from that of the greater part of the country in a number of striking ways that are rooted first of all in the uniqueness of the terrain.

Sir Francis Drake sighted the Pacific coast of Canada in 1579 and claimed it for Queen Elizabeth I. Juan Perez, the Spanish commander sailing off the Queen Charlotte Islands, encountered canoes filled with Haida Indians. But it was Captain James Cook who was the first white man to land on these coasts, when he put into Nootka Sound in 1778.

British Columbians do not live on open plains like the Prairie peoples or in the relatively human-scale landscapes that emerged in the Maritimes and Québec and Ontario once the farmer had impressed his image on the countryside. They live in the midst of what the nineteenth-century Liberal leader Edward Blake described with some horror as "a sea of mountains", the succession of great ranges — the Selkirks and the Monashee, the Cascades and the Coast Mountains — that continue in gigantic parallels four hundred miles from the Divide until the last of them dips its fjord-bitten feet into the islanded waters of the Pacific. As Roderick Haig-Brown said, "The first almighty fact about British Columbia is mountains." Apart from a small amount of dryland plateau like the Cariboo and Chilcotin region, all that the rain-forest-covered mountains leave for British Columbians to inhabit are narrow valleys and river deltas and offshore islands. These provide such scanty footholds that only a tiny fraction of the province is arable and more than three-quarters of the people live in a twentieth of its area, mostly in Vancouver, in the lower Fraser valley and on the southern tip of Vancouver Island in the neighbourhood of Victoria. The two larger cities account for well over half the population of the province, and though the rich fruit-growing valley of the Okanagan is fairly thickly populated, with orchards and vineyards clambering over the dry hillsides, there are few important concentrations of people elsewhere in the province. Kamloops

Accompanying Captain Cook was the artist John Webber, who drew many scenes of Nootka Indian life, including this interior of a longhouse, with the fish hanging from the rafters and the cooking hearth in the middle of the floor.

in the southern and Prince George in the northern interior are regional farming and lumbering centres with around thirty thousand inhabitants, and Prince Rupert is a fishing centre on the northern coast with less than twenty thousand residents. For the rest, British Columbians live in small mining and logging towns and even smaller farming and ranching villages scattered wherever a cultivator can gain a toehold or a hundred cattle can graze or an exploiter can find something to tear from the surface or the interior of the earth.

British Columbia does in fact depend far more on exploiting its natural resources, renewable and non-renewable (timber, fish, minerals, fossil fuels, and hydro power) than on agriculture (like Saskatchewan) or industry (like Ontario). Even its major industries, such as smelting and paper-making, depend very directly on natural products. This has been one of the causes for the extraordinary mixture of "types" one encounters in British Columbia, from the flamboyant ranchers of the Cariboo to the God-intoxicated Doukhobor farmers of the Kootenays; from the ruthless lumber and mining barons who live in great Vancouver mansions to the equally tough loggers and miners with their labour traditions largely inherited from the radical "Wobblies" who moved here early in the century; from the English snobs who still prevail in parts of Vancouver Island to the hard-line democrats of the mining settlements in northern areas (where the climate resembles that of neighbouring Yukon) and of the fishing settlements far up the coastal inlets; from the Chinese, who came to work in the mines and on the railways and are now

Much of our knowledge of Coast Indian life in the early days of contact with Europeans we owe to the painter Paul Kane, who set off overland from Toronto in 1846, and drew many vivid sketches of the plains Indians as he wandered to the Pacific, where, among many other items, he drew this study of "Medicine Masks of Northwest Coast Tribes".

In the twilight of the Coast Indian culture the photographer E.S. Curtis captured, by careful stage-managing, many of its characteristic elements. Here he portrays a wedding party arriving in full ceremonial regalia, sailing in painted and carved canoes.

The painting of spruce-root hats with heraldic designs was one of surviving arts of the Coast that Curtis recorded.

breaking into Canadian finance and politics, to the Sikhs, largely involved in the timber industry, who worship beside the Fraser in a starkly beautiful temple designed by Canada's leading architect, Arthur Erickson.

At first sight there may seem to be little in common between the people of the interior who often still live something very close to a frontier existence, and the inhabitants of Vancouver and Victoria, where the bland, rainy climate combines with nearby mountains and sheltered waterways to provide a uniquely hedonistic existence, the renowned lotus life of the shores of the Gulf of Georgia where, as Paddy Sherman once boasted, "we are able to golf, ski, sail, climb mountains, garden ten months every year," and where, as Rupert Brooke observed, the mountains change colour "every two minutes in the most surprising way" and nature "is half Japanese". Yet these people all share one common attribute, and this is a strongly developed individualism, a collective image — if one may talk so paradoxically — of themselves as loners in a world of loners. The traditions of Man alone against the wilderness — of the prospectors and hand loggers, of the settlers in remote valleys and the fishermen risking their lives single-handed in small gill-netters — linger among the descendents of such men and are even acquired by those who only came over the mountains a few years ago. In a similar way, the memory of bitter industrial struggles has left its mark. The traditions of the I.W.W., the militantly syndicalist Industrial Workers of the World who flourished on the Coast in the early days of the century, are not forgotten by British Columbian labour activists, who sometimes sing a song — "Where the Fraser River Flows" — written by the famous American worker bard Joe Hill to celebrate a tough strike in 1912.

Where the Fraser River flows, each fellow worker knows,
They have bullied and oppressed us, but still our Union grows.
And we're going to find a way, boys, for shorter hours and
better pay, boys,
And we're going to win the day, boys, where the Fraser
River flows.

British Columbians see themselves as divided from the rest of Canada by geography — there is always a mountain to be circumvented if one travels any distance — by traditions, by personal interests and even by class interests, and this has always made them a politically volatile people, not to be tamed by the mass Canadian parties whose organizations are based on the Ontario-Québec axis. Instead they are liable to give their loyalities rather capriciously to populist local leaders — like John Oliver and Duff Patullo, like the Bennetts and Dave Barrett — with whom they can make some kind of personal identification. It was significant that when a national poll was held recently to find who was the man most hated by Canadians, Pierre Trudeau won hands down in

Curtis also photographed this mask of the Sisiutl, the mythical double-headed snake which was the feared guardian spirit of Kwakiutl warriors.

British Columbia, beating even Idi Amin, which is a fairly typical sign of the distrust national leaders inspire beyond the Divide. On the other hand, if Trudeau's apparent arrogance has often angered British Columbians, significantly few of them took any exception to their own flamboyant premier W. A. C. Bennett's habit of declaring "I'm plugged in to God!"

Part of the fractionable character of British Columbian society can, of course, be attributed to historical causes and especially to the fact that the province had its own separate history of settlement by sea from Britain and Asia and by land from California even before it entered Confederation; that early identity has by no means been submerged by the Canadian overlay. When the colony joined Canada in 1871, the island capital of Victoria was undoubtedly more English in its way of life than any other part of Canada, and long continued so, while the main dissident element in the city was American rather than Canadian, for most of the merchants had come up from San Francisco bringing with them a Californian style of architecture that can be seen in the buildings that survive from the gold rush period of the 1850s and 1860s.

The guardian spirit myths of chief clans were recorded on poles erected before the houses of the Coast Indians. Already, in this Bella Coola village, the houses have become modernized — built of sawn planks with windows and doors instead of being windowless buildings of split cedar planks, but the heraldic motifs and the carving styles of the poles remain as they were when Cook landed.

There were Canadians in British Columbia before Confederation, as there had been on the Red River, but again they were a minority that played a small part in pre-Canadian official life and did not determine social attitudes, at least on Vancouver Island. The situation has not changed as radically as might have been expected. "British Columbian" certainly does not, in the 1970s, mean the same as "British" or anything near it. Yet it conveys in a subtle way the idea that here is another province in its own way *pas comme les autres*, and it is edifying to observe how quickly immigrants from England and other European countries, and even eastern Canadians who elect to make their lives beyond the Divide, tend to think of themselves as British Columbians first, as Canadians second — just as the Québecois and the Newfoundlanders are inclined to identify primarily with what Spaniards, with the special eloquence of a traditionally regionalist group of peoples, refer to as the *patria chica*, the little fatherland.

Not that British Columbia is even a single *patria chica*. History and topography and local loyalties fragment it, so that the island, the lower

The most prestigious ceremonial garments of the Coast Indians were the costly Chilkat blankets, woven by Tlingit tribes in Alaska, but traded all down the coast. The heraldic designs of the blankets were drawn on boards by male artists, and then the blankets were woven by women from goat's wool. Dancing tunics were also made in the same way by the Chilkat weavers. The original design of the Chilkat blanket is said to have been originated and then forgotten by the Tsimshian of British Columbia.

mainland and the interior are distinct mental as well as physical zones, and within the interior the people of the Okanagan are sharply different in outlook and lifestyle from the people of the Kootenays. Farther north there is little in common between an Indian cowboy from the Cariboo and an Indian fisherman from the Queen Charlottes.

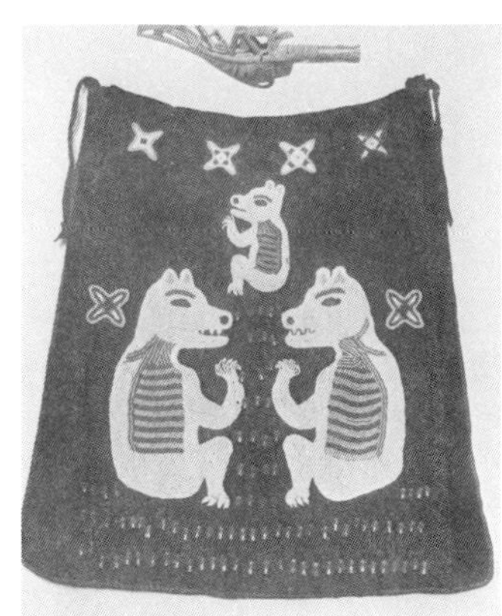

This robe and raven rattle were used by a Kwakiutl chief when he danced at the potlatch feasts where he would entertain and make generous gifts to the guests who came to witness some ceremonial event, such as his assumption of a title or raising of a pole.

To ask how all this came about leads one back into the haphazard history of the discovery and settlement of the province. Sir Francis Drake may have seen it, though he certainly never set foot here, when he sailed up the Pacific coast of North America in 1579, naming it New Albion. The spanish mariner Juan Perez was certainly there in 1774, and on July 20 of that year he encountered the Haida Indians, when a great canoe almost as long as his ship put out from the shore and others followed, with people clad in sea otter robes and conical hats of reeds dancing in the prows and scattering eagle down on the water in welcome. Perez did not land, and four years later Captain James Cook and his crew became the first Europeans to set foot on British Columbian soil when they landed at the village of the great Nootka chief Maquinna on Vancouver Island. Cook too, on that March day in 1778, was welcomed by a dancer, the chief himself, wearing alternating masks and his bear-skin whale-hunter's robe, but he was perhaps even more impressed by the extraordinary sense of property that became immediately evident in the behaviour of the Coast Indians.

> I have no where, in my several voyages, met with any uncivilized nation, or tribe, who had such strict notions of their having a right to the exclusive property of everything that their country produces, as the inhabitants of this Sound. At first, they wanted our people to pay for the wood and water that they carried on board; and had I been on the spot, when these demands were made, I should certainly have complied with them. Our workmen, in my absence thought differently; for they took but little notice of such claims; and the natives, when they found that we were determined to pay nothing, at last ceased to apply. But they made a merit of necessity; and frequently afterward, took occasion to remind us, that they had given us wood and water out of friendship.

With the coming of steel tools brought by the sea traders, the Coast Indians — originally great carvers in wood and horn — branched into metalwork, and this silver napkin ring, said to have been made by the great Haida artist Charles Edenshaw in the late nineteenth century, is a fine example of the craft.

British Columbians have not changed greatly; whoever encounters them for the first time today finds them hospitable, sometimes recklessly so, as the Indians were at potlatch time, but conscious of property and proud of their possessions.

The first white man actually to acquire land in British Columbia was Captain John Meares, who, in 1788, gained possession of a lot at Nootka from Maquinna, and there erected a post and even built a small ship, the *North West American*. By 1789 the Spaniard Martinez displaced Meares and erected a fort that lasted until the Spanish withdrawal under the Nootka convention in 1795.

The first white settlements in British Columbia were the forts in the northern part of the province, established by Simon Fraser in the early years of the nineteenth century, such as Fort St. James, founded in 1806. In 1828 Sir George Simpson, governor of the Hudson's Bay Company, reached Fort St. James on his trans-continental tour, and was welcomed by James Douglas, later the first governor of Vancouver Island and British Columbia.

But if the seamen built earliest in British Columbia, the Montreal fur traders who followed Mackenzie's 1793 pioneer overland journey to the Pacific, created settlements that have lasted until today, all of them in the cold and still thinly populated north of the province, the region of short summers and hard long winters known then as New Caledonia. In 1804 Simon Fraser established Fort McLeod and in 1806 Fort St. James; there are still lakeside villages on both these sites. In 1807 he founded Fort George, which is now part of Prince George, hence the oldest of the larger British Columbian towns. In this area agriculture west of the Rockies first began, when the trader Daniel Williams Harmon, a dour and practical Vermonter, cultivated potatoes and turnips, carrots and barley to supplement the dried salmon that was the regular diet of his men, and found that such species grew marvellously in the clear, brief northern warmth.

After 1813, when the Americans abandoned Fort Astoria at the mouth of the Columbia, the North West Company, and later the Hudson's Bay Company, began to concentrate on the coast. First, in 1825, Fort Vancouver was built on the north bank of the Columbia in the hope that it would give the British a fair claim to what is now the state of

The fur traders used the great rivers of British Columbia as their thoroughfares, but the canyon of the Fraser they found too dangerous as a trade route. It was finally rejected after George Simpson and Chief Trader Macdonald descended it at great peril in 1828.

After the Oregon Boundary Treaty of 1846, the Hudson's Bay Company had to move its Pacific Coast headquarters from the Columbia River (Fort Vancouver). A suitable site was found at Camosun harbour on the south end of Vancouver Island, and Fort Victoria was built there in 1843. This water colour of the Fort was made in 1854.

For those who came to British Columbia by land before the railways were built, the Rockies, and the ranges beyond them which Edward Blake called "a sea of mountains", seemed not only a Great Divide, but an almost impassable barrier, and attempts to cross them, like that of the Overlanders of 1862, were full of perils. William G.R. Hind in this painting of the "Foot of the Rocky Mountains" shows how grand and indifferent the country must have seemed to these exhausted travellers who long ago had exchanged Red River Carts for pack animals.

Washington. Then, when it seemed likely that the forty-ninth parallel would become the international boundary, with Vancouver Island entirely British, the Company moved north, founding Fort Langley on the lower Fraser in 1827, Fort Simpson near Prince Rupert in 1831 (to provide a bastion against Russian penetration southward), and, in 1843, as the new Pacific coast headquarters, Fort Victoria on Vancouver Island. When Vancouver Island became a Crown Colony in 1849, Fort Victoria was its capital; it is now the capital of British Columbia. Fort Langley was to have a brief spurt of distinction as the capital of the newly created colony of British Columbia in 1858, but soon lost the glory to New Westminster and has lived on as a gracefully old-fashioned riverside village with the fort itself reconstructed as a national monument.

In Fort Victoria and Fort Langley the Hudson's Bay Company began to depart from its old dependence on the fur trade, and in the process initiated all the province's essential industries. Two of them, lumbering and fishing, were taken over from the Coast Indians who were already building fine cedar houses and catching and preserving large quantities of salmon; in 1848 a sawmill at Victoria began to export sawn timber to San Francisco, and Fort Langley exported barrels of salted salmon to the Sandwich Islands. The next year mining began in the coal deposits of Fort

Beyond the mountains the Overlanders came to the dense rainforests, clogged with the deadfalls of centuries. Not all those who followed this route to the Cariboo gold mines reached their destination. Some of them died of sickness, of starvation, of drowning in the swift rivers, and there were those whom even cannibalism did not save.

Rupert and shortly afterwards at Nanaimo. And, through its subsidiary, the Puget Sound Agricultural Company, the Hudson's Bay Company established several farms in the oak-studded parkland around Victoria, while the few English gentleman farmers who arrived as independent settlers were relegated to farms in remoter parts of the island.

To carry on these various operations, coal miners from Staffordshire and Scotland, and English farm workers and labourers were brought on the long voyage around Cape Horn, as were the bailiffs, the doctor, the chaplain, and the schoolmaster who, together with the Company's officers and the gentlemen settlers, formed the small upper class of the new colony. These immigrants created the nucleus of a white population in British Columbia, for many of them, like the little German-English doctor John Sebastian Helmcken, founded families that would play an important role right down to the present day in British Columbian life. Altogether, there were about a thousand of them by the early 1850s, of whom between four and five hundred were living in Fort Victoria or in whitewashed log houses outside its stockades.

The tiny capital, with all its apparatus of colonial government (Governor, Council, even an Assembly elected with difficulty because of the shortage of qualified voters) became a strange combination of the primi-

The Fraser Valley gold rush of 1858 transformed Victoria from an isolated fur trading post into a busy commercial town, its harbour filled with shipping, as shown in this 1860 painting by H.O. Tiedemann.

The Fraser Valley gold rush precipitated the creation of the Crown Colony of British Columbia in 1858, and the law-and-order problems of a previously uninhabited land now flooded with miners from California resulted in the appointment as Judge of a flamboyant English barrister, Matthew Baillie Begbie, who tirelessly rode on horseback through the mining country, sometimes holding court without dismounting, and ensuring that the lynch law so often dispensed in the American mining camps was not transplanted to the Canadian west.

The first capital of British Columbia in 1858 was Fort Langley, the Hudson's Bay Company's post on the Fraser, but in 1859 it was superseded by the new settlement of Queensborough (quickly renamed New Westminster at Queen Victoria's orders) which Colonel R.C. Moody and his Royal Engineers regarded as a defensible site. This photograph was taken three or four years after foundation and a little while before New Westminster became the capital of the united colony of Vancouver Island and British Columbia in 1866. In 1868 New Westminster was superseded by Victoria as the British Columbian capital.

tive and the sophisticated. The streets were notoriously muddy, and at certain seasons the place took on a barbaric aspect when the beaches were lined with the ragged encampments of Haida and Kwakiutl Indians from the north, who had the reputation of being proud and violent. Yet the social amenities of early Victorian life were at the same time enthusiastically observed, class distinctions were maintained, and the naval officers whose ships often anchored in the nearby harbour of Esquimalt helped to give an air of elegance to the succession of balls and parties.

It was with increasing difficulty that the Company maintained its hold and preserved the semblance of a fur-trading society, for, despite all discouragements, individual settlers found their way to the Island and into the Assembly, and there was a great deal of criticism in Britain of the paternalistic way James Douglas, both Governor of the colony and the Company's Chief Factor, carried out his two potentially contradictory roles.

The end of this early colonial phase came far more quickly than any resident of Vancouver Island can have expected. Gold was discovered in the rivers of the interior, and the news filtered down to San Francisco, which was filled with miners longing for a new field of prospecting since the California diggings were no longer profitable for a man without capital. On April 25, 1858, as the people of Victoria were leaving church after Sunday morning service, they saw an American side-wheeler, the *Commodore,* nose its way into the harbour. Shortly afterwards some four hundred and fifty miners streamed ashore, the vanguard of the twenty-five thousand men who in that summer passed through Victoria on their way to the gold-rich bars of the Fraser Canyon.

It was a cosmopolitan migration, as Colonel Moody, who became Commissioner of Lands and Works, later described it: "ENGLISHMEN (staunch Royalists), *Americans* (Republicans), Frenchmen, very numerous, Germans in abundance, Italians, several Hungarians, Poles, Danes, Swedes, Spaniards, Mexicans. . . ." Out of the first four hundred and fifty, there were sixty British subjects and about a hundred Americans by birth, including some forty blacks who had been persecuted by Southerners in California. The remaining three hundred were Europeans who had arrived late in California and wanted to try their luck elsewhere. During that first season few people arrived either from Britain directly or from the Canadian and Maritime provinces.

Life in Victoria and on the mainland, which had hitherto been merely a fur-traders' territory, was changed beyond recognition. At Victoria the miners stayed, until they could get passage to the diggings, in a large tent encampment, but to serve them the merchants who arrived from San Francisco built a whole new commercial town to which many of them transferred their bsinesses. Within six weeks more than two hundred stores had been established. Theatres and newspapers made their appearance, including *The British Colonist,* which bitterly criticized the political ascendancy of the Hudson's Bay Company and the miniature family compact which linked a surprisingly large number of the colonial officials, maritally or otherwise, with Governor and/or Chief Factor, James Douglas. The *Colonist,* still published as *The Daily Colonist* in Victoria, was edited by the colourful Amor de Cosmos, a Nova Scotian disciple of Joseph Howe, originally named William Alexander Smith, who, while he was working as a photographer in the California goldfields in 1854, had changed his name by act of the state legislature. "I desire not to accept the name of Amor de Cosmos because it smacks of a foreign title, but because it is an unusual name and its meaning tells what I love most, *viz.*, order, beauty, the world, the universe." De Cosmos became a fervent advocate of British Columbia's entry into the Confederation of Canada, and for a brief and stormy period in the 1870s he was Premier of British Columbia, but at heart he was a chronic dissenter. As early as 1870 he expressed very eloquently the inclination to defy centralized authority that is endemic in British Columbian politics.

> I would not object to a little revolution now and again in British Columbia, after Confederation, if we were treated unfairly; for I am one of those who believe that political hatreds attest the vitality of a State.

James Douglas — whom even the Victorians nicknamed Old Squaretoes — was a strong man as well as a staid one, and he acted decisively to show the miners that they were subject to British law and that there would be no repetition of the circumstances that led to the American acquisition of Oregon by population movement. The territory

More than any other individual, **Amor de Cosmos** was responsible for British Columbia entering the confederation of Canada. He founded a newspaper — *The British Colonist* — that represented the democratic opposition to the autocratic rule of Governor James Douglas. In 1860 De Cosmos issued his first demand for the union of British American colonies, and from that time, in his paper and (from 1863) as opposition leader in the legislative assembly, he carried on a double campaign, for confederation and for responsible government. He led the movement for uniting the colonies of Vancouver Island and British Columbia, which took place in 1866. In 1871 British Columbia entered confederation, gaining responsible government at the same time. De Cosmos became a federal MP, but from this time his career lost impetus. Though they shared a love for the bottle, Sir John A. Macdonald gave him no federal office, and though he became premier of British Columbia in 1872, De Cosmos resigned soon afterwards when rioters invaded the provincial legislature in protest against his administration. Gradually he dropped out of political activity, and at the end of a lonely old age died mad in 1897.

As the gravel bars of the Fraser River were worked out, the prospectors spread north and east of the Coast Range into the Cariboo. The gold-bearing gravels of William's Creek were found by 'Dutch William' Dietz in 1861, but the town that sprang up around the diggings was named Barkerville after Billy Barker, the Cornish miner who in 1862 struck it rich on the Barker Claim, and made a fortune of $600,000, which he quickly lost. Though he prospected for decades afterwards, he was not lucky a second time, and died destitute in 1894 in the Old Men's Home in Victoria.

of New Caledonia was transformed into the colony of British Columbia, and Douglas governed it energetically, keeping order with the assistance of Judge Matthew Baillie Begbie, a British lawyer who rode tirelessly through the wilderness to hold his courts (in which he appeared suitably wigged and red-robed) wherever the miners temporarily settled; and building roads through the wilderness with the help of Colonel Moody and the Royal Engineers.

Moody's great achievement was the building of the wagon road through the Fraser Canyon as far as the diggings in the Cariboo, where in 1861-62 Barkerville became the centre of another great rush. By this time travellers began to notice that there were far more miners from Britain, from Upper Canada, from Nova Scotia. The first Chinese had also arrived, working as laundrymen and labourers and panning the tailings left by the white miners for the vestiges of gold that remained. For a few months Barkerville was the most populous community in North America west of Chicago, but then the mining became too difficult for the man who relied merely on his hands and his experience, and the greater part of the population drifted on the waves of later rushes to other centres, leaving in its trail a series of ghost towns, many now so long decayed into the bush that hardly a trace remains.

Population fluctuated wildly during these early times, and it is likely that during some years of the late 1850s and early 1860s there were as many as sixty thousand people in British Columbia. By the time the colony entered Canada in 1871 the transients, including most of the American miners, had departed, and there were little more than ten thousand white inhabitants. Yet the infrastructure of a society had been established. To the towns like Victoria, Kamloops, Hope, Yale, Fort Langley, which owed their origins to the fur trade, had been added those established by Colonel Moody, such as New Westminster, Lytton, Lillooet, and Quesnel. Roads and trails of varying quality probed northward to Barkerville and eastward to the new goldfields north of the international boundary. Agriculture had been developed not only in the lower Fraser valley, where three hundred farms now existed and dairying had been started around Chilliwack; but also in the Okanagan, where the Oblate fathers had established the first orchards, and in the Cariboo drylands where the earliest ranches were in operation. Pioneer canneries were already at work, and the Coast Indians were beginning to feel the pinch of alien competition in harvesting the great salmon runs that had once made them so wealthy. Logging had become a major industry on both Vancouver Island and the mainland, where Burrard Inlet, with its magnificent harbour, was already a sawmilling centre exporting dressed timber not only to California but also to Australia and South America.

British Columbia entered Confederation with a promise of a railroad from Canada, and more than once during the 1870s and early 1880s its citizens threatened to secede because the Dominion had not kept its

Washing the gold of the Cariboo required elaborate wooden flumes to bring the water down out of the hills, and the same water worked the wheels — like that on the Davis claim at Williams Creek, which pumped the seepage from the deep galleries that were eventually dug at bedrock level.

In 1871 British Columbia entered Confederation. One of the conditions was that a railway should be built connecting this remote western province with eastern Canada. The first survey parties to prospect the route began work immediately, and on July 22, 1871, this photograph was taken in Victoria of a joint party of railway and geological surveyors.

promise. But at last the Canadian Pacific Railway was complete. In 1885, in the rainy heart of the Monashee range, the last spike was hammered in by Lord Strathcona, and the first train made its way to the coast through cuttings and tunnels and over dizzying trestles made largely by the battalions of Chinese engaged by the contractor Andrew Onderdonk.

The end of steel was made beside the deep waters of Burrard Inlet. The fur trade had created Victoria, the gold rush had created New Westminster, but the shrewd brain of the American-born William Van Horne, railway magnate and impeccable connoisseur of painting, created Vancouver. Josiah Stamp had established a great sawmill on the south shore of Burrard Inlet, which later became a centre for the settlement of Hastings Mill. In its shadow a retired sea captain, "Gassy Jack" Deighton, ran a bar, and a little later, somewhat west of Hastings Mill, he built the Deighton Hotel. Its environs became known — and still are known — as Gastown, in memory of the convivial Jack Deighton, but in more polite official circles the locality was described as Granville until, in 1886, at Van Horne's insistence, it was incorporated as Vancouver.

One of the world's most superb harbours, a scenic as well as a mercantile bonanza, ensured Vancouver's future; ninety years ago it offered the key to an all-British rapid route to the China coast; today it is Canada's most important seaport, fulfilling at least in part the prophecies that it would become "the Constantinople of the West." Within two years it had become a city of eight thousand people with two daily newspapers; Victoria was left behind and New Westminster far behind. In a very few years the poet Bliss Carman would be chanting:

Tyre and Sidon — where are they?
Where is the trade of Carthage now?
Here in Vancouver on English Bay,
With tomorrow's light on her brow!

After many delays, and threats of secession on the part of British Columbia, serious construction of the Canadian Pacific Railway got under way with the appointment of the American William Van Horne as General Manager. Van Horne was largely responsible for the creation of British Columbia's largest and Canada's third city when he decided that the terminus of the CPR should not be Port Moody, as originally planned, but Granville, farther down Burrard Inlet, which in 1886 became Vancouver; Van Horne chose the name.

In 1889, with extraordinary foresight, the city fathers, led by Mayor David Oppenheimer, dedicated Canada's most splendid civic park, the peninsula known as Stanley Park with its natural forest and lakes and its seafront perimeter walk seven miles long — to the use of people of "all creeds and colours."

Unfortunately the good intentions expressed in that dedication were imperfectly maintained, for while the fugitive American blacks who came in 1858 among the first participants of the Fraser valley gold rush were given a fair welcome and became a recognized part of the community with a durable settlement on Salt Spring Island in the Gulf of Georgia, British Columbia established a sad record of anti-Asian discrimination. The Chinese, as we have seen, arrived first from California as camp followers of the Fraser valley gold rush of 1858. They were reinforced in the early 1880s when the two thousand "coolies" were brought in to build the CPR. They established large Chinatowns in Victoria and Vancouver and small ones in the gold-mining settlements; they cultivated truck gardens in the suburbs. As low-paid gardeners, houseboys, cooks, and laundrymen they offered middle-class British Columbians a standard of living and leisure not far below that of imperial servants in India or Malaya. But they aroused the anger of organized labour by competing as labourers, miners, and fish cannery workers, and it was the nascent trade unions — particularly the Knights of Labour — who fostered demands for the exclusion of "orientals" and encouraged xenophobic talk of "the yellow peril."

Agitating through demogogic politicians like Amor de Cosmos, the British Columbian workers persuaded the federal government to impose an iniquitous $500 poll tax on Chinese immigrants. Even this did not end the flow of Asian immigrants around the turn of the century, and in 1903 alone not only fifteen hundred Chinese, but two thousand Sikhs and eight thousand Japanese entered the province. All these groups established lasting communities, the Chinese moving farther into market gardening, the restaurant business, and store-keeping, the Japanese applying their skills as fishermen, and the Sikhs working mainly in sawmills. The situation provoked bitter riots and afterwards discriminatory legislation which eventually stemmed the flow of Asian immigrants until in very recent years the prohibitions were relaxed. The situation came to a dramatic head in 1914, when a shipload of 376 angry Sikhs — British subjects to a man — was escorted out of Vancouver by His Majesty's cruiser *Rainbow*. Worse was to come in the Second World War. In 1942 all the Japanese on the coast of British Columbia — even if they were

Yale on the Fraser River had been an important transshipment point during the gold rush, since passengers left the river steamers there to continue by road to Cariboo through the canyon. When railway construction began it was once again a wild and busy town, as Henry Fairfax's drawing suggests.

Local labour for building the CPR through the mountains of British Columbia was scarce, and Andrew Onderdonk, the contractor for this section, imported thousands of Chinese labourers. Many of them died during the period of construction, but many of them survived to form the basis of the West Coast Chinese community.

The Canadian Pacific Railway was completed when the last rails were laid in 1885 in the Monashee Mountains. But the real last spike was not that driven by Lord Strathcona on the ceremonial occasion well known from the publicity photographs; full spiking of this section of track was carried out after the train carrying the CPR notables had passed over it.

naturalized or Canadian born — were forcibly evacuated and resettled in the ghost mining towns of the interior while their property in houses, fishing boats, and farms was sold for derisory sums to greedy whites. Racial hostility has not entirely vanished even now among British Columbians, but in general the Chinese, the Japanese, and the Sikhs have been accepted as part of the very varied mosaic of peoples that history has created in the province.

Even now more than two-thirds of British Columbians are, as the stubbornly retained name of their province suggests, British by descent. From the early 1860s, when American influence began to wane, there was a tendency for the British-born and the descendants of those who came directly from Britain to remain dominant on Vancouver Island while Upper Canadians and Nova Scotians took the lead on the mainland, especially in New Westminster and the Cariboo.

Americans continued to arrive with the successive gold rushes of the nineteenth century. They came to Rock Creek and Big Bend, to Omenica and Cassiar, and, when large deposits of silver and base metals were found in the Kootenays at the turn of the century, miners flowed over the border and introduced the militant syndicalism of the American northwest. But these were tides that always ebbed, leaving small residues behind; more important were the steady infiltration of eastern Canadians over the Divide (particularly after the CPR was completed), and the successive waves of immigrants direct from Britain which have continued right down to the present.

The first railway station in Vancouver was in the Scottish baronial style much favoured in Canada during the late nineteenth century. In this photograph it is shown decorated for the visit in 1901 of the Duke and Duchess of York, who later became King George V and Queen Mary.

There were, for example, the Englishmen who came during the Edwardian era to establish fruit farms in the Okanagan and elsewhere. When I arrived on the coast in 1949 one was still shown the dying orchards of Walhachin near Kamloops and told the pathetic story of the Englishmen who planted them and then, in 1914, departed to a man and never returned. But there were others who stayed and left their descendants. A type of Englishman familiar on the coast until the Second World War was the remittance man, son of a well-off family (oddly enough there were no remittance women) who had disgraced the family name in some way and was paid an allowance to stay away. Malcolm Lowry was perhaps the most celebrated of the remittance men, but many Victoria and Vancouver families were founded by one, though to admit to having a remittance man father or grandfather has become rather like admitting to a bend sinister in one's armorial bearings. Very different from the ineffectual remittance men (against whom were directed the famous job advertisements reading "No Englishman need apply!") were the working-men who brought with them from England their trade-union traditions and before and after the First World War laid the foundations of a labour movement in British Columbia. And different again have been the sahibs from India and the taipans from the China coast who have found in British Columbia, as the Empire has faded away, a more congenial refuge than a small flat in Kensington or a cottage in Cornwall.

Finally, when several hundred thousand British immigrants entered Canada after the Second World War, many of them professionals and skilled technicians, the largest number settled in Ontario, but British Columbia was a close second, and there are areas of Victoria and of West and South Vancouver where the British-born families are still ascendant.

This kind of ethnic pocketing is a phenomenon encouraged in British Columbia by the topographical divisions of the land. Parts of the lower Fraser valley are settled almost entirely by late-migrating Mennonites of German descent who fled from the Ukraine in the 1920s. In some valleys of the Kootenays most of the people are Doukhobors who still speak Russian among themselves though their fathers crossed the mountains seventy years ago. The smelting town of Trail in the Columbia valley is largely inhabited by northern Italians who came fifty years ago, while Maillardville near Vancouver is a town of Québec French whose fathers came to work in sawmills here sixty years ago. The island of Sointula, between Vancouver Island and the mainland, is inhabited by Finns, the descendants of a group of socialists who, about seventy years ago, founded a short-lived Utopian community of a thousand people. Swiss mountain guides settled at Golden in the Rocky Mountain trench, while in 1956 the whole faculty and student body of a Hungarian forestry college fled their country and affiliated themselves to the University of British Columbia until the students had graduated and been absorbed into the local forest industry.

More diffuse migrations have been those of the Swedes, who drifted northwest out of the western United States to work in the British Columbia woods, and the Norwegians who came as fishermen and found the British Columbian fjords even more majestic than their own. There are also many fishermen of Dalmation descent, and Dutch nurserymen, and Germans who have transformed the eating habits of the region with their food shops and sausage factories and restaurants. German and Dutch immigrants from the period after the Second World War are often to be found in the farming districts and particularly in the Fraser valley and the Okanagan. The Mediterranean migrants who came after them are more likely to be found in the larger cities, where they create their own enclaves, so that Commercial and East Hastings streets in Vancouver form a Little Italy, with many people from Sicily and Calabria; the far west end of Broadway is the centre of a Greek sub-culture; Fraser Street is largely dominated by Sikhs and East Indians from Uganda; and Cambie Street, once a largely Jewish area, has been taken over to a great extent by younger Chinese moving out of the old Chinatown centred on East Pender Street.

The Slav and Mediterranean minorities in British Columbia are not so large proportionately as the Latins in Ontario and Montréal or the Slavs in the Prairies. Of all the regions west of Prince Edward Island, British Columbia probably comes nearest in its population ratios to the

Roderick Haig-Brown was a man of many parts and many reputations. Even before he became a writer, during the years after he left England for the Pacific Coast at the age of seventeen, he moved from occupation to occupation, gathering — as logger, trapper, guide, fisherman and farmer — the experience he would use when he began in the early 1930s his long literary career. Haig-Brown was a fine amateur naturalist, as he showed in books like *Silver: The Life of an Atlantic Salmon* and *The Western Angler*. He was an ardent conservationist long before the environmental movement gathered impetus in the 1960s, and for years carried on energetic one-man campaigns against the promoters of pulp mills, hydro projects, and other spoilers of the wilderness. He was a dedicated public servant, acting for many years as stipendiary magistrate at Campbell River, and later as Chancellor of Victoria University. He was a good wilderness novelist *(Timber* and *On The Highest Hill)* and writer of children's books *(Starbuck Valley Winter* and *The Whale People)*. But most of all he will probably be remembered as one of Canada's finest essayists, recording with great sensitivity the life of places on the edge of the wilderness, in books like *Measure of the Year, A River Never Sleeps* and *Fisherman's Spring*.

Next to the Parliament Buildings of British Columbia and the Vancouver Court House, the best known of F.M. Rattenbury's buildings was The Empress Hotel in Victoria, which he designed for the Canadian Pacific Railway and which opened for business in 1908.

Samuel Maclure, a sensitive landscape painter as well as an architect, was an active contemporary of Rattenbury, though he designed mainly houses, and left many examples of his work in the patrician areas of Vancouver and Victoria. This hallway of the Roderick Sutherland House, built between 1912 and 1913 is a good example of his work, which derived a great deal from the arts and crafts tradition stemming from William Morris and Philip Webb in England.

Anglo-Celtic-Germanic ideal of the days before Clifford Sifton. Yet the special character of life there really depends, not on any dominant majority culture, which hardly exists, but on the sheer variety of minority cultures — native Indian, Asian, and European — and on the splendid natural obstacles that fragment the land almost to the degree of fantasy.

Certainly there is both fantasy and an awareness of the frightening splendour of the natural world to be found among British Columbian writers, as there is among British Columbian painters. Emily Carr provided the bridging point, since she not only expressed in her paintings the brooding dread of the coastal rain forests and the brilliance of the coastal waters, but she also distilled into a series of warm and perceptive autobiographical volumes, including *Klee Wyck*, *Growing Pains*, and *The Book of Small*, the essence of life in Victoria and in remote Indian coastal villages half a century ago. Emily Carr's paintings and her writings, apart from their intrinsic merits, are invaluable for what they have to tell about the way British Columbians are inclined to see their land.

Much of the best prose written in British Columbia has been concerned with coming to terms with the land, often through the typical occupations of the region. One of the best early British Columbian novels was a logging story, Martin Allerdale Grainger's *Woodsmen of the West,* and some of the finest essays written in Canada are contained in Roderick Haig-Brown's books, such as *A River Never Sleeps* and *Measure of the Year,* which describe the natural environment seen through the eyes of a naturalist and environmentalist. Perhaps the most intriguing of recent British Columbian autobiographies has been *The Curve of Time,* M. Wylie Blanchet's record of living off the land and sea in the coastal inlets during the Depression.

Even among the prose writers who are less directly concerned with the practical details of living, the British Columbian landscape is a compelling presence. Malcolm Lowry, who found his Hell in Mexico, found his Paradise on Burrard Inlet, and celebrated it in novels like *October Ferry to Gabriola* and stories like "The Forest Path to the Spring". Other kinds of British Columbian environment, like the dry country of the interior, were the intrusive settings of novels like Ethel Wilson's *Hetty Dorval* and *Swamp Angel,* and Sheila Watson's *The Double Hook,* while in *Tay John* Howard O'Hagan wrote a telling myth of the Rockies. At the same time Ethel Wilson, in books like *The Equations of Love* and *The Innocent Traveller,* and Earle Birney in *Down the Long Table,* evoked the varying aspects of Vancouver life, its cosmopolitan quality, its contrasts of wealth and poverty, of gentility and frontier populism, of gentleness and violence.

British Columbia has always attracted poets, and in recent years Earle Birney, Dorothy Livesay, P. K. Page, Margaret Atwood, and Al Purdy have all lived and worked here for short or long periods, while there have always been groups of working poets in Vancouver

Emily Carr was a great painter and a fine writer, and in these two roles she presented a splendid evocation of the coastal waters and forests of her native British Columbia. Carr waited long for recognition. After years of what seemed unproductive student wanderings, she settled in Victoria, where she was better known as keeper of an eccentric boarding house than as a painter until, at the age of 56, she had her first exhibition of paintings — rain forest scenes and Indian encampments — which won the attention of the Group of Seven and launched her belated career. But her often arduous travels on the Pacific Coast in search of paintable scenes left Emily Carr with impressions which she felt paint was insufficient to express, and a few years before her death she began to write, in rapid succession, a series of books of vivid recollections of Victoria and the coast as she had seen them. *Klee Wyck,* the first of them, appeared when she was seventy. Others followed — *The Book of Small* and *The House of All Sorts* — and when Emily Carr died in 1945 there was still enough for several other books that appeared posthumously. She was a splendid example of the kind of artist who waits for the right forms that will release her genius, but after that release works with the passion bred of a sense of time being short and precious.

and Victoria, and even in small inland towns, who are often very little known east of the Rockies but who produce good and original work, usually published in local magazines like the *Malahat Review* and the *Capilano Review.* In poetry also the themes of an overbearing landscape and of a mingling of cultures and peoples, including the Asians and the Coast Indians, have been strongly dominant. Susan Musgrave's poems inspired by Coast Indian legends, Dorothy Livesay's *Call My People Home,* a long poem on the Second World War expulsion of Japanese from the coast, and Earle Birney's mountain poems, such as "David", are examples reflecting these varying aspects of life in a region where, as Birney put it in "November Walk Near False Creek Mouth", we live, in relation to the rest of Canada,

in the last of warmth
and the fading of brightness
on the sliding edge of the beating sea.

British Columbia's economy has always been based mainly on its natural resources — first gold and base metals, then fish and lumber, and in more recent years oil and natural gas. These photographs show geologists searching for signs of oil in the Rockies, and exploratory drilling for oil at Fernie in the Selkirks.

CHAPTER TEN

The Vulnerable North

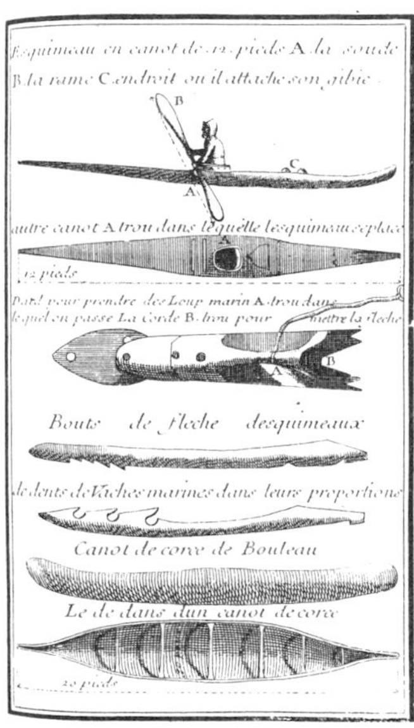

What Canadians call "The North" begins at the sixtieth degree of latitude and includes the vast Arctic Archipelago. Altogether it includes about forty per cent of the total land area of Canada and more than half of its fresh-water area. This great wilderness of mountain and tundra, of lake and sub-Arctic bushland is populated by about one person to every twenty-five square miles. In the 1971 census the combined populations of the Northwest Territories and the Yukon Territory, into which the north is divided, were approximately fifty-seven thousand, and seventy-thousand — about a total of 0.3 per cent of the Canadian population — would be a reasonable estimate for today. It is unlikely that the north was ever more thickly populated, given the scarcity of food that made the nomad native peoples travel great distances during each year in their search for sustenance.

This may be a tiny fraction of the Canadian people, but for many reasons it is a highly interesting one, since this is the only region of Canada in which the native peoples still form a considerable proportion of the population. It is also the only region of Canada whose status is still that of a colony, for neither the Yukon Territory nor the Northwest Territories enjoys the responsible government that Canadians and Nova Scotians won over a century ago. Ultimate decisions regarding the territories are made in Ottawa, and the way the north is governed is strikingly similar to the way India was once governed by Britain.

There is a difference in population between the Yukon and the Northwest Territories which is due mainly to the accidents of history. Never have the Northwest Territories — at least in their present form — experienced the kind of mass invasion which constituted the last great gold rush of history, when in 1898 a hundred thousand men and women set out on a fantastic Odyssey over tall mountain ranges and by cruel waterways to find their fortunes in the Klondike diggings beside the Yukon. Perhaps a half of them eventually reached Dawson City, the one really large town in northern history, which sprang into existence in a few months and lived hectically for two or three years in the eye of the world as one of the last great sprees of the century. By 1901 the spectacular fortunes had been made and spent, the whores and the sharpers and the entrepreneurs had departed, and most of the miners had gone on to seek other and more illusory Eldorados, leaving the theatres and the music halls and the gambling houses deserted. The gold rush left enough

The unique hunting techniques of the Inuit and such highly specialized inventions as the kayak fascinated eighteenth century geographers and were often illustrated in their treatises.

people enamoured of northern isolation to create a permanent population, even if a small one, and eventually, when Dawson City shrank into a greying ghost town, there were sufficient people in Whitehorse, attracted by the building of the Alaska Highway in 1942, to provide a new capital. Today about a fifth of the twenty thousand residents of the Yukon are Athapaskan Indians.

In the Northwest Territories, on the other hand, well over half the more than forty thousand inhabitants belong to the native peoples: Inuit, Indian, and a few Métis, descendants of those who drifted northward after the defeat of the rebellion on the Saskatchewan River in 1885. Moreover, it is the native peoples who are the permanent residents, for if there is one common characteristic among the whites in the Northwest Territories it is their custom — however long they may stay in the north — eventually to depart. Few whites are born and fewer die in the territories. Some go there for short terms of duty, and some, especially the missionaries, may perform their whole life's work there, but they are almost always born "outside" (the northerner's term for the rest of Canada) and, however reluctantly, they will almost always leave the north to die outside.

Surprisingly few of the people who work in the Northwest Territories are even born in Canada. Most of them, from the beginning of northern exploration, have come from Europe. There is an old tradition at work here. Rupert's Land was administered by the Hudson's Bay Company from London, and the Company's ships sailed directly into the Bay, avoiding what was then Canada. Unlike the North Westers, the Hudson's Bay Company did not recruit its servants in Québec or from the Métis of the Prairies, but preferred engaging Orkneymen and tended to pick Englishmen as its officers. After the two companies were united there were also many Scots, but there were never many Canadians.

Even after Rupert's Land was absorbed into Canada in 1870, Canadians continued to leave the Arctic to outsiders; they had plenty of land south of the sixtieth parallel to settle and exploit. To give an example of the kind of situation that still exists, let me instance Baker Lake in Keewatin, the eastern of the two Northwest Territories (the other is Mackenzie). When I went there a few years ago it was a settlement of five hundred and fifty Eskimos with about sixty whites (including families) — whose number would be doubled during the short season when summer workers came in. Trade was still entirely in the hands of the Hudson's Bay Company, whose storekeeper was a Scot, while his two young assistants were English. The Roman Catholic missionary was Belgian and his Anglican counterpart English. The administrator, the highest government officer, was Anglo-Irish. The nurse in charge of the hospital was Hong Kong Chinese, and the foreman of the public works depot a Trinidadian. The teachers were divided fairly equally between British-born and Canadian-born, and only the RCMP officers were entirely

Arctic explorers in the nineteenth century passed through waters already frequented by fur traders, as exemplified in the encounter which Peter Rindisbacher recorded in his drawing entitled 'Fortunate meeting of HBC ships Prince of Wales & Eddystone with Capt. W.E. Parry's ships Hecla and Griper, July 16, 1821'. Parry was at the beginning of his 1821-3 expedition and Rindisbacher was on his way to the Red River when he witnessed the meeting.

In 1821 Rindisbacher also drew "from nature" this sketch of an Inuit family.

The oomiak or woman's boat, used by the Inuit for travel and transport, drawn by Captain Lyon, RN, in 1824.

Canadian in origin. Moreover, those who saw themselves as having lasting commitments to the north, like the missionaries and the traders, were all non-Canadians; the Canadians came on short-term assignments, and it was said that many left before they were over. I found a similar pattern in other Arctic settlements, and even in Yellowknife, the capital of the Territories, I encountered an astonishing collection of people from the corners of the known world: people like, for example, Peter Baker, an octogenarian Lebanese whose Arab name had been forgotten, and whom the Indians called Orange because fifty years ago he had sailed into the Great Slave Lake in a scow loaded with golden fruit they had never seen before, and who was elected by the people of Yellowknife — Indians and whites alike — to represent them on the Territorial Council.

It may be true, as Brian Moore said, that the north which makes Canada the second largest country on earth is "all important to the Canadian's self-image", if only because "its brooding presence over the land is a warning that Canadians have not yet conquered their universe." It may also be true, as André Siegfried said, that the north is "the background of the picture without which Canada would not be Canadian." Even more true was the ironic remark of J. B. McGeachy, a personality of the golden days of radio, that "We sing about the north but live as far south as possible."

White men are few in the north and usually transient; they also came late, so that it was well into the twentieth century before any effective penetration was made of the Arctic Archipelago, which until that time was so rarely visited that Canadian sovereignty seemed precarious.

The north is geographically divided into the zones which are generally called Arctic and sub-Arctic, and the dividing line, which is the tree line, does not follow the latitudes but runs northwest from about sixty degrees in the neighbourhood of Churchill on Hudson's Bay to about seventy degrees in the Mackenzie Delta. South of this line lies the boreal forest of small trees and scrub, where the caribou winter and the Athapascan people, the Dené, hunt and live. North of it lies the tundra, the Barren Land, where the caribou go in summer. The Indians fear this treeless wilderness, the territory of the Inuit, who, in the days before the coming of the white men, spread their almost invisibly thin web of

In 1829-33 John Ross and his nephew James Clark Ross carried out the historic expedition on which they discovered Boothia Peninsula and named it after the financer of their expedition, the gin distiller Angus Booth. In 1831, on the west side of Boothia, James Clark Ross located the Magnetic Pole. Among the many illustrations to John Ross's account of their expedition was this picture of Inuit and their igloos.

occupation northward to the Arctic Sea and the Archipelago as far as human life could be carried on. More than that, they adapted themselves to the rigours of northern life, and even learnt, as that uniquely adaptable species Man has always done, to see the beauty of the life into which destiny had thrust them, as did the anonymous Inuit who composed the song Knud Rasmussen recorded fifty years ago:

> And yet, there is only
> One great thing,
> The only thing:
> To live to see, in hunts and on journeys
> The great day that dawns
> And the light that fills the world.

The Yukon Territory is almost entirely within the tree line; so is the southwestern triangle of the Northwest Territories, including the Mackenzie valley and the watersheds of Great Slave Lake and Great Bear Lake. It was to this region, among the Dené Indians, that as traders the white men first came. In 1731, writing the entry on Canada in that celebrated bible of the Enlightenment, the *Encyclopédie*, Denis Diderot remarked that "this immense country" has "no known boundaries to the north, where it meets the cold lands where European avarice and curiosity have not yet penetrated." A generation later, after the British had replaced the

The Rosses were held in the ice for four years on their 1829-33 expedition, and in 1833 Captain George Back was sent on a search expedition. He went overland and descended the Back River (then called the Great Fish River) to Chantrey Inlet, and there he drew these sketches of the "Esquimaux of the Thleweechodezeth".

French as the lords of Canada, European avarice and curiosity found their way in.

Cuthbert Grant, the Métis trader employed by the North West Company, had established a temporary post on Great Slave Lake in 1786, three years before Alexander Mackenzie descended the Mackenzie River to the Arctic, but only with the dawning nineteenth century were the first permanent posts established in the area. In 1804 Fort Simpson, for long the centre of white activity on the Mackenzie, was established. Other posts followed in the early years of the century — Fort Resolution and Fort Rae on Great Slave Lake, Fort Franklin on Great Bear Lake, Fort Liard on the Liard River, and Fort Good Hope and Fort Norman on the Mackenzie — creating a trading network by which the furs could be collected at Fort Simpson and taken over the brigade routes from Lake Athapaska to Montréal or, in later years, to Hudson's Bay. During the 1840s Robert Campbell established a series of posts in the Yukon, but after the Tlingit Indians from the Alaskan coast, who claimed middlemen trading rights in the area, burnt down Fort Selkirk in 1851, the Hudson's Bay Company abandoned the territory for half a century.

There was no attempt at settlement connected with these trading ventures, though gardens were grown at Fort Simpson in which the vegetables waxed luxuriant in the long days of the brief northern summer.

When the rival Hudson's Bay Company and North West Company were united in 1821, George Simpson became the Governor of the new concern. Known as the Little Emperor for his autocratic ways, he reorganized the Company and made many arduous tours over its domain, from Montréal to the Pacific, to maintain efficiency. Under his rule the Company moved towards the high Arctic, establishing posts on the Mackenzie and Yukon rivers.

Yet on Indian — and later on Inuit — life in the north the presence of a few white men wreaked changes that were irreversible and by no means entirely beneficial. Sir George Simpson, the famous Governor of the Hudson's Bay Company, exhorted his staff in 1821 to make the Indians dependent so as to ensure that they would remain assiduous in providing furs for the trade, and the effect of this policy was admirably defined by R. A. J. Phillips, a contemporary northern administrator with an unusually long knowledge of the Arctic.

> It was this pressure towards dependence on the white man that most profoundly altered the character of the North wherever the trader came to settle. The orbit of operations of the Indians, and later of the Eskimos, was changed. The rifle enabled the hunter to get as much game as before, without having to roam so large an area — for a while. The desire to range about the land was now reduced by the wish to be within easy reach of the permanent trading-post. As Simpson foresaw, the Indian trapper became dependent on the white man's goods, and subordinate to his wishes. When the natural economy disappeared, no one, on his own, could recapture it. The Indian's dependence on the trader for tobacco, tea, calico, and cooking-pots was serious enough, but his need for ammunition became vital.
>
> (*Canada's North*, 1967)

The trader, with his goods that so quickly became indispensable, represented only the first of several waves of white intrusion into the north. The missionaries followed close on the heels of the fur trade. The Catholics established a mission on Great Slave Lake in 1852, but the same year they lost a race with the Anglicans for Fort Simpson, which in 1874 became the centre of the vast diocese of Mackenzie, presided over for many years by that great northern traveller, the ascetic Bishop William Carpenter Bompas.

The churches nominally converted most of the Dené and later the Inuit, though their efforts to stamp out shamanism and such pagan customs as the Inuit drum dance have not been entirely successful. But

Throughout the northland the fur traders and their voyageurs *travelled in the large* canots de maître; *in such a canoe Mackenzie descended the river that bears his name to the Arctic Ocean.*

their work extended far beyond proselytization. It was they who helped both the Dené and the Inuit to become literate in their own tongues by creating grammars and syllabic scripts of the native vernaculars, and until very recent years all the schools and all the hospitals in the North West Territories, and many in the Yukon, were operated by missionary organizations. Thus the churches in their own way played as decisive a role in the transformation of the north as did the fur traders.

A curious trinity was completed when the searchers for fur and the hunters of souls were followed by those who hunted and searched for gold.

Already, in the 1870s, the prospectors were moving into the Yukon region, overland in a northerly direction from the exhausted diggings of British Columbia and upriver from Alaska, which had by now become American territory. In 1875 there were a thousand miners in the area, and in the succeeding years they followed small rushes backward and forward across the international boundary until the late summer of 1896, when George Carmack and two Indian friends made the strike at Bonanza Creek that began the Klondike Rush and led to the Yukon being named a separate territory in 1898. Mining — in recent years silver and lead, copper and zinc, rather than gold — has kept a permanent white population in the Yukon, many of them wage earners in the hard rock mines, but a large proportion still the kind of solitary wanderers who, like the alchemists of old, are in their own way searching for something more precious in terms of experience than gold itself.

It was not until the coming of air transport into the north in 1921, and the evolution of that extraordinary breed of men, the bush pilots, that the search for minerals spread into the North West Territories. "The

Sir George Simpson's last public act was to welcome at Lachine the Prince of Wales, later King Edward VII, on his tour of Canada in 1860. On this occasion he presented him with a birchbark canot de maître.

whole history of the Canadian North," said Hugh Keenleyside, "can be divided into two periods — before and after the aeroplane." The change began when fighter pilots of the Royal Flying Corps, demobilized at the end of the First World War, began to seek ways in which their skill and their desire for adventure could be put to use. As early as 1919 the air ace "Wop" May established the tiny airline whose planes began to fly up the Mackenzie valley. In 1921 regular flights with mail were being carried into the Arctic, and charter services were offered by a variety of tiny outfits manned by pilots whose names have now become famous in the history of the north; May himself, "Punch" Dickens, Grant McConachie. Journeys that had taken weeks or months could suddenly be completed, with some risk, in days or even hours.

Prospectors who had been daunted by the thought of travelling by foot and sleigh for endless miles over the open tundra welcomed the mobility which the plane offered them. In the 1930s gold was found at Yellowknife in large enough quantities for the only real town in the north to appear on the shores of Great Slave Lake, while beside Great Bear Lake Gilbert La Bine discovered the uranium deposits of the El Dorado mine. But the most formidable mineral gift of the Canadian north may yet be the oil which Alexander Mackenzie noticed seeping through the banks of the Mackenzie when he explored the great river almost two hundred years ago. No use was made of northern oil until the first wells went into operation near Fort Norman in 1921. In more recent years the discovery of great new fields in the Mackenzie delta and in parts of the Arctic Sea has already subjected the north to the activity of a new kind of prospector and exploiter whose presence — through the development of oil wells and pipelines — threatens to change even more radically than

In 1865 when **William Carpenter Bompas** was ordained in the Church of England at the age of thirty-one, he heard that a sick priest on the Yukon needed relieving, and volunteered for the task, thinking it would mean just a brief though doubtless interesting trip to the Canadian North. But the North trapped him in chains of love, as it has trapped many others, and he died there more than forty years later at Cariboo Crossing. By the time he reached Canada the sick priest had recovered, and Bompas was given charge of the mission at Fort Simpson on the Mackenzie. It was a vast parish of several thousand square miles, but Bompas — with no previous wilderness experience, took well to the life of hard travelling, and spent years going from one Indian camp to the next, acting as priest, teacher and doctor. He learnt the local languages and prepared primers of Beaver and Cree. In 1874 he was appointed, over his own protests, bishop of the new diocese of Athabaska, including all the Northwest and Yukon territories; in 1891 he became bishop of Selkirk, the Yukon section of the old diocese, and shortly afterwards tended the spiritual needs, such as they were, of the Klondike miners. There were many priests as dedicated and hard-working as Bompas, but despite his humility he struck the Victorian imagination as *the* Bishop of the North.

any other past wave of intruders the way of life of the northern peoples and the very ecology of the land.

The first to come from the east, after the probing voyages of the Norsemen, were sixteenth-century Europeans in search of the Northwest Passage to Cathay. In 1576 the Elizabethan adventurer Martin Frobisher advanced as far as the bay in Baffin Island that now bears his name. He returned to tell his adventures to Queen Elizabeth, who gave the Arctic an evocative name that dropped out of use — *Meta Incognita* — the unknown goal. Frobisher was back at Baffin Island in 1758 to load his ship with glittering rock that turned out to be iron pyrites, to receive an Inuit arrow in his buttock, and to be treasured in the folk memory so securely that almost three hundred years later, in 1861, Charles Hall not only found the relics of the buildings Frobisher had erected but also discovered that the Inuit talked of the Elizabethan sailor's visit as if it had happened within the recent past.

A long series of navigators followed Frobisher on the same vain search. John Davis sailed in 1595, discovering what we now call Davis Strait between Greenland and Baffin Island, and in his tiny vessels (one of fifty and the other of thirty-five tons) encountering the alarming aspects of nature in the Arctic:

> The lothsome view of the shore, and irksome noyze of the yce was such, as that it bred strange conceits among us, so that we supposed the place to be wast and voyd of any sensible or vegitable creatures, whereupon I called the same Desolation.

Davis returned safely, but Henry Hudson, who set sail in 1609, was less fortunate. His men mutinied and he and his son and seven other members of the crew were set adrift to die in a small boat in Hudson's Bay. Robert Bylot was one of the mutineers who brought Hudson's vessel, the *Discovery,* back to England. Because men with knowledge of the seas leading towards the Northwest Passage were so scarce his crime was ignored, and he went back with William Baffin in 1615 and 1616 to explore and map the seas around what is now Baffin Island. A few years later, in 1619, in an attempt to duplicate the achievements of the early Norsemen, the Dane Jens Munk sailed with Danish and Swedish ships in search of the Northwest Passage. He sailed into Hudson's Bay, wintered off the mouth of the Churchill River, saw most of his men die of scurvey, and passed through a depth of despair where he became, as he said, "like a wild and lonely bird." He recorded in his diary: "Herewith goodnight to the whole world and my soul into the hand of God." Yet Munk and two of his men recovered and sailed their boat back to Norway. Munk survived to die serving under Gustavus Adolphus in the Thirty Years War. And then there was Captain Thomas James, who sailed in 1631, and whom Canadians know because James Bay was named after him, but who lives in literature for his vivid travel account, *The Strange and*

The greatest stimulus to exploration in the Canadian Arctic was provided by one of the notable polar tragedies. Sir John Franklin had already carried out two important explorations of the northland, when in 1845 he set out on his third venture, this time to discover the North West Passage. He sailed in the Erebus *and the* Terror, *which were caught in the ice off King William Island.*

Franklin's disappearance aroused an extraordinary furore in Britain, and many expeditions went out during the next decade, some of them planned by the Arctic Council of the Admiralty (portrayed in this painting by R. Pearce) and others financed by Lady Franklin. In the process many of the gaps in the North West Passage were filled by the searching navigators.

It was a Hudson's Bay Company's surgeon, Dr. John Rae, who eventually discovered in 1854 the first relics which bore on Franklin's fate. Rae represented a Canadian philosophy of exploration — by imitating the natives and living off the land — that was the opposite of Franklin's method of moving in with naval ships crammed with stores but crewed by men inexperienced in Arctic survival. The evidence Rae discovered suggested that some of Franklin's men had turned cannibal, and for this he was attacked, particularly by Lady Franklin. Dickens defended him.

Dangerous Voyage of Captain Thomas James, one of the books that gave Coleridge the material for his *Rime of the Ancient Mariner*. "We had Ice not far off about us," said James, "and some pieces, as high as our Top-mast-head," and in Coleridge's poetic alchemy this became:

> And now there came both mist and snow,
>   And it grew wondrous cold:
> And ice, mast-high, came floating by,
>   As green as emerald.

None of them found the Northwest Passage, which would only be traversed in the twentieth century, first by Roald Amundsen, who took three winters, from 1903 to 1906, going through it from east to west, and then by Henry Larsen on the RCMP vessel *St. Roch*. Larsen took two winters, going from west to east, but then travelled the passage from east to west in a single season in 1944. By this time it was evident that the Northwest Passage was impractical as a route for trade. Its early sixteenth- and seventeenth-century explorers had little lasting effect on the country or on the lives of the Inuit with whom they made occasional contact, but they opened the way for the first line of exploiters of the far north — the whalers in search of baleen, the so-called whalebone that eighteenth- and nineteenth-century European ladies used to keep their figures trim.

The first Dutch whalers entered the eastern Arctic at Davis Strait as early as 1719. By the mid-century there were hundreds of boats engaged in the trade, and, like the early Newfoundland fishermen, they appear to have probed into many icy channels before the explorers who actually took the credit. The whalers not only decimated the sea mammals of this region and, later, of the western Arctic, but had an irreversible effect in

The discovery of gold on the Klondike led to the greatest gold rush in history, which peaked in 1898. On the banks of the Yukon River arose the instant community of Dawson City, which at its peak boasted a population of 25,000.

many ways on the lives of the native residents. They spread tuberculosis and venereal disease to a people who had always led remarkably healthy lives so long as they could find food. The whalers also introduced trading, since they were on the lookout for furs as well as baleen, and the winter skin of the Arctic fox, commonly known as the silver fox, fetched high prices in Europe. Tempted by the goods the whalers offered, the Inuit turned to trapping as well as their traditional subsistence hunting, and the result was a pattern of dependence similar to that of the northern Indians. Metal utensils replaced stone cooking utensils and oil lamps, canvas tents replaced hide shelters, wooden whaleboats replaced umiaks, and tea and tobacco took their places on the Inuit list of necessities.

In 1906 a cheap metal substitute for the whalebone in corsets was invented, and almost overnight the Arctic whaling industry vanished. A few years later the fur traders from the Mackenzie valley began to press into the north, and found the dependency they needed was already established in large parts of the Arctic. The Hudson's Bay Company made a first tentative beginning of trade among the Inuit when its post at Aklavik was established shortly before the Great War, and in the 1920s traders spread along the shores of the Arctic seas, into the islands of the Archipelago and into the Barren Lands, the dreaded tundra.

It was the Barren Lands Inuit who in the short run seemed to benefit, but in the long run suffered most, from the changes which the arrival of the traders wrought in their way of life. They depended on the caribou, whose flesh they ate and preserved, and whose skin provided clothing and the tents they used in winter as well as summer. They shot the animals with bow and arrow and slaughtered them in large numbers at river crossings during the great annual migrations, but they never killed enough by such methods to reduce seriously the caribou population.

Gold rushes were crowded occasions, but the prospectors who made the discoveries that started them off were solitary wanderers, like this man panning the river gravels. Tucked up around his hat is the veil which was often necessary in this land of mosquito and blackfly.

The men who rushed to the Klondike came from all walks of life. They included writers who kept a record of their experiences and artists who sketched the scenes they encountered, like Alfred Boultbee who drew 'Cabins on the Klondike Flats.'

Canadian merchants attempted to cash in on the gold rush, as Eaton's did with their special Klondike mail-order clothing advertisements, but Canadians on the whole were disgruntled — as a Toronto Globe cartoonist emphasised — with the small profits that came to them from this activity in their own territory. Large numbers of the prospective miners were outfitted in Seattle and travelled by American boats to Skagway, and most of those who took large fortunes out of the Klondike were Americans.

When the rifle was introduced to them, it seemed to offer abundance — an assurance that the old cycle of feast and famine would come to an end. But the replacement of the seasonal feast conditions by an orgy of killing not only reduced drastically the number of caribou, but also disturbed their migration routes, so that by the 1950s there was serious starvation among the Barren Lands Inuit. In an attempt to remedy the situation, the government herded the Inuit into village settlements like Baker Lake and Rankin Inlet. There the people were supposed to adapt themselves to modern life without any real means to do so. Handcrafts were introduced; for a short period a mine operated at Rankin Inlet and the Inuit, used to the long northern night, showed themselves well-adapted to work underground. But all too many of the Barren Lands Inuit were condemned to a demoralizing pattern of a few months of temporary summer work each year and a long winter of welfare payments.

The intervention in the lives of northern native peoples which began in the 1950s was the culmination of a long and reluctant involvement in the region on the part of the federal government, which for decades had been as alarmed as most individual Canadians by the very magnitude of the north — of its problems as well as its possibilities. The idea of the north as a vast consumer of men and of money had been implanted in the minds of mid-nineteenth century people by the drama of Sir John Franklin's lost expedition and the expensive series of searches that followed, and it died very slowly among Canadian politicians and the Canadian people. Not until 1898 did any real administration of the north even begin, and then it was done mainly by the North West Mounted Police, which was keeping order on the Klondike. In 1903 a Mounted Police post was established on the Mackenzie at Fort McPherson and in 1904 another was situated at Herschel Island in the Arctic Sea. From 1905, when Saskatchewan and Alberta were carved out of the old North West Territories, until 1920, the Commissioner of the Territories and the Comptroller of the Mounted Police were the same person. Even after this close identification of administration and policing came to an end, the

But Canada did at least take the precaution of defending its frontier. A North West Mounted Police Post was established and equipped with maxim guns at the head of Chilkoot Pass, to turn away suspicious characters and those who came with insufficient stores, while the police detachment in Dawson City under the famous Sam Steele, kept order in the goldfield, rigorously maintaining the Lord's Day Act, but turned a benevolent blind eye to the prostitutes plying their trade on Paradise Alley.

North West Territories (though not the Yukon) were still to all practical intents and purposes a fief of the Mounted Police, since in almost every settlement the only public official was the policeman who also acted as stipendiary magistrate and jailer, relief-officer, registrar of vital statistics, census-officer, and any other role that proper administration of his several thousand square miles of ice and tundra might involve. Until after the middle of the present century, the federal government was content with this situation which, whatever may be said for the conscientiousness and capability of individual officers, created the paradoxical situation of a police state, whose people had no democratic rights, within the boundaries of a democratic confederation.

This, of course, constituted an even more authoritarian system than the British had developed in India, for there the police were locally subordinate to the civil authorities and took no part in the judicial process. But there is little evidence that until quite recently questions of this kind seemed important to those who distantly ruled the north, and in 1953 when the Department of Northern Affairs and National Resources (to be succeeded in 1966 by the Department of Indian Affairs and Northern Development) began to create an administrative network that took over all but police functions from the Royal Canadian Mounted Police (as the North West Mounted had become), its motivations were paternalistic rather than libertarian — to make sure that people did not

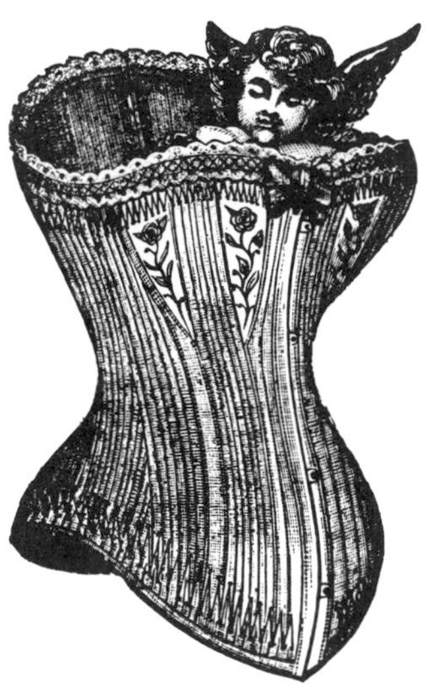

CORALINE.—Price $1 and $1.25 a pair.

Those wise and gigantic beasts, the whales, have always been the victims of human greed and even of the whims of fashion. During the Victorian age ladies' fashions were based on the wasp-waist, which demanded the confinement of the body in corsets stiffened with 'whalebone', actually the horny substance through which certain whales filter the kril on which they feed. Early in the twentieth century, the invention of synthetic substitutes like 'Coraline' susperseded whalebone. The whaling industry of the Arctic, which had existed since the eighteenth century, came to a sudden end.

Unlike the Coast Indians of British Columbia, the Inuit did not traditionally hunt the larger whales. But — except for the Barren Ground Inuit who depended mainly on caribou — they relied chiefly for their food on marine mammals. Among these were the beluga, or white whale. In 1865 George Simpson MacTavish photographed a harpoon-wielding Inuit with the beluga he had killed on Little Whale River, which runs into Hudson's Bay.

The Eskimos were traditionally carvers of soapstone and, like this artist photographed by E.S. Curtis in 1927, of the ivory of narwhals and walruses.

starve but not to make sure that they continued their chosen way of life without interference. Indeed, the coming of the welfare state to the north had meant a heightened and systematic interference with customary ways of life through the workings of the relief system (which finds it convenient if people are settled and not nomadic) and also through a type of education designed to assimilate the native peoples into the society developed in the rest of Canada, in what the northerners see as "outside."

As for the northern people themselves, recent years have produced a marked shift in attitudes and actions. Even a decade ago, when I first travelled in the region, Indians and Inuit alike were still notably passive in accepting whatever the white men wanted to impose on them, though it amounted to a drastic transformation of their nomadic and rulerless way of existence. The only people to protest at that time were a few anthropologists and a few white men who had lived long in the north as missionaries and traders and who admired the old native ways with their premium on courage and initiative, the qualities paternalism first erodes.

During the last few years, however, a great change has taken place, largely through the influence of movements which began among the native peoples of the United States and southern Canada. Because they are proportionately so numerous among the scanty northern population, the Inuit and the local Indians have been able to influence official policies more than native peoples elsewhere in Canada. Unlike the native peoples of Alaska they have not yet received satisfaction of their massive land claims, which involve hundreds of thousands of square miles, but they have been able to force the modification of plans for developing the oil resources of the north in ways that would harm the environment and the local fauna. It is unlikely that the Mackenzie valley pipeline would have been abandoned in 1977 if Justice Thomas Berger had not immediately beforehand, on his one-man commission of enquiry, heard such sensibly stated opposition from the local Indians.

These circumstances have brought to the fore a new kind of Indian and Inuit, self-confident and adept in gauging how to embarrass the white authorities, with their mixed motives of benevolence and acquisitiveness. But whether this amounts, as some native spokesmen in the North West Territories (and in the Yukon and Ungava as well) suggest, to a defence of the traditional native way of life, is problematical. The life the native people now live, and which they want to defend against the encroachments of oilmen and other latter-day intruders, is in fact the dependent life of the fur-trading days, based on a combination of hunting and trapping, oriented partly to subsistence and partly to trade, and leaving the Indian or the Inuit, however freely he may move within his environment, keyed into a white man's world. The native people must accept the white man's products in order to live wearing clothes, using equipment and ammunition, and consuming tea and flour, tobacco and alcohol. There is, in the emergence of native leaders more educated and

Eskimo carvings first became widely known outside the Arctic in the 1950s through the efforts of James Houston, and the making of them quickly became a minor industry, especially among the people of the Barren Ground who were threatened with starvation through the failure of the caribou herds. Early Eskimo stone carvings had been small and simple, usually animal figures that could be held in the hand and which were linked with hunting magic. But later Eskimo artists have branched into larger sculptures of human figures, like 'Mother and Child' and of fantasy beings, like Samoutik's 'Mask of Death' and Philipussee's 'Naked Giant'.

eloquent than their fellows, an even profounder social change, for no such leaders flourished in the original anarchic world of the north, where tribes did not exist and the nomadic family was the basic unit. Irreversible change has come belatedly to the north. The same forces that turned the people of the outside from the country to the city are even more rapidly turning the people of the north from wandering neolithic hunters into twentieth-century settled people. The transition that took millenia in Europe has here been telescoped into a few decades.

It seems inappropriate to write of Inuit carvers in the terms of ordinary biography, since they came out of the timeless world of the primitive hunter and in many cases were confronted only when they were men and women of forty or over by the time-bound world of Canadian society. **Tiktak** was one of these hunters, born about sixty years ago, learning his hunting skills in the traditional way, leading a nomadic life dependent on the movements of the caribou herd. During the 1950s the caribou diminished and also changed their migration route. There was starvation in the Barren Ground, and when I met Tiktak he sang me an Inuit song of that time, "The Hungry Camp." The Inuit were resettled in places along the west shore of Hudson's Bay, and it was at Rankin Inlet that Tiktak began, about 1960, to carve the sculptures for which he is well known. Eskimo artists are highly individual, and Tiktak's penchant is for human figures with highly stylized faces that — unconsciously of course — resemble archaic Polynesian sculpture. In our terms Tiktak is a great artist, but one attaches the epithet with diffidence, remembering the humorous, hospitable man who was humble about his art and much more interested in talking about how much better food had tasted when one hunted it for oneself in those lost days of free wandering in the Barren Ground.

That the North continues changing is due largely to world shortages of oil. Traces of petroleum were observed by Alexander Mackenzie when he descended the Mackenzie River in 1789, and since that time the exploration teams have been investigating and the rigs have been going up, particularly in the delta of the Mackenzie. The changes these developments will cause in the local ecology and in the lives of the Inuit are unpredictable but are likely to be serious and may be disastrous.

III A Canadian Identity

Long after the Plains Indians acquired horses, and even after they had adopted European dress, they clung to the simple carrying device of the travois, *two long poles attached to the horses's back, with a platform for goods between, and the ends trailing on the ground. Even before they had horses, the Indians used a smaller* travois *that was dragged by dogs.*

CHAPTER ELEVEN

Unity Without Uniformity

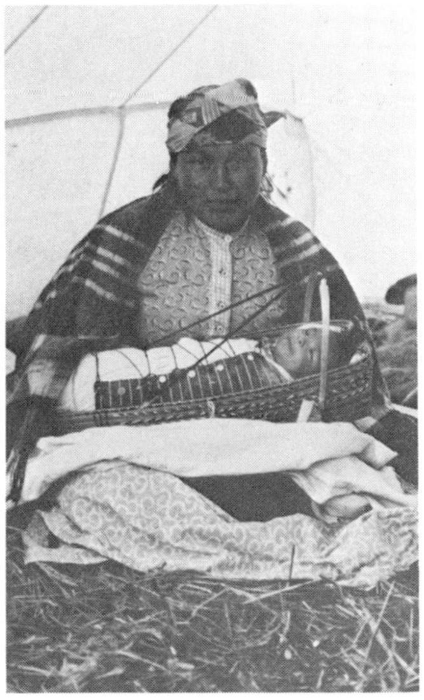

This late nineteenth century Coast Indian woman carries her child in a cradle of basketwork.

The search for unity in diversity is inevitable in a country as large as Canada and as varied in its physical conformations and its history. Now, as I am writing this book, the idea of unity seems urgent in a special political way because of the presence of a separatist government in one province, Québec, which is threatening to take the steps needed for independence. Goldwin Smith declared long ago that "The father of confederation is deadlock," but the problem has always been there — it was there even before Confederation — of how to reconcile the very real common interests that draw Canadians together with the historical and geographical imperatives that tend to separate them. It was because the founding fathers recognized the tension between these two aspects of Canadian life that in 1867 they created, not a centralized nation-state on the European model, but a confederation of former colonies who entered into a compact of limited unification. But they discovered the cement that would hold the compact permanently together. What Henri Bourassa said in 1907 rings a surprisingly familiar sound in our ears seventy years afterwards:

> There is Ontario patriotism, Quebec patriotism, or Western patriotism, each based on the hope that it may swallow up the others, but there is no Canadian patriotism, and we can have no Canadian nation when we have no Canadian patriotism.

Since Confederation there has always been in Canadian political life a significant oscillation between periods when the federal government, forgetting the true spirit of Confederation, has sought to take the greater part of power into its hands, and periods when the provinces have reacted and have insisted on a greater decentralization of powers and functions. Paradoxically, rigidity at the centre has always seemed a greater danger to unity in Canada than independence on the verges. Between Ottawa and Quebec City, between centralist Trudeau and separatist Lévesque, to quote the example that is most in Canadian minds at this moment of writing, it is not easy to decide which has most imperilled the true unity of our country. My personal reading of the situation leaves little doubt in my mind that when a confederal society runs into trouble it is usually because the dynamic equilibrium which should unite its parts has been disturbed by the effort to create an over-riding authority instead of a system of co-ordination between equal

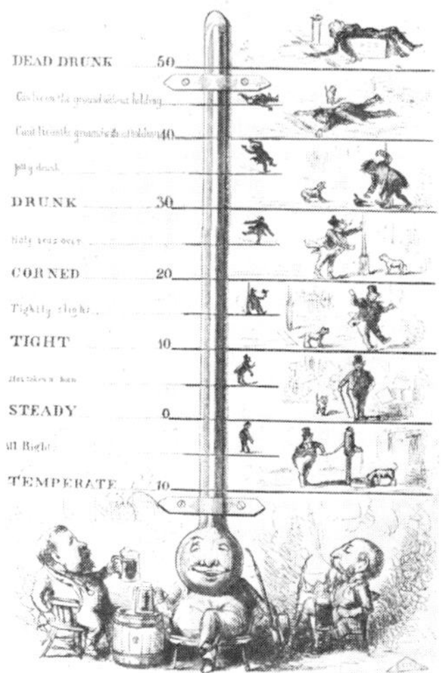

In Canadian as well as in American history there has been a kind of symbiosis between alcoholism and temperance. The periods of heaviest drinking were also those when the advocates of prohibition were hard at work, and the great campaigns against booze swept the Canadian Prairies when the saloons were most crowded, during the days of railway construction and first settlement in the Prairies. Women particularly were active in the temperance campaigns, and leading feminists like Nellie McClung were also leading prohibitionists. During the first world war they succeeded in imposing prohibition everywhere but in Québec, but afterwards it was realized that restrictive laws created more problems than they solved and most of Canada went 'wet'. The controversy at its various stages gave good fodder for cartoonists, like the deviser of 'The Inebriometer.'

partners. Therefore I regard Pierre Trudeau as perhaps the leading enemy of a workable Canadian unity, and René Lévesque as perhaps its greatest friend, since he has awakened us to the perils of an artificial constitutional unity that will not take into account the various — though not always different — needs and aspirations of Canada's regions.

Inevitably, given a common history more than a century long, and common perils, even common enemies, there are many aspects of Canadian life which show a unity that complements the diversity I have shown in tracing the regional pattern of Canadian life. It is a unity whose manifestations are usually unofficial, often undeliberate, and which may often express itself in ways that seem more diversified than in reality they are. In writing of these aspects of their existence which Canadians share, I begin with the most basic factor of all, the moral ambience, which is expressed in religion, in daily human relations, and, by extension, in the social, economic, and political aspects of Canadian life.

Canadians, I would say, are less a spiritual people than a people in whose lives formal religion has played and continues to play a considerable role. I am not suggesting an absence of spiritually awakened individuals or even groups of people; they certainly existed among the dedicated missionaries and nuns of New France, among the evangelical New Lights who followed Henry Alline in late eighteenth-century Nova Scotia, among Mennonites and Doukhobors, among the Methodist circuit riders of Upper Canada, among little sects of enthusiasts, and in unexpected corners of the great organized churches.

But, except perhaps for the early seventeenth-century period in a Québec dominated by Bishop Laval, ours has never been a society permeated by spirituality like that of the European middle ages or of relatively recent Tibet. Canadians may go to church regularly, as many still do; they may defer to the spiritual authority of their priests or pastors; they may be seized with pentecostal fires. But, unlike the United States, Canada does not put "In God We Trust" on its coins; efforts to create established churches have dismally failed and attempts by the existing churches to influence non-religious affairs have always in the end created resentment. This happened even in devout Québec, where hardly a voice was raised in protest when the Catholic Church was deprived of its influence in education and its power over local trade unions during the Quiet Revolution of the 1960s.

Canadian religions dramatically exemplify much unity of feeling accompanied by a complete lack of uniformity in observance. Canada is generally regarded as a Christian country but, quite apart from the growing number of professed agnostics, a fair-sized minority of Canadians adhere to religions other than Christianity, and if their numbers seem small spread over the whole population, they are often important in localities where they congregate, like Chinese and Japanese Buddhists and Indian Sikhs in and around Vancouver, and Jews in Montrẽal and

Red Square, Michael Snow

Morning Snow, Ivan Eyre

Snap No. 12, Harold Town

January, Alex Colville

Winnipeg. There are growing numbers of Moslems and Hindus and Confucians, and among the native peoples there has been a melding of Christian and pagan elements into movements such as the Indian Shaker Church, whose dancing and bell-ringing ceremonies flourish among the Salish Indians of British Columbia. There have also been attempts among the Ojibways and the Prairie Indians and the Coast Indians of British Columbia to recreate pre-missionary Indian religions, particularly the cults of spirit dancing.

Traditional crafts were long practiced in Québec. This woman was hand-spinning in 1930. In recent years there has been a revival of hand-weaving.

The Roman Catholic Church is by now the largest religious community in Canada. It commands the adherance of about forty-five per cent of the population, and one can no longer plausibly draw a line between a Catholic Québec and a Protestant English Canada. The postwar migrations from Mediterranean Europe have notably increased the Catholic presence in Ontario, British Columbia, and to a lesser extent, the other Canadian provinces.

Perhaps the most remarkable feature of Canadian Protestantism has been an early and successful example of ecumenical unification. At the time of Confederation the three leading Protestant Churches, more or less equal in numbers, were the Methodist, the Presbyterian, and the Church of England in Canada. In 1955 the Church of England sought to dispel the impression of being a relic of colonialism by changing its name to the Anglican Church. In part this move was inspired by the strength its rivals achieved through the accord which in 1925 established the United Church of Canada by bringing together the Methodist Church, about two-thirds of the Presbyterian Church, and the small Congregationalist Church. A fraction of the Presbyterians stubbornly refused to unite with people they regarded as imperfect Calvinists, while the entire Baptist movement stood aside and remained an independent group between the three large and socially acceptable churches — Catholic, Anglican, and United — and the more extreme fundamentalist and pentecostal groups whose influence grows rapidly in the rural districts and in the working-class urban areas of western Canada and Ontario.

Work on the farm in Québec during the 1920s.

There is a predictable mixture of hypocrisy and genuine fervour in Canadian religious practice, and here the English heritage is strong. Many people keep up their attendance at Anglican or United churches because they feel it is expected socially, or because it may be professionally expedient, or merely because in our atomized urban world they are lonely and the Church is the last vestige of the mutually protective pioneer society. Among the smaller sects, which have a sense of chiliastic urgency and exact a more active involvement, the level of genuine enthusiasm and inner commitment is always a great deal higher. And then, an essential part of the Canadian ecclesiastical scene, there are the churches whose survival is largely bound up with that of an ethnic tradition — the Greek Orthodox Church and the Doukhobors among Russians, the Uniate Catholic Church among the Ukrainians, and the

Settlers with their belongings seeking a home in Alberta before the first world war.

To learn English was one of the first needs of the European immigrants. These Galician girls — nowadays we would call them Ukranian — attended a village school in Alberta.

Lutheran and Mennonite churches among Germans. In such situations the power of racial nostalgia is often hard to distinguish from a genuine spiritual devotion.

If one is to judge by the census returns, all Canadians adhere to churches of one kind or another; very few of them have the negative conviction that makes them register themselves as of "no religion." The number of church members is, of course, much lower than the census figures (which are virtually useless as a guide to actual religious commitment) would indicate, and how much influence the churches really have on contemporary Canadian moral standards is hard to estimate. Has Puritanism really declined with the ebbing of the kind of active expression of faith so common in an earlier Canada? Does the loosening of manners and morals so dramatized by the media mean that there has been a basic change in Canadian ethics?

In reality the contrast we now see in terms of past and present has always existed in Canada as a polarity between the Puritan and the libertine, with a middle ground of compromise, now perhaps broader than it once was. Throughout early Canada there was always the contrast between the strict manners of the settlements, where stability was an essential virtue, and the liberated manners of the frontier, where adventurousness was an asset. This existed when the comparison was between the *habitant* living under the tutelage of his village priest, and the *coureur de bois* living his free life among the Indians, and it continued when the *habitants* were replaced by the citizens of towns established across Canada as settlement spread and the ways of the *coureurs de bois* were followed by other men who made their lives in the wilderness, whether as trappers, as miners, or as lumbermen. Very often, when towns emerged on the edge of the frontier, the respectable life represented by well-attended churches would go on in one part of the community while, as happened in Dawson City, recognized red-light districts existed elsewhere. On the edge of the frontier there have always been places known as "Saturday-night towns," where the proper and the timid surrendered the streets to the wild and the wayward as loggers and miners streamed in for a weekend away from the rigours of the camp and the bunkhouse. Perhaps nobody expressed the curious symbiosis between the pious, puritanical aspect of Canadian life and its libertine opposite more felicitously than the famous Camillien Houde, mayor of Montreal for the quarter of a century between 1928 and 1954. Commenting on his policy of running a wide open town, Houde remarked: "As long as we keep a good balance between prayer and sinning, I know my city is not going to sink into wickedness."

I believe that in practice, even during the high Victorian era, Canada kept, like Mayor Houde's Montreal, "a good balance between prayer and sinning", and that the situation is not greatly different today. The puritan element, represented most openly by the fundamentalist Christian sects, may be comparatively small, but its influence radiates and seems to be increasing after a decade or so of what may have been wrongly interpreted as a revolution in sexual and other kinds of behaviour. There is a libertine fringe whose unconventional and occasionally alarming behaviour distresses a large section of Canadian society, as does the increase in pornography, an inevitable result of a more tolerant attitude throughout the Western world towards what is produced in the arts and the media.

But I suspect that the section of society whose members want nothing more than to live in relative affluence and peace, the middle section which is neither libertine nor puritanical and which is perhaps larger than it has been in the past, has not fundamentally changed. We are told that there are more divorces, and that fewer marriages are lifelong, and both these things are true, but divorce is easier to obtain and people are no longer under the same compulsions to continue marriages which they recognize to be failures; the number of actual failed marriages may not have increased. Similarly, more young people tend to live together without going through the religious or legal formalities of marriage, but often such relationships turn out to be as enduring as the formal marriages they so closely resemble. We hear a great deal also of the dual problems of drug abuse and alcoholism. But social problems often come into prominence merely because they are recognized, and it is doubtful whether more Canadians are alcohol-addicted than in the past, although there is no doubt that drugs are more easily available and that their non-medical use has spread. This use is largely responsible for the increase in violent crime and for the fact that many Canadian towns are less safe than at any previous time, at least within living memory. But most Canadians are less conscious of the degree of physical insecurity which this situation creates than they are of the less-defined and more ominous threat of insecurity in their personal lives which the economic condition of Canada has aroused in recent years.

One can say, in general, that in formal terms Canadian life has become less constrained, but that the essential moral conformation of the nation has not changed greatly. What has happened, as it has in many other countries, is that a fringe society has emerged, separate from the traditional criminal classes, whose rejection of conventional standards of social morality has led to an increase in violence and an appearance of social instability. These in their turn have brought a hardening of authoritarian inclinations among Canadians in general, to the extent that a majority of Canadians would now probably favour a return to such social ferocities as the death penalty, whose abolition not many years ago was welcomed as an enlightened and progressive step. In matters such as this, recent years have shown a widespread retreat from the liberalism (in the unpartisan sense) that in the early post-war era seemed to be permeating Canadian attitudes.

Many of of the settlers who came after the 1890's belonged to the Slav peoples who were unwilling subjects of the Austro-Hungarian Empire.

Itinerant German bands, playing Strauss, Léhar, Von Suppé and other popular composers, were a regular feature of Winnipeg streets in the days before the first world war aroused prejudice against anything German — even music.

Since the second world war, immigrants have tended to come in waves, with the British usually predominant, but in second place the Dutch, then the Germans, then the Italians. Among the later important groups have been the Portuguese.

Discussions of the moral fibre of a society take one inevitably into areas where the morality becomes social and verges on the economic and political — areas which embrace attitudes to work, class relations, the extent of collective responsibility for the needs of individuals and of society in general, and the political-economic patterns to which such questions lead.

In Canada, as elsewhere, a great deal has been said about the decay of the Puritan work ethic. Workers, it is said, have ceased to be conscientious and reliable; the task is no longer regarded as its own reward. I would say rather that what we have seen decaying over the past generation has been not so much the Puritan ethic as the pioneer ethic, and that the decay has been going on since the years of the Great Depression. While there was land to be cleared and a new life more free and abundant than that of the Old World to be created by individuals and small communities in the wilderness, a willingness to work without thought of immediate reward was a necessary virtue. This was the basis of the pioneer work ethic rather than any imperative derived from the classic European connection between Puritan concepts of duty and the rising capitalist system.

This pioneer work ethic was eroded in two ways. First, no more than a generation after the Prairie settlers had firmly established themselves, and most of Canada's arable land had been brought under the plough, the Depression ensued; the products of pioneer toil became unsaleable, life resumed its old precariousness and the work ethic seemed irrelevant. After the Depression ended, the age of rapid technological change began, and a younger generation was quick to recognize that grinding toil was not necessary for survival. Increased mechanization also tended to diminish the interest of the individual job and the value of acquiring manual skills. This has contributed to what often appears to be a casual attitude towards work and its responsibilities among younger Canadians.

But whether this attitude is entirely outside the Canadian tradition has again to be questioned. The idea of a calling whose skills took years to master and which one followed for a lifetime did not transplant well from Europe to Canada. Pioneer life demanded an ability to master many skills less than perfectly, rather than one skill perfectly. The impracticability of dedicating oneself to a single lifetime working role (which meant that the apprenticeship system was never strong in Canada) combined with the temptation to wander in a great and empty land to produce a remarkable occupational as well as a geographical mobility among Canadians. In Europe to have done many kinds of work is regarded as a sign of fecklessness, and the term *Jack-of-all-trades* is a derogatory one, but in Canada shifting from one calling to another is regarded as a sign of adaptability, and people talk with pride of the tasks they have done.

And, of course, there are always the exceptions, the people who swim against tides. As in the past there are many Canadians — those who are craftsmen or artists or seers by temperament and genius — whose dedication to their work is total and disinterested. Everywhere in Canada one encounters people of this kind; people whose vision has led them to decline both profit and the challenges of the mobile life to become potters or playwrights, violin-makers or marginal farmers, not always merely for personal satisfaction, but also with a half-articulated sense of the opportunities for self-realization in a land as vast and unpopulated as Canada in this age when machinery can provide for the basic needs

Among the industries that in recent years have absorbed many immigrants is the construction industry.

The age of near-affluence indeed hovers uncertainly around us, and its economics have in recent years eroded in Canada the classic connection between work and class that formed the basis for radical social criticism in nineteenth-century Europe. Yet class remains important in Canada, and virtually inescapable, even if it does not manifest itself in the old European way. It is true that attempts to create imitation European societies, with the traditional hierarchy of monarch, aristocracy, gentry, and honest labourers were never successful in Canada. The few great French nobles who came to La Nouvelle France under the *ancien régime* were high officials who planned to go home when their terms of office came to an end, and the element of mobility provided by the fur trade prevented the emergence of a static feudal order. Even before the Conquest of 1759 the *habitants* impressed foreign visitors with their lack of docility. Attempts in Upper Canada to naturalize an English rural order of gentry, farmers, and labourers likewise failed because the Loyalists were too American to tolerate it. So Canada became a monarchy without an aristocracy, and the populist strain in the North American tradition led to an angry rejection of the British tests of title and accent as determinants of a man's social worth. Mrs. Moodie and other genteel immigrants of the 1830s as well as the English remittance men of later generations encountered the same resistance to the pretensions of the Old Country upper classes, and an English cultured accent still grates on Canadian ears in a way that English and Scottish regional accents do not. There were some Victorian Canadians, like the former Oxford professor Goldwin Smith, who lamented that with the pretensions of gentility the sense of *noblesse oblige* had also vanished from Canadian life.

> There are in Canada — said Smith — no social materials for a House of Lords, nor is there anything like that independent gentry which has furnished the conservative element in the House of Commons. The leading men in Canada are commercial, and cannot leave their business offices for Ottawa, or if they do, it is on business of their own.

This does not mean that Canadian society is classless. Manners may be freer than in the Old World, but no-one who visits Canadian cities and observes how clearly divided are the districts where the rich and the poor live can imagine that a genuine social or economic equality exists. The Canadian standard of living is among the highest in the world, and

probably the poorest of the country's people are rich in comparison with most of the inhabitants of India and Bangladesh. But the fact remains that among Canadians there are vast disparities of income. As I write I have just glanced at a salary survey published by *Weekend* magazine which reveals that while a cement finisher in Halifax earned $9,000 last year and a day-care assistant in Toronto $9,391 (neither being in the lowest range of incomes), the president of Massey-Harris earned $401,660, the chairman of Alcan Aluminum earned $388,250 and the Chairman of Seagram's earned $325,674.

It is true that some old forms of class distinction have been eroded, in Canada and elsewhere, some blue collar workers have attained incomes and standards of living as high as those of many professionals, and as industrial militancy has led many white collar workers — including academics — to make common cause with other workers in the trade union movement. Such changes, however, have not eliminated many notable forms of inequality: the fact that a tenth of the Canadian labour force is at present unemployed and an eighth of Canadians live below the official government poverty line; the divergence in standards of living between Newfoundland at one extreme and British Columbia and Alberta at the other; the dramatically underprivileged status of Indians, Inuit, and especially Métis; the great mass of people who have become superfluous in a mechanised and profit-based society and whose presence the transformation of Canada into a welfare state has merely emphasized.

Nor does the absence of an aristocracy in the traditional sense mean that Canada is a country without ruling elites. The rich do not merely have privilege; they have power as well. Thirteen years ago John Porter published a remarkable book, *The Vertical Mosaic*, in which he demonstrated that Canada was in fact ruled by a closely interconnected group of about two thousand people, with less than a thousand controlling the principal financial and industrial corporations and the rest scattered in politics, bureaucracy, the universities, the labour movement, and the media. None of the economic elite was a woman, an Indian, an Inuit, an Asian. Eighty per cent were British in origin and ninety per cent were Protestant. At that time, though French Canadians were prominent already in the political elite, they formed less than seven per cent of the men controlling banks and industries. There have been changes in the composition of the ruling elites, with more French Canadians moving into positions of bureaucratic and industrial power, but the power of the elites as such has not diminished. A small group of about one ten-thousandth of the population still makes the major decisions that affect the lives of Canadians, and makes them as often as not in the privacy of exclusive social clubs or of mansions secluded in large grounds and anachronistically well-staffed with servants. Not formally recognized, class is a potent factor governing the lives of all Canadians.

The peculiarities of Canadian economic life are closely connected with the political structure of the country; Canadians find themselves operating in a half-world between American and English values and methods. On the formal level, Canada is a parliamentary democracy on the model of Westminster, and not a presidential system like that of the United States. There is no division such as the Americans have between the legislative and the executive branches of government, and the Governor General, who as the Queen's representative is titular head of state, maintains in the splendid isolation of Rideau Hall a studied avoidance of more than formal and symbolic duties.

To the federal Parliament in Ottawa and to the ten provincial assemblies Canadians elect their respresentatives, and, under the accepted theory of responsible government, the majority party in each house forms the government whose ministers are picked from among the chosen members. Here too formality and symbolism are important, though they are tied to the reality rather than the semblance of power; Parliament is conducted with the ceremonial evolved in Westminster centuries ago, and the throne speech, the robed Speaker, the arcane duties of Black Rod, fit in with Ottawa's Gothic architecture and the bear-skinned and scarlet-coated guards who parade on its lawns to convey a sense of traditionalism which puzzled an astute observer like Thoreau more than a century ago, when he wondered why Canada "wild and unsettled as it is" should seem "an older country than the States." He formed the impression that:

> All things seem to contend there with a certain rust of antiquity, such as forms on old armour and iron guns, the rust of convention and formalities. If the rust was not on the tinned roofs and spires, it was on the inhabitants.

Yet in some respects the ceremony one sees in Canada may be deceptive, for Canadian political life is far from being a replica of the British. This is partly because the two larger Canadian political parties, the Conservatives and the Liberals, though they bear British names, are nearer in structure and function to the multiple-interest parties of the United States, the Republicans and the Democrats, with the same kinds of territorial bases (Liberals in Québec, Tories in the west) and the same wide spectrums of political standpoint, so that a Tory radical like John Diefenbaker would be considerably to the left of a reactionary Liberal like Otto Lang. However, the strict bipartisanship of American politics is not reproduced in Canada, where the political situation is complicated by the fact that strong minority parties exist — the social democratic New Democratic Party and the Social Credit Party — and often elect enough representatives to hold a balance of power when there is a minority government, and to ensure the kinds of progressive legislation which have made periods of minority government some of the most

The Japanese came to Canada in considerable numbers about the turn of the century, and settled largely in British Columbia, where they became fishermen, farmers and market gardeners. After the attack on Pearl Harbour in 1941, 22,000 Japanese — many of them Canadian born — were deported inland from the Coast; their property confiscated and sold. No specific charge of disloyalty was laid against any person of Japanese origin throughout the war, and since that time the incident has been regarded with shame by most Canadians. The Japanese salvaged their lives, and the scars of that time have grown faint but have never entirely faded away.

For many years Canadian immigration laws were racially biassed, and few Chinese were allowed to enter the country. Now, however, the rules have been liberalized and there has been a considerable influx of Chinese immigrants, mainly via Hong Kong.

productive in Canadian political life. Between a fifth and a quarter of Canadians vote regularly for such parties, and this disinclination to fit into set political patterns is emphasised by a well-known Canadian tendency for electors to vote differently in provincial than in federal elections.

Canadians often vote in federal elections on grounds of principle rather than in the hope of seeing their party forming an actual government, and they express their strong regional feelings by electing governments provincially that are likely to disagree with the federal government on matters of local policy. Thus the variety of the country emerges strongly in its political patterns; a British Columbian or a Newfoundlander feels his regional identity as strongly as he feels his Canadian nationality, and his interests in one role may modify his interests in another.

For this and for other reasons a very large proportion of Canadians avoid partisan allegiances that tie them beforehand, as is witnessed by the high proportion of uncommitted answers given in political opinion polls. Thomas Chandler Haliburton gave expression to a wide spread Canadian feeling when in the 1840s he declared that "politics makes a man as crooked as a pack does a pedlar, not that they are so awful heavy, neither, but it teaches a man to stoop in the long run."

The fact that the third Canadian party has been for forty years one professing democratic socialism is perhaps the feature that most of all distinguishes Canadian from American politics. And the presence of this socialist party, regionally strong enough to have held control in the early 1970s of three western provinces (British Columbia, Saskatchewan, and Manitoba), reminds one that long before any socialist party appeared, Canada had begun the evolution that has led to a partially socialist system in which the state in many areas competes with non-governmental capitalist corporations.

Canada has two major railways, the privately owned Canadian Pacific and the publicly owned Canadian National; it has two major airlines, the privately owned Canadian Pacific Airlines and the publicly owned Air Canada; its broadcasting system is divided between the publicly owned Canadian Broadcasting Corporation and a variety of private networks; the National Film Board runs a film-making operation parallel to those of privately financed groups.

This unusual situation arose from the necessities of a large and thinly populated country with comparatively undeveloped industries but ample natural resources; transport and communications on a large scale were essential for its development, but there was not sufficient private capital to underwrite them. In the early years of the last century, when Upper Canada was being settled, governments provided the canals necessary for defence and commerce. After Confederation a trans-Canadian railway was needed, and even the privately owned Canadian Pacific was not built without heavy public subsidies in cash and land. When the two other trans-Canadian railways, the Canadian Northern and the Grand Trunk Pacific, proved economically unviable, they were bought out by the federal government and in 1919 combined as the Canadian National. With such precedents, Canadians naturally took it for granted in later years that the government would intervene to make sure that adequate communications were ensured, and so Air Canada and the CBC were created but — and this is the special characteristic of Canadian near-socialism — not as monopolies; competing private enterprises were always encouraged to emerge and flourish.

The relaxation of the immigration laws has also encouraged the immigration of West Indian blacks.

Thus powerful governmental corporations rival powerful private corporations — largely American-owned — in dominating the economic lives of Canadians. And this seems to have followed from the geographical necessities that dominate Canadian history. Individual farmers, miners, and loggers started the country's great industries, but publicly owned or subsidised transport was needed to ensure the full development of the country. Thus a tradition of public interference in economic life was established, and over the years it has led to the growth of an immense governmental apparatus which many Canadians regard with distrust and find conflicting with their image of themselves. They are accustomed to seeing themselves as one of the most liberated nations on earth, and in recent years they have discovered that in reality they may belong to one of the most over-governed countries of the western world. The growing reaction to this situation is likely to have a considerable influence on the changes in the structure of Canadian political life which the near future will inevitably bring about. The wind, as it now blows, is set towards increasing devolution and decentralization, the direction of true confederacy.

Jack Shadbolt, Guardian.

CHAPTER TWELVE

The Life of the Arts

Emily Carr,
Potlatch Welcome.

Culture is one of the most protean words in the English language. If one accepts the venerable authority of the Oxford English Dictionary, it first appeared — like *cult* — as a derivation of the Latin *cultus,* meaning worship, and here there is a special Canadian irony, since the two major cultures of our country, accepting the later definition of the intellectual and artistic aspect of civilizations, are linked with strongly differing religious traditions; with the Catholicism of Québec and its underlying strain of Jansenist puritanism, and with the Protestantism of English-speaking Canada with its dominant strain of Scottish puritanism.

Yet to trace the cultural patterns of Canada only in terms of a French-English duality means an excessive simplification of the artistic and intellectual development of a country which has justly taken some pride in being a "mosaic" of many cultures rather than a melting-pot society on the American model.

Already, in an earlier chapter, I have referred to the native cultures of Indians and Inuit which were stimulated rather than destroyed by the first appearance of the white men; this was especially true of the Coast Indian and the Inuit cultures. In the case of the Coast Indians, the period during which they produced their best work — among the most monumental and also among the most exquisite sculptures ever created by a primitive people — was in the 1870s and 1880s. This happened after the fur traders had provided an abundance of metal tools which not only allowed the carvers to produce much greater quantities of artifacts by speeding up work processes, but also tempted them to more daring complexities of design and to a more elaborately executed finish. This renaissance, as brief as most cultural movements, had expired before 1920. In recent years the Coast Indians have rediscovered their own traditions, but the work they have been doing tends to be trapped in the old conventions and shows little originality of design. Perhaps in recent decades the most important contribution of the Coast Indians had been that which their arts have made to a wider tradition; Emily Carr and Jack Shadbolt, the most important painters to emerge from western Canada, were both greatly influenced by the forms created by Coast Indian carvers.

It is hard, at the moment of writing, to assess the condition of Inuit art, which a decade ago seemed a highly vital tradition. It is an ancient tradition, developed within a singularly unorganized society. Among the

Mordecai Richler

Matt Cohen.

Alden Nowlan.

Inuit there were no elaborate ritual fraternities like those which fostered the arts of the Pacific coast; instead there existed a loose network of family groups, nomad hunters in cruel landscapes. Long ago, in the distant Dorset culture, carvers were making tiny bone sculptures, and for the last millenium and more, since the pre-white-contact Thule culture, Inuit have been making portable and personally evocative carvings from caribou antler, walrus ivory, and soft stone. The earliest of these carvings may have fulfilled the same magical purposes as did the palaeolithic cave paintings of Lascaux; that is, they were representations of animals devised to attract members of the species that the sculptor hunted. They were small, made to fit the palm of the hand that carried them and fondled them, so that its grease gave them a special patina. During the nineteenth century early travellers brought back Inuit carvings that found their way into the ethnographic collections of museums (the British Museum has some superb early specimens), but the outside world was hardly aware of this almost secret artistic tradition until 1949, when James Houston brought some Inuit sculpture from the Arctic and began to organize its sale on a commercial basis.

Within a very few years the art world of Canada became aware of this haunting culture of a barren land, and the first effect was highly stimulating. For two decades the Inuit carved industriously, in stone, in petrified whalebone, in caribou antlers; they produced an immense number of works. They abandoned their traditional miniaturism and produced massive carvings in a variety of forms they had never before attempted; Canadian connoisseurs created "masters" in a culture that had never known the western concept of "artist," and some carvers sold their work for very high prices. Subsidiary arts were developed: pottery, printmaking, appliqué textile work, all using recognizable Inuit motifs. A proportion — inevitably a small proportion — of the works so produced were of remarkable quality, and were recognized as such in exhibitions that toured western Europe, the Union of Soviet Socialist Republics, and the United States. But already, less than thirty years after the art of the Inuit was discovered by other Canadians, there has been a commercial vulgarization that reflects the way the traditional hunting life — which originally inspired the carvers — has receded into the past. Other manifestations of Inuit culture, such as the songs that describe the vicissitudes of a nomad existence in the far north, and the shamanic drum dances, are following the igloo and the skin kayak into extinction, and it seems unlikely that the art of Inuit sculpture will survive except as an increasingly meaningless commercial craft.

There is no doubt that the basic duality of Canadian society at the time of Confederation in 1867, and the persistence of such a strong French-speaking culture, encouraged other European minorities to retain their cultures, often in very militant ways, for in recent years the Ukrainians and other fairly numerous minorities have agitated for their mother tongues to be given equal status to French and English in a multicultural society. The most numerous of the minority groups in Canada are the Germans, and their traditional customs and festivals survive across Canada, from Lunenburg, where they first settled in the 1750s, to Vancouver where many immigrants settled after the Second World War. Other minorities such as the Italians and the Portuguese in the large eastern cities, the Icelanders in northern Manitoba, the Russian Doukhobors in the mountain valleys of British Columbia, and the old Chinese and Sikh communities in Vancouver and Victoria have retained their languages; they remember their native songs and dances with a great deal of nostaligic dedication, and most of them maintain their own churches or temples. Writers from such minorities — especially the Germans, Hungarians, Ukrainians, and Icelanders — publish poems and fiction in their mother tongues, and there are ethnic journals and publishing houses to sustain them. But the only minority apart from the French that has really influenced Canadian cultural life outside its own little ethnic world is the relatively small Jewish group, which has produced not only some of Canada's best composers, but also a remarkable group of English-language writers, including novelists like Mordecai Richler and Adele Wiseman, Norman Levine and Jack Ludwig, and poets like A. M. Klein and Irving Layton, Leonard Cohen and Joe Rosenblatt.

Adele Wiseman.

The development of the major cultures in Canada, French and English, really falls into two phases; a colonial era when motherland traditions are adapted rather uneasily to the conditions of a new environment, and a national era when the culture takes on a distinctive character which its artists, abandoning irrelevant traditions, seek to express.

Irving Layton.

At the same time, there is a significant difference between the French and the English traditions. The French brought with them a living peasant tradition, and so, we have seen, did the English, Irish, and Scots who came during the seventeenth and eighteenth centuries to Newfoundland and the Maritimes. But this peasant culture of the villages and outports survived only in the isolation of early pioneer existence and it had little influence on the literate colonial culture of the nascent towns and cities, where people sought to create in a strange environment a replica of the world from which they had come. It took a long time for immigrants to recognize that in their efforts to subjugate alien environments they were in fact creating new societies for which new forms of expression were appropriate.

The consequence of this situation is — as the Canadian poet Louis Dudek has said — that English-Canadian literature "begins with decadent romantic lyric and with the lees of late eighteenth-century sentimental poetry imported from Europe." Early poets like Oliver Goldsmith, Charles Heavysege, and Charles Sangster — the "dear bad poets" as James Reaney once called them — showed no originality of form and

Gwendolyn MacEwen.

William Berczy,
Blind Man's Buff.

very little response to the special nature of the Canadian environment. They were usually most interesting when they were most unconsciously comic, like James Gay, the self-styled poet laureate of Canada, who wrote to Tennyson on terms of equality, and addressed Queen Victoria with true colonial rodomontade:

> Hail our great Queen in her regalia;
> One foot in Canada, the other in Australia.

Early French-Canadian poets, like Octave Crémazie and Louis Fréchette, are somewhat more interesting because they show at least the passionate resentment of a people anxious to redress the humiliation of their conquest in 1760.

As for early Canadian fiction, the tone for the first century was already set by the book generally regarded as the first Canadian novel, Frances Brooke's *The History of Emily Montague* (1767), which very significantly is concerned with garrison life. *Emily Montague* is in fact a

Thomas Davies,
A View of Chateau Richer Church.

Joseph Légaré,
Les Ruines aprés l'Incendie du quartier St. Jean vue vers l'Est.

Paul Kane,
The Death of Omoxesisixany or Big Snake.

novel of manners that might easily have been written about a small town with a nearby military camp in eighteenth-century England if it were not for a few French characters and above all for the Canadian winter, which Mrs. Brooke, an acquaintance of Dr. Samuel Johnson, experienced with undisguised horror: "The rigour of the climate," she remarks "suspends the very powers of the understanding; what then must become of those of the imagination?"

In early Canada the best writing, like the best painting, was descriptive and narrative, the vigorous, functional prose of explorers like Samuel Hearne and David Thompson, whom we have already encountered. Such writers were so involved in the pressures of experience that they utilized literary conventions rather than accepting their domination. For rather similar reasons, the best writings to emerge from the settlements of Canada at the same era were those which set out to display in factual or satiric terms the actualities of current Canadian life.

Two of the most remarkable examples are the English sisters, Susanna Moodie and Catharine Parr Traill, who were disappointed in their hopes of duplicating the lives of the English squirearchy in the woodlands of early nineteenth-century Upper Canada, and wrote their books out of a bitter experience of trying to sustain gentility in a pioneer environment. Because of this intensely personal involvement, Mrs. Moodie's *Roughing it in the Bush* and *Life in the Clearings* and Mrs. Traill's *The Backwoods of Canada* seem much more authentic than any novel written at the same period in presenting the picture of real life during the 1830s on the pioneer verges of Upper Canada. In the Maritimes it was satire rather than documentation that brought authenticity. Thomas Chandler Haliburton, in *The Clockmaker; or, the Sayings and Doings of Sam Slick of Slickville* (1836), and Thomas McCulloch, in *Letters of Mephibosheth Stepsure* (1860), were frustrated reformers who tried to laugh their neighbours out of their follies and prejudices by creating, in sketches for periodical publication, a comic yet very realistic picture of the Atlantic provinces on the verge of the Victorian era.

Most early Canadian painting that survives is the work of uninspired imitators of academic styles. Among the exceptions are the vigorously primitive *ex votos* produced by Québec village artists to celebrate apparently miraculous events in the lives of their patrons, and the works of the very few men of visual sensibility who went into the wilderness and recorded their impressions on the spot. Perhaps the best of these was Thomas Davies, a topographer attached to the British army who executed some naïve and vividly coloured water-colours of Canadian landscapes during the 1750s and 1760s which are interesting as historical documents and pleasing as paintings but which also capture something of the mythical resonances of the northern wilderness. Unfortunately, in an age before *plein air* painting became respectable, there could be a considerable gap between an artist's original perception and his finished work, and a striking example in early Canada was that of Paul Kane. In 1844 Kane travelled across the Prairies to the Pacific Coast with the aim of studying and recording the native Indian cultures before they died out. When he returned he painted a series of vast canvases which portrayed Indian life in an artificially heroic manner. Only recently have the actual sketches which Kane painted on small pieces of board come to light; they reveal a far more original painter than one had imagined from his finished works, with a sharp eye for mood and movement and a fresh sense of colour, all of which he subdued to please a Victorian public in Toronto and Montreal that was accustomed to academic painting and to a false image of the "noble savage."

If Canadian painters and writers offer little of real interest before the late nineteenth century, the situation in music and drama was even less inspiring. They flourished indeed, but as performing rather than creative arts. There were many orchestras of amateur musicians, and a theatre would be one of the first buildings to indicate that a village was turning into a town, but the music, the plays, and often even the musicians and

Charles Mair (left) with Charles D. Roberts, 1927.

players, would be imported. No original Canadian play or musical composition of even the slightest interest has survived from this period.

Canada's evolution into a nation and the emergence of a true Canadian tradition in at least some of the arts were almost coterminous. With the so-called Confederation Poets of the 1890s, such as Charles G. D. Roberts, Archibald Lampman, and Duncan Campbell Scott, there is at last the effort to find a way of responding directly to Canadian experiences and of recognizing the special qualities of the Canadian environment. Roberts and Lampman write evocatively of rural life in the Maritimes and Ontario; Scott finds poetry in his observations of Indian life in the northern wilderness. With such poets and with their tragic French Canadian contemporary, Emile Nelligan, the garrison mentality opens its gates, the pioneer fear of the land seems to dissipate, and a literature based on a true national sentiment begins to emerge.

Yet if the content of these poets is Canadian, they are still using the idiom and the tone of European writers; their sound is that of the Romantics and the Symbolists. It is really with Stephen Leacock that a true Canadian tone — ironic, self-deprecating yet subtly arrogant — begins to appear in the satiric sketches of Upper Canadian life that make up books like *Sunshine Sketches of a Little Town* (1912) and his sharp attack on urban plutocracy, *Arcadian Adventures with the Idle Rich* (1914).

But it was in painting that the most dramatic breaks towards a modern style and a distinctive Canadian outlook emerged. The earliest major Canadian painters were remarkably unalike except in the illuminating vision with which they perceived the Canadian setting. Ozias Leduc was a self-taught Québec church decorator who came by chance on the work of the French Impressionists and in a small village of the Laurentians created still lifes and landscapes of other-worldly limpidity. James Wilson Morrice, who came of a wealthy Montréal family, was eventually accepted by Matisse and the other French painters of his time as their equal, but before that he had seen and portrayed the light and colour of Canadian cities and rivers undimmed by academic lenses.

Stephen Leacock.

On the experiments of Leduc and Morrice the most famous school of Canadian painters, the Group of Seven, based their practice. There were really eight painters involved, for Lawren Harris, A. Y. Jackson, Arthur Lismer, Frederick Varley, Frank Carmichael, Francis Hans Johnston, and J. E. H. MacDonald were closely associated between 1913 and 1917 with Tom Thomson, who shared their preoccupation with a visual re-exploration of the Canadian landscape, using the styles and techniques of the Impressionists, of Cézanne, and of Art Nouveau. Thomson, perhaps the most talented member of the movement, drowned in 1917; A. Y. Jackson, its best-known master, survived until 1974. Pushing far into the wilderness, these men observed and recorded the forms and colours of the Canadian landscape as had never before been done by painters; they established a colour range so vibrant and an interpretation of natural form so compelling that most educated Canadians are still inclined to see their country with a vision shaped by these remarkable men.

Ozias Leduc,
L'Enfant au Pain.

Unfortunately the Group of Seven's influence on Canadian painting was heavy and lingering. Only a few other painters of importance emerged from their shadow in the first decades after their appearance — notably David Milne and Emily Carr — and it was only in the late 1930s that a group of French-Canadian painters broke away from local influences and figurative traditions to embrace the modernist experimental trends that flourished in Paris and later New York. Notable among them were Alfred Pellan and Paul-Emile Borduas, Jacques de Tonnancour and Jean-Paul Riopelle, the only contemporary Canadian who also enjoys a great reputation as a leading painter in France.

James Wilson Morrice,
Winter Street with Horses and Sleighs.

From the Second World War onwards Canadian art has shown a superficial inclination to follow the movements that rise and fall in the international art world, and a simultaneous and more deeply flowing nativism, so that even in the work of nominally non-figurative painters one sees Canadian landscape and its natural world acting as a source of images and forms. During the past generation there has been a great increase in the number of practicing artists, and names have emerged and disappeared bewilderingly, but a number have forged adaptable and durable styles that outlast fashion, that merit international recognition and yet remain identifiably Canadian. Among the generation that ap-

Tom Thomson,
Algonquin Park

A.Y. *Jackson,*
Early Spring, Quebec.

J.E.H. MacDonald, Falls, Montreal River.

peared in the 1950s and 1960s the most notable figures were Jack Shadbolt, Harold Town, Tony Urquhart, Gordon Smith, William Ronald, Ronald Bloore, Michael Snow, Toni Onley, Kazuo Nakamura and the illuminist realists, Alex Colville and Jack Chambers. It is significant that there is no single centre of painting in Canada; the names I have mentioned are those of artists who paint and exhibit their work across the country from Vancouver to Halifax, and the regional nature of Canadian painting has been emphasized by the new school, responsive to Asian influences, that has arisen on the west coast, represented especially by Jack Wise, Roy Kiyooka, and Lin Chien-shi. Graphic arts, and crafts such as pottery have flourished recently, particularly in Québec and British Columbia, and architecture as a public art has been finely developed.

A great deal of modern Canadian architecture, perhaps inevitably, has followed the international idiom that derives from masters such as Le Corbusier, Walter Gropius, and Mies van der Rohe, but in recent years it has been a weakening line of inspiration responsible for the characterless

Arthur Lismer, September Sunlight, Georgian Bay

Lawren Harris, Lake Superior.

Jean-Paul Lemieux, Lazare.

Alfred Pellan,
Femme d'une Pomme.

Alex Colville,
To Prince Edward Island.

Raymond Moriyama.

Central Library, Toronto, designed by Raymond Moriyama.

white towers and black towers that Canadians now tend to regard as alien intrusions in their towns and cities.

The more sensitive, and the more definably Canadian kinds of building have been those whose architects have recognised that Canada is indeed becoming a country of town dwellers, but that it has also a series of greatly differing terrains, and that buildings must be designed not only to harmonize with these landscapes but also with the traditions and local lifestyles of the Canadian regions.

The lower slopes of the mountains outside Vancouver and the coastlines of Vancouver Island, for example, have provided spectacular residential sites which tested the abilities of architects to build houses well related to the environment. Arthur Erickson, Geoffrey Massey, and Ron Thom, among others, gained practice in such domestic work before they embarked on great imaginative tasks like Erickson and Massey's mountain-top Simon Fraser University in Burnaby, Erickson's fine Lethbridge University, responding to the natural forms of rolling hills and deep coulees in southern Alberta, and Ron Thom's academically appropriate Massey College in Toronto. Other remarkable examples of recent Canadian architecture have been Mario Pei's spectacular

If Canadian architecture has an international image it is due largely to the achievements of **Arthur Erickson.** After a wandering youth, which included a wartime stint in India and solitary wanderings in the Middle East, Erickson settled down in the late 1950s to teach architecture in Vancouver and to design houses, made of local materials and full of light, that fitted lyrically into their settings on cliffsides over British Columbian seaways. The other, monumental side of Erickson's architectural talent became evident in the early 1960s when he designed Simon Fraser University on top of Burnaby Mountain, a unified campus superbly integrated into its hillcrest setting and looking into the heart of the Coast Mountains. Later, straddling a deep Alberta coulée, he built the equally spectacular Lethbridge University. He has designed a magically mirror-walled Canadian pavilion for the 1970 Osaka exhibition, government buildings in Saudi Arabia, a pure-lined Sikh Temple in Vancouver and a tall-aisled Museum of Anthropology to house the great totem poles at the University of British Columbia. His Courthouse Complex of low, controlled skylines and hanging gardens has transformed the centre of Vancouver, halting the march of black-walled highrises, and he has designed a new town in Kuwait whose building is in the lap of political uncertainty. The variety of his designs is immense: the one constant element is an unrivalled sense of the kinship of the building to the terrain it inhabits and expresses.

underground-aboveground Place Ville Marie in Montreal, Raymond Moriyama's Ontario Science Centre, imaginatively terraced into the Don Valley in Toronto, John C. Parkin's Art Gallery of Ontario, again in Toronto, and Moshe Safdie's modular residential building, Habitat, which was built in Montreal for Expo in 1967.

Recent imaginatively planned urban renewal projects have shown the deep interest among modern Canadian architects in preserving the essential characteristics of cities. An integrated structure covering three blocks of downtown Vancouver, like Arthur Erickson's courthouse project, challenges with its low elevations and careful use of space the idea that the hearts of towns must necessarily grow upward to the exclusion of light and air and hence of vegetation.

Dorothy Livesay.

In the modern age literature in Canada has followed a development rather like that of the English and American traditions, beginning with the vivification of poetry, proceeding to fiction, going on to criticism, and culminating in drama.

The vital period for Canadian poetry was the 1930s, and the dominant English-Canadian poets then were E. J. Pratt, A. J. M. Smith, F. R. Scott, A. M. Klein, and Dorothy Livesay. All but Klein and Pratt are alive and still writing. Pratt wrote epics in a rather conventional manner, and his poems on historic themes — the Jesuit martyrs *(Brébeuf and his Brethren*, 1940) — or the building of the Canadian Pacific *(Towards the Last Spike*, 1952) — gave a historical foundation to the new Canadian poetry and complemented the modernism of younger writers like Smith, Scott, and Livesay, who were influenced by the English poets of the 1930s and given to a very individual combination of satirical social criticism and lyrical celebration of the wilderness landscape. During the 1940s a vigorous school of even younger poets, influenced by Ezra Pound and William Carlos Williams, evidenced a shift towards American literary attitudes; the most active were Irving Layton, Louis Dudek, and Raymond Souster, all of whom have remained influential figures in the Canadian literary world. Later the American and British styles were melded into a local and genuinely Canadian style in which poets played interesting variations on expressing the experience of being Canadian. Significant of growing maturity has been the strengthening of individual voices and sensibilities and the lessening self-consciousness of their Canadianism, even though most Canadian poets are political nationalists of one kind or another. Among Canadian poets writing vigorously today P. K. Page, Earle Birney, Phyllis Webb, Leonard Cohen, Al Purdy, Margaret Atwood, Alden Nowlan, George Bowering and Gwendolyn MacEwen are the most interesting established names and Michael Ondaatje, Patrick Lane, Tom Wayman, and Dale Zieroth are among the best of the younger poets. Lately the younger poets have been deeply concerned with finding ways of expressing the relationship between the physical quality of the land and its historic resonances. Like painting, poetry has become steadily more regional in its inspiration.

Al Purdy.

Prairie novelists were the first in Canada to capture the distinctive flavour of regional life, and this was due to the powerful impact of the vast landscapes and climatic extremes of the Canadian plains. The first major Canadian novelist was Frederick Philip Grove who wrote a series of massive, flawed novels about the struggles of Prairie farmers against nature and their own passionate deficiencies. *Settlers in the Marsh* (1925) most typically expressed his gloomy, Zola-esque view of existence, but his masterpiece was *The Master of the Mill* (1944), in which the successive transformations of the mill symbolically portrayed the industrialization and dehumanization of Canadian society.

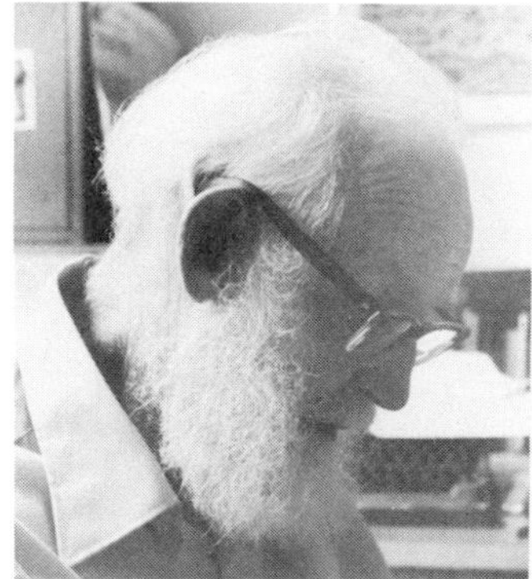
Earle Birney.

The first internationally known Canadian novelist was Morley Callaghan, a very urban writer best known for the series of moral parables — such as *They Shall Inherit the Earth* (1935) — which he disguised as novels of Toronto life.

Hugh MacLennan's first novel, *Barometer Rising* (1941), started a career that made him the leading Canadian novelist of the 1950s and at the same time established the theme of Canadian national consciousness he explored in his later novels, laying special importance on the Anglo-French relationship, whose precariousness he prophetically foresaw and explored in *Two Solitudes* (1945) a title which gave Canadians the phrase by which they have ever since described their own cultural divisiveness.

Phyllis Webb.

Jack McClelland.

Mel Hurtig.

A vital element in the literary explosion of the 1960s and 1970s was the emergence of a publishing industry which, while never strong financially, was energetic in publishing Canadian books and fostering Canadian literary talent. Most prominent in this revolution, among older publishers, was McClelland and Stewart, which **Jack McClelland** inherited and transformed into the major publishing house for Canadian creative writing, with Margaret Laurence and Margaret Atwood, Matt Cohen and Rudy Wiebe, Irving Layton and Leonard Cohen, Earle Birney and Al Purdy all appearing in his lists. An equally significant development was the emergence of small avant garde presses like House of Anansi, Press Porcepic, Oberon Press and Coach House Press, specializing in poetry, short stories, experimental fiction and other genres previously thought financially disastrous. Yet another trend of the period has been the appearance of regional publishing houses which take on national status, like Hurtig Publishers, operated by **Mel Hurtig** in Edmonton, and Douglas and McIntyre in Vancouver.

MacLennan was technically a very conservative writer, and conservatism was the mood of Canadian fiction until the late 1950s, when Sheila Watson produced her single novel, *The Double Hook* (1959), which established poetic fantasy as an enduring element in Canadian fiction. Another new element was the satire of manners, which Mordecai Richler developed with extraordinary vigour in his good novel of Montreal Jewish life, *The Apprenticeship of Duddy Kravitz* (1959). These and other trends including anarchistic social criticism and a dash of nationalist polemic, have combined to make Canadian fiction much more vivacious and experimental than in the past, and in the work of one novelist, Margaret Laurence (her last novel *The Diviners* being perhaps her best) it has reached a level of major fiction comparable with the best in other traditions. Other excellent contemporary Canadian novelists include Robertson Davies, Margaret Atwood, Marian Engel, and Matt Cohen, while the short story has been developed into a particularly expressive form by writers like Hugh Garner, Hugh Hood, Alice Munro, and David Helwig.

In Québec, the literary progression has been remarkably similar to that of English-speaking Canada, with the kind of changes one expects in a looking-glass image. First there was the poetic movement of the 1930s and early 1940s, led by Saint Denys Garneau, Anne Hébert, and Rina Lasnier, which departed radically from the imitation of romantic and symbolist models among Québec poets up to and including Nelligan. This was at least on the surface a non-political movement, expressed in highly subjective verse, yet it was political in the negative sense that it reflected the boredom and resigned despair which overcame so many of the best intellects of Québec at that time. A new mood appeared in the later 1950s, inspiring the younger writers who rebelled against English-Canadian economic domination, against the spiritual power of the church, and in favour of a new Québec nation. Gilles Henault, Roland Giguère, Jean-Guy Pilon, Fernand Ouelette, and Pierre Trottier were typical of the earlier phase of this movement; a more radical group, gathered around the magazine *Parti pris,* set out to create a literature written in the Montreal dialect of *joual*. In this way they rejected the literary model of Paris as well as the political supremacy of Ottawa.

Until long into the 1930s, the fiction of Québec was rural and sentimental; it idealized the peasant world in which the priest's word was law. An era of more realistic fiction began when Philippe Panneton, writing under the name of Ringuet, published *Trente arpentes* (1938) and mordantly portrayed the decay of traditional agrarian Québec. Gabrielle Roy continued Ringuet's work in novels like *Bonheur d'occasion* (1945) which dealt with the movement from the country towards the cities and presented the pattern of social malaise that urbanization created. Younger novelists paralleled the younger poets by extending this social motif into the political sphere, and many recent Québec

With seven books of verse, three novels, a book of short stories and a volume of literary theorizing *(Survival)* to her credit since she began publishing with *The Circle Game* in 1966, **Margaret Atwood** has been one of the most prolific Canadian writers to emerge into prominence recently, yet her work has never shown the looseness of thought and texture that often comes from copious writing. It remains tight, poised, ironic and above all aloof, whether in novels like *Surfacing* or books of verse like *Power Politics*, and this is one of the secrets of her success. There is a Protean quality about Atwood as a person; she courts celebrity yet shuns it; she seems subjectively to identify with her women characters yet publicly repudiates the possibility; she writes passionately about women's wrongs yet denies being a feminist; she argues that cultural colonization from the south is the greatest peril to Canadian arts yet portrays anti-Americans satirically. In all this she follows a politics of the creative person, which is not to get involved in political processes but to give the revelatory images of the human condition in our time that will help us see into and through topical issues into a self-integrative state of mind, a middle way of wisdom.

Alice Munro.

Marian Engel.

Marie-Claire Blais.

Roberton Davies.

The Toronto Symphony Orchestra.

novels have dealt with themes of separation and terrorism, while others combined social satire with poetic fantasy. Among recent French-Canadian novelists some of the most interesting have been Yves Thériault, Gérard Bessette, Hubert Aquin, Marie-Claire Blais, Roch Carrier, and Jacques Godbout.

There has been a great recent flourishing in the more public Canadian arts, such as theatre, music, ballet, and opera, though in some of these fields creativity has lagged behind performance and interpretation. The past of theatre and music in Canada was not distinguished. It is true that during the nineteenth and early twentieth centuries there had been a degree of improvement from the Upper Canadian days when John Lambert reported in 1810:

> It may be easily conceived how despicably low the Canadian theatricals must be, when boys are obliged to perform the female characters; the only actresses being an old superannuated demirep, whose drunken Belvidears, Desdemonas and Isabellas, have often *enraptured* a Canadian audience.

Canada has shown itself by no means lacking in acting and musical talent, and the list of Canadians who have made notable careers for themselves on the stage in London and New York and in Hollywood is long, including names like Raymond Massey and Mary Pickford and Walter Huston. But before the Second World War there were few professional theatres and only two symphony orchestras in the whole of

Karen Kain and Frank Augustyn in the National Ballet of Canada production of Elite Syncopations, *choreographed by Kenneth MacMillan.*

Members of the Royal Winnipeg Ballet at home in Centennial Concert Hall, Winnipeg.

Canada. "There is no future for an actress in Canada," said that fine performer Toby Robins as late as 1968, "The Meccas are elsewhere." Those players and musicians who remained in Canada had to depend on the CBC for a living, and for most of them the pickings were thin. "Canada," said Robertson Davies in those bleak days, "demands a great deal from people and is not, as some countries are, quick to offer a pleasant atmosphere or easy kind of life."

The situation began to change after 1945, when massive emigration from European countries brought many people skilled in the performing arts, and the movement was given impetus after the Canada Council was formed in 1957. Now the Canada Council gives more than $10,000,000 every year to support theatres, opera companies, orchestras, etc., and provincial arts councils and municipalities, following its example, provide even more grants. As a result there are now orchestras in all the major cities; regional centres like Vancouver and Edmonton as well as the metropolitan centres of Toronto and Montréal now have regular opera seasons; there are a number of professional ballet companies such as the Royal Winnipeg Ballet, the National Ballet, and Les Grands Ballets Canadiens. The annual Shakespearian Festival at Stratford, Ontario and the Shaw Festival at Niagara-on-the-Lake are international events, while theatres such as the Théâtre du Nouveau Monde in Montreal, the Citadel Theatre in Edmonton, the Neptune Theatre in Halifax, and the Playhouse Theatre in Vancouver maintain high professional standards and form the nuclei for clusters of experimental theatres such as Tarragon Theatre and Theatre Passe Muraille in Toronto. Canadians, indeed, have become far more devoted than in the past to the performing arts, and recent statistics show that more people now attend arts events than attend spectator sports events.

At the same time, there is not a great co-ordination between performance and creation in Canadian terms. Theatres and orchestras rarely perform Canadian works, and the fault does not lie entirely in a public taste for internationally acknowledged works or a contempt for local creations. Though there have been some exceptions (such as Barbara Pentland and Harry Somers) musical composition in Canada has not been greatly original or inspiring, and good Canadian operas are few, a notable exception being *The Night Blooming Cereus,* for which the poet James Reaney wrote the libretto and John Beckwith the music.

Similarly, until the 1950s, there were very few stage plays written by Canadians. It was the Canadian Broadcasting Corporation that kept drama alive by commissioning radio plays; there were too few theatres to make writing for the stage worthwhile. Even when theatres did multiply in the later 1950s, dramatists were slow to change to the stage, and theatre managers were just as slow to experiment with Canadian plays when audiences seemed to have a thirst for the experimental European and American plays they had not yet had a chance to enjoy. The situation

The Annual Shaw Festival, Niagara-on-the-Lake — Merrilyn Gann as Gloria Clandon *and James Valentine as* Valentine *in Shaw's* You Never Can Tell.

Lyn Vernon as Joan in the Canadian Opera Company's 1978 production of Tchaikovsky's Joan of Arc.

Festival Theatre, Stratford, Ontario

Though it is not easy to decide why, the Maritime provinces during the last quarter of a century have become a stronghold of high realism in painting, just as they were a stronghold of romantic regionalism in poetry during the 1890s. The leading high realist in the Maritimes, and perhaps in all Canada, is **Alex Colville,** a Toronto-born artist who has lived most of his life in New Brunswick. In his carefully composed paintings, with their meticulous brush-work, Colville seeks to capture action in arrested moments, and in paintings like *Horse and Train* and *Hound in Field* he has created some of the most haunting images of our time. Few contemporary painters have so admirably evoked the multiple resonances of visual images.

by the 1970s has changed greatly. Canadian plays are being written and performed and even published. Among the more remarkable writers in this dramatic upsurge have been James Reaney with his fantastic verse plays like *The Kildeer* and *Colours in the Dark,* George Ryga, John Coulter, and John Herbert, whose *Fortune and Men's Eyes* (1970) won international acclaim; and, among the younger, more experimental writers, Carol Bolt, Sharon Pollock, David Freeman, David French, Beverley Simons, and Michael Cook.

In French Canada the development of a local drama came earlier than in English Canada, largely through the efforts of Gratien Gélinas to create, during the 1940s, a popular theatre. Gélinas himself was the first important French-Canadian playwright. He has been followed by many younger writers, and the theatre has taken its place beside the novel and poetry as a vehicle for expressing political disaffection. Its value in this direction lies in the fact that it is more public than poetry and more direct in its appeal to an audience than fiction. The more energetic younger playwrights in Québec include Michel Tremblay, Robert Gurik, and Jacques Barbeau. Their plays are being translated into English more quickly than Québec fiction or poetry, and in the theatre in general, more than in any of the other arts, a cross-fertilization seems to be taking place. On the stage at least, Canada's "two solitudes" seem to be in dialogue.

Theatre Passe Muraille's production of Les Canadiens.

CHAPTER THIRTEEN

Canadians at Leisure

It is hard to tell whether average modern Canadians, who are basically urban, enjoy more leisure than their rural forebears. A Canadian today, employed by others, is likely to work on five days and between thirty-five and forty hours a week. He or she receives at least ten days paid leave a year, usually more, and enjoys the statutory holidays which vary from province to province but which average about nine days a year. Christmas and Good Friday are religious holidays everywhere in Canada. American historic links are shown in the October observance of Thanksgiving, introduced by the Loyalists, and the early September celebration of Labour Day — as distinct from the European celebration of May Day as a workers' holiday. The strong Scottish links are shown by the fervent celebration of New Year's Day.

National Canadian holidays with a somewhat political flavour are Canada Day — formerly Dominion Day — held on the first of July to celebrate the implementation of Confederation on that day in 1867, and Victoria Day in May, commemorating the British monarch who played the greatest personal role in Canadian history. Almost every province has its own special holidays. Epiphany, Ash Wednesday, and Ascension Day are all celebrated in Catholic Québec, but the province's most important holiday is St. Jean Baptiste Day, a somewhat nationalistic occasion when French Canadians celebrate their patron saint. On St. George's and St. Patrick's days the English and Irish founding peoples of Newfoundland commemorate their respective origins. On Discovery Day, August 17, Yukoners celebrate with appropriate sourdough sports the finding of gold on the Klondike River in 1895. Some of the ethnic groups celebrate their own holidays. Burns' Night is an occasion for feasting wherever Scots are gathered, but perhaps the most colourful minority celebrations occur on Chinese New Year in February, when the Dragon Dancers weave their grotesque way through the streets of Victoria, Vancouver and Toronto, and Peter's Day when the Russian Doukhobors in the Prairies and in British Columbia gather for great choral festivals to commemorate the acts of resistance to the tsars of Russia that eventually led them through great persecutions to their final settlement in Canada.

With all these holidays, it has been estimated that every employed Canadian enjoys a minimum of 124 days of leisure a year and many of them enjoy more, though self-employed people, like farmers, small storekeepers, artists, and independent craftsmen still work from neces-

Native Canadians were given to sports and games, and these were often associated with gambling. Lafitau in the seventeenth century represented a kind of Iroquois ball game that may have been a kind of hockey, and Paul Kane in the mid-nineteenth century found the Plains Indians playing a game with obvious ritual significance called Alcoloh.

Rocky Saguniuk, a new ice hockey star with the Toronto Maple Leafs, plays a game which first appears in history as a winter entertainment of British garrison soldiers in the early nineteenth century, but ultimately it may well derive — as lacrosse certainly does — from Indian ball games.

sity or choice far longer hours than those customary in most employments. One has to balance these figures against the circumstances that in the rural past imposed long periods of leisure on many Canadians. Prairie farmers, excepting those who reared stock as well as growing wheat, enjoyed and still enjoy a long work-free winter in which today, if the crops have been good, they are inclined to spend a fair amount of time away from home in warmer climates. The Prairie summer, on the other hand, is a time of long working hours on the farms; equipment is often used by floodlight after dark, and school holidays are traditionally arranged to fit the days of the past when every hand was needed for the harvest. In construction work there have always been layoffs due to the hard winter weather of the Prairies and central Canada, while the logging industry is particularly susceptible to climatic interruptions, not only in the depth of winter but also at the height of summer, when lack of rain can lead to the woods being closed for long periods. Fishing in British Columbia, which is dominated by the annual salmon runs, has always been a highly seasonal occupation, as it was when the Coast Indians could store enough preserved food from their summer's catch to give them a winter of leisure and ceremonies. Even mining, when it was a matter of placer work in the river gravels, was usually abandoned during the winter, and gold rush camps waxed and waned according to the seasons. Thus Canada has a tradition of seasonal periods of idleness which Canadians have been inclined to turn into times of enjoyable or productive leisure.

They accomplished this in many ways. The life of the arts, which we have discussed, is one of them. Before the arrival of cinema and radio, Canadians were much inclined to make their own music and to organize amateur theatricals, particularly in small and remote communities which the touring professional companies did not reach. Amateur poets flourished in the small towns of Upper Canada and in the mining settlements of the Cariboo and the Klondike, and some of them produced work of spectacular badness, like the famous James McIntyre, whose

If Indian ball games find their descendants in modern Canadian sports, so do the methods of transport which the Indians handed on to the fur traders. As the voyageurs *faded into history, canoeing became a favourite Canadian pastime, and gatherings of the Toronto Canoe Club in the 1890s would attract many ardent boaters. Ladies too participated, like this team of the Carleton Place Canoe Club, paddling a modern* canot de maître *two abreast like the boatmen of the past.*

"Ode on the Mammoth Cheese", written to celebrate a 7,000-pound cheese made in 1884 at Ingersoll, Ontario, achieved its own kind of immortality with verses like:

> We'rt thou suspended from balloon,
> You'd cast a shade even at noon,
> Folks would think it was the moon
> About to fall and crush them soon.

Today, after a hiatus when media — the cinema, radio, and later television — seemed to be turning them into a captive and passive audience, Canadians are participating in the arts as they never before have, whether as the audience at live presentations, or as amateurs, many of whom take professional instruction at evening classes in towns all over the country or at summer schools of the arts such as those held in Banff and at Emma Lake, Saskatchewan.

Many Canadians are enthusiastic followers of sports events. There are many more people active in sports than there are people who attend professional events as spectators, although millions of Canadians do become spectators indirectly by watching ice hockey or football on television. Some Canadian sports are indigenous, developed by earlier generations coping with the problem of filling in time during long and workless winters. Lacrosse is the oldest Canadian game still being

European fashions and crazes also helped to shape the ways in which Canadians entertained themselves, and in 1810 George Heriot, an artist who was also deputy postmaster-general of British North America, drew this Rowlandsonian sketch, 'Minuets of the Canadians', which portrayed the colonial gentry amusing themselves.

played. It was based on an Indian game called baggataway which was played along the shores of the St. Lawrence before the French arrived. Lacrosse became so popular in early Canada that in 1867 it was adopted as the national game, but it soon began to wane before the vogue for another game that may have been borrowed from the Indians — ice hockey. In something near to its present form, ice hockey is said to have first been played by British soldiers seeking to relieve the monotony of winter garrison duty. It was not accepted as an authentic sport until the 1860s, and only in 1880 was the first enduring team, that of the McGill Hockey Club, established. Shortly afterwards ice hockey leagues came into existence, and in 1893 the Governor General, Lord Stanley, bestowed an official blessing on the game by presenting the Stanley Cup, since then the leading competitive award in ice hockey. No game more deeply arouses Canadian passions than does this fastest of all team sports, as was shown by the deep sense of pride aroused in 1972 when Canada defeated Russia in an ice hockey series.

Other games which Canadians follow with a great deal of commitment have their origins elsewhere. Notable among these is the American game of baseball which, like ice hockey, has caught the national imagination to the extent that it figures greatly in Canadian fiction, notably in the works of writers such as Morley Callaghan and Hugh Hood. As a summer game it has greatly outrivalled the English game of cricket. Canada is the only Commonwealth country not to have adopted cricket with enthusiasm. The English forms of football — soccer and Rugby — are played, but here again the more boisterous American football is most popular. In sports, indeed, Scotland has made a greater mark in Canada than has England, since golf is very popular, especially in Nova Scotia and British Columbia, and curling is a great winter sport in the Prairie provinces and even in Arctic Canada.

The Victorian age, with its cold baths and open windows, was a more rigorous time, and round about 1850 Canadians of both sexes were developing their muscles with the Indian Club.

Much Canadian leisure activity, as befits a country with a small population and much land, tends to be unstructured, and often it is solitary. To own one's own house is a characteristically Canadian ambition, and a majority of Canadians eventually achieve it, even though the beginnings and ends of their adult lives may be lived in apartments and the middle years spent extricating themselves from mortgages. Many people spend much of their leisure time working on their houses (a fair number of Canadians even build their own carpentered dwellings), or in their gardens; the English-style gardens of west coast cities like Vancouver and Victoria, blessed with mild winters, are among the most beautiful in the world.

The wilderness, which in many ways plays a great role in the Canadian consciousness, is also important for its influence on the patterns of leisure activity. The vast spaces of this largely untamed environment provide a setting for many outdoor sporting activities. Skiing is most popular in the mountains of British Columbia and Alberta and in the Laurentian hills of Québec, and in recent years many people have been deserting the crowded slopes of the resorts for cross-country skiing. The Rideau Canal in Ottawa is almost as thickly populated with winter skaters as are the canals of Amsterdam, and tobogganing and sleigh-riding are favourite pastimes in Québec, where an air of event and leisurely ritual is given even to some domestic winter and early spring occupations, such as "sugaring off" in the maple sugar bushes. Sailboats and speedboats figure largely in the leisure patterns along the British Columbian coast, in the Maritimes and on the Great Lakes, while canoe tripping is popular in the Shield country with its networks of lakes, small rivers, and portages.

Thanks to Canada's unparalleled abundance of fresh-waterways and lakes, as well as the intricate salt-water channels of all its coasts,

Among the imported sports that Canadians practiced, those derived from Scotland have been durable favourites. Canadians, like the Ontarians of 1894, are still partial to golf as a means of taming waistlines, and curling, which is here shown as a feature of the Montréal Midwinter Carnival at the turn of the century, is a favourite game from Niagara northward to the shores of Hudson's Bay.

fishing is a sport pursued in all parts of the country from the Arctic down to the American border and, although millions of Canadians and many thousands of tourists go fishing every year, there are still untouched lakes populous with fine fish; the salt waters have unfortunately become depleted by the commercial fishing that in eastern Canada has been going on for almost five centuries, and it is no longer possible, as it was in Cabot's day, to catch cod merely by dipping a bucket over the ship's side.

Hunting is a less favoured occupation than fishing, and may be declining in popularity, for many people, conscious of ecological problems, now content themselves with observing and photographing animals and are concerned with ensuring the preservation of wild species, in the hope that the disaster of the bison's virtual extermination on its native Prairies will not be repeated. Other large animals, like the musk ox and the Barren Grounds grizzly, have been near the verge of extinction, and even the polar bear and the caribou are imperilled by over-hunting and by the disturbance of feeding grounds and migration paths through the exploitation of natural resources. Yet if hunting tends to be more restricted by law as well as less popular, many thousands of people do still hunt, from the rich American tourists who travel expensively with guides and much equipment, to the Prairie man who drives out from his

In most countries which were formerly part of the British Empire, English sports are still ardently followed. But cricket, fanatically played in India and Australia, hardly exists in Canada, and the kind of football played in the Olympic Stadium, or on Taylor Field, Regina, where our photograph shows the Saskatchewan and Ottawa Roughriders opposed, is an import from the United States. Soccer and rugby, the English kinds of football, are almost as seldom played as cricket.

home into the country with his shotgun and his dog for a day shooting the wild ducks and wild geese along the local sloughs.

Fishing and hunting, the serious occupations of the early Canadians, are part of the mystique of the wilderness which is strong in modern Canadian minds. Having lost the need to fight against the dread of the wild that is part of the settler syndrome, Canadians have returned vicariously to the attitudes of the fur traders and explorers who, long before the settlers arrived, moved through the forests and the mountains and the tall buffalo grass of the roadless Prairies as through their natural elements. This is not to say that Canadians are willing to duplicate the actual journeys or the wilderness living conditions of the fur traders — though some on occasion do. But in summer cottages fringing most of the accessible lakes in the Shield country and the northern parts of the Prairie provinces, in cabins on the shores of islands off Nova Scotia and British Columbia, and in summer camps where Canadian children are sent for an annual toughening-up, the past is romantically re-evoked in direct contact with nature, accompanied by a modicum of pioneer hardship.

There are some social critics who look with considerable scepticism at the pretensions they see exhibited in such behaviour. Frank Underhill, a caustic-penned historian, once argued that:

A whole complex of activities that test the human will at various levels are associated with the Canadian mountains, which stretch eastward from the modest heights of the Laurentians to the grandiose summits of the Rockies. The more daring mountain lovers climb the rockfaces of the British Columbian ranges, or perform difficult feats on skis. Those who are content to absorb the landscape without glory follow less perilous pursuits like trekking (here shown at the foot of the Athabaska Glacier in the Jasper National Park), horse-riding (at Lac Rond in the Laurentians) or cross-country skiing (at Muskoka in Ontario).

The artistic cult of the North is, as a matter of fact, pure romanticism at its worst, and bears little relation to the real life of Canada. Far from seeking inspiration among the rocks and winds, the normal Canadian dreams of living in a big city where he can make his pile quickly and enjoy such urban luxuries as are familiar to him in the advertizing columns of our national magazines.

However, since Underhill wrote those words a generation ago, the normal Canadian not only dreams of living in a big city, he actually does so, and this means that his dreams take other directions. Perhaps the cult of the wilderness has never been so strong as it has become now that the average Canadian is an urban man.

In the form which the Canadian wilderness mystique now takes, the park systems of the country play a notable role. The federal system began when hot springs were discovered in 1885 at Banff during the construction of the Canadian Pacific Railway, and ten square miles of the mountains was reserved as the first National Park. Now more than 50,000 square miles are reserved in areas which range from the great series of parks that includes most of the Rocky Mountain chain, to seacoast parks on Vancouver Island, Prince Edward Island, and Newfoundland; from Wood Buffalo National Park in Alberta where the last sizeable herd of wood bison lives under natural conditions, to Arctic parks on Baffin Island. The National Parks are geographical in character, intended to preserve still unspoilt natural areas that are representative of various regions in Canada. In this role they are supplemented by the 115,000 square miles of provincial parks, perhaps the best known of which are Algonquin Park in Ontario, where Tom Thomson and the Group of Seven painted some of their best work, and Laurentide Park in Québec.

Such parks meet two somewhat different needs. One is to allow Canadians and foreign tourists to travel through areas of the country that are in an almost natural state and to see in their appropriate habitat wild animals that elsewhere have fled before the encroachments of humanity on their environments. Many people each year can see mountain sheep and mountain goats with no greater effort than that involved in travelling the mountain highway from Banff to Jasper. Some areas are preserved as wilderness where even roads cannot penetrate and only *bona fide* naturalists are allowed to observe the otherwise undisturbed patterns of wild nature.

There are, of course, considerable stretches of Canada outside of the parks where the indigenous wildlife of Canada can still be seen, and these are not all in the North. As Edward A. McCourt said in his book, *Saskatchewan*, "Fine herds of antelope — a glorious sight on the skyline of a far-off ridge or hill — roam all the way from the border north into the country of the Great Sandhills." But such wildlife is often dependent on the ultimate stronghold of a reserve to which it can retreat, and McCourt

Few Canadians any longer depend for subsistence on hunting or fishing, but — whether one regards it as atavistic or not — the urge towards these activities continues. Men still paddle their canoes through lonely lakes of the Shield in the hope of killing moose. In other lakes Canadians still catch the gigantic fish that most anglers merely dream of, and those who still see fishing as the solitary man's occupation cast their flies into remote white waters like those of the Montreal River Falls near Lac la Ronde in northern Saskatchewan.

Wherever there are larger stretches of water, from the bays of the Maritimes through the Great Lakes to the sounds and inlets of British Columbia the sails billow in thousands from the masts of yachts owned by weekend navigators.

In most of Canada the open water of summer is replaced by the frozen water of the long winter, but even then sails are not abandoned

tells of the herds of antelope streaming down into the Cypress Hills, which are now a provincial park, as soon as the hunting season starts.

Canadians who do leave their urban environments to spend their leisure travelling in their own country are inclined to travel in time as well as space. In recent years the vogue in Canadian history, which has produced so many books and magazine features on past events, has also been expressed in the inclination not only to read of what happened, but also to see where it happened and to get some physical sense of the realities behind history. To satisfy this need a whole series of historic parks has been created. Nearly a hundred of them are federally administered, and these range from the great reconstructed fortress of Louisbourg on Cape Breton Island to the remaining gold rush buildings of

The Rideau Canal was built between 1826 and 1832 from the Ottawa River to Kingston on Lake Ontario as a route by which troops and artillery could be transported, well out of reach of the American border. It was never used for military purposes, but the four miles of the Canal that run through Ottawa itself are not only a fine park in summer, bordered by lawns and flower beds, but in winter are used by half a million skaters.

Dawson City, and from old fur-trading posts like Rocky Mountain House and Fort Langley to such unspectacular but historically important sites as the shallow excavations at L'Anse aux Meadows which mark the Norse settlement in Newfoundland almost a millenium ago. Other historic sites are operated by the provinces. In some of these, like Upper Canada Village in Ontario, and Barkerville in British Columbia, the visitors can not only visit authentic buildings of a period, but can also see the life of that period re-enacted, with its sounds and smells as well as its sights. There is no doubt that in recent years Canadians — who for so long seemed a people without a past — have so entered into the spirit of their history that many of them are not only intrigued but also moved to see a lost way of living taking shape before their eyes, even though they themselves may not always be the descendants of settlers.

If Canadians today devote more of their leisure to exploring their heritage in space and time, they have also become more conscious during recent decades of the perils that threaten this heritage and of the need to protect it. Environmental groups seeking the minimum disturbance of ecological balances and the minimum pollution of the environment, and conservationist groups seeking the preservation of historic sites and buildings have flourished as never before during the past decade in Canada, and, in fact, have gained a degree of success which would not have been likely in past generations. Governments have introduced measures of stricter environmental control, and in varying degrees have enforced them. Environmentalists — often in alliance with groups of native peoples whose hunting or fishing terrains must be defended —

Exhibitions have always played a role in the summer entertainment of Canadians, but none quite so spectacularly as Expo 67, on St. Helen's Island in the middle of the St. Lawrence off Montréal. The spectacle of the Montreal Olympics (below), was matched by the financial drama surrounding the construction of the Stadium itself.

OPPOSITE:
Tangible evidence of the past is immediately available from many historic sites across the country. One such site is the reconstructed French fortress of Louisburg on Cape Breton Island in Nova Scotia, where the rooms are furnished in the rococo styles of the last years of the ancien regime *in Canada.*

have been able to halt exploration operations in the wilder parts of Canada and have even managed to gain the diversion of pipelines in areas — for example, the Mackenzie Valley — where it was evident that the ecological balance might be destroyed.

But in Canada, which economically is still so dependent on the exploitation of natural resources, there is an inevitable conflict of interests on environmental issues. Often the person whose leisure time is spent travelling in the unspoilt wilderness is dependent for a living, directly or indirectly, on logging or mining or oil or transport or the construction of roads or airfields or pipelines, all of which are in the hands of corporations whose primary interests lie in exploiting and therefore changing the environment, usually for the worse. Environmental controls are opposed not only by industrial corporations but often also by the trade unions who tend to accept more than they did in the recent past the argument that where jobs are threatened environmental damage has to be accepted.

Clearly this is one of the most urgent problems that Canadians now face. What ways can be devised to prevent the industries which make life easier for us from destroying the environment that gives meaning to the increasing leisure time technological advances may offer us? And if ways cannot be found, must we — as many environmentalists argue — turn our backs on technological progress, on the whole concept of a growth economy, and accept a lower material standard of living, hoping to gain a higher quality of existence in compensation?

In my view few Canadians have at present any answer to the first question, yet equally few are ready to say yes to the second. The wilderness is still imperilled, and still unconquered, as it always has been. But can that remain a permanent contradiction in Canadian life?

CHAPTER FOURTEEN

Canada Identity Crisis

> He wants to be different from everyone else
> and daydreams of winning the global race.
> Parents unmarried and living abroad,
> relatives keen to bag the estate,
> Schizophrenia not excluded,
> will he learn to grow up before it's too late?
>
> Earle Birney
> "Canada: Case History: 1945"

In modern terms Canada is an old country — at 111 years of age as I write these lines it is very much senior to most of the countries that make up the United Nations. Yet the sense that the country has never grown out of national adolescence, and that its people have never decided what they are or who they are as Canadians, continues to perplex both sympathetic outsiders and self-critical Canadians. J. B. Priestley, a shrewd observer of national characteristics, noted in his introduction to an English anthology of Stephen Leacock's writings that: "The Canadian is often a baffled man because he feels different from his British kindred and his American neighbours, sharply refuses to be lumped together with either of them, yet cannot make plain his difference." Though Priestley concerns himself only with Anglophone Canadians, there is little doubt that French Canadians — whether Québecois or Acadians — experience a similar identity crisis when they try to establish their distinctiveness, either in relation to the North American cultures among which they live or in relation to the culture of twentieth-century France.

W. L. Morton, the Canadian historian, was not very far from Priestley when he remarked that "A Canadian is someone who knows he is going somewhere, but isn't sure where." I confess that on one occasion of bewilderment, of which I am reminded every time I look into *Colombo's Canadian Quotations,* the only foolproof definition of a Canadian that occurred to me was that he was "a North American who does not owe allegiance to the United States or Mexico." And Marshall McLuhan, in one of his more impudent moods, flatly declared that "Canada is the only country in the world that knows how to live without an identity."

The question of a Canadian identity has certainly obsessed the media and the politicians and a great many ordinary, thinking Canadian people in the past in rather the same way as the question of Canadian unity obsesses them today. My own conclusion on the subject is perhaps already suggested by the fact that I have devoted more than half this book to the discussion of Canada's regions: in other words to the presentation of Canada as a country whose very nature is contained in the fact that it has as many faces as a Buddhist deity. An identity can in real life be many-faceted; a unity can find its reality in diversity. And when we have a country so large and so varied in the origins of its people that many-faceted diversity is its very nature, we have a country *pas comme les autres,* a country whose identity crisis really seems to lie in an attempt to cling to the illusion that uniformity and unity are the same thing and equally desirable, neither of which, of course, is true.

What do we really mean when we talk so much of a Canadian identity? To a great extent it depends on what we mean by *identity,* and here the *Oxford English Dictionary* is, as always, helpful in the range of meanings it offers: a range within which one can find room for the notable changes that have taken place in Canadian attitudes towards Canada during the generations since Confederation.

There are recondite algebraic denotations of the word *identity* which have little relevance to the condition of Canada or to the outlook of that great majority of Canadians who are not mathematicians by vocation. But the first two meanings that the OED gave and carefully dated seemed to me — in their appearance of mutual contradiction — to mark out with extraordinary fidelity a shift in our views of ourselves and our land that has occurred within the last generation. The first definition, which dates from 1570 when Canada was still a place visited mainly for the cod fishing, is: "The quality of being the same; absolute or essential sameness; oneness . . ." The second, which dates from 1638, when the first settlers were already established on Canadian soil, is amazingly divergent: "Individuality, personality", modified, apparently in 1683, to extend the meaning of *identity* to include "individual existence." It seems to me that if we take those two definitions in their proper order we find a pretty faithful reflection of the change in our own intentions when we talk about "Canadian identity."

Almost thirty years ago, when I at last returned to Canada after decades of life in Europe, I was soon aware of a kind of tremulously dawning self-consciousness among Canadians that made discussions of their "identity" a favourite topic of conversation and writing. This seemed to me novel and curious, because the English and Welsh, the Scots and French among whom I had been living never talked about their identities or those of their countries, perhaps because — whatever personal or national disasters might befall them — they were never in any doubt as to what history had made them. Among Canadians at that time, however, it seemed a question of lost people, people without a common past or common traditions that had lasted more than a few years, seeking something outside their own local and personal lives with which to identify themselves.

World events were destroying the British Empire in the form it had retained longer than any living man could remember; the old ideas of Imperial Federation that had once been so attractive to Canadians were moribund. Canadians had fought a second time — and many of them had died — for a mother country with which they found to their growing astonishment they no longer had very much in common.

In the nineteenth century it had taken a man of rare foresight to declare, as Amor de Cosmos did in 1882, for the severing of the British connection. It cost de Cosmos his parliamentary seat in Victoria and ended his political career when he said:

> I see no reason why the people of Canada should not look forward to Canada becoming a sovereign and independent State. . . . I was born a British colonist, but do not wish to die a tadpole British colonist. I do not wish to die without having all the rights, privileges and immunities of the citizen of a nation.

Sir John A. Macdonald fought to the end of his career on the declaration that he would live and die a British subject, but in our age another Conservative leader, John Diefenbaker, found it necessary to amend Macdonald's statement and declare — as he did in 1967 — "A Canadian I was born, a Canadian I will die."

Canada of Confederation and Canada after each of the two great wars belonged to different eras and different worlds. Canadians were beginning to realize, as the British elements were becoming an absolute minority in their demographic mosaic, that the old identifications were no longer valid. This recognition was made formal from the Canadian side when we established in 1947 a definite Canadian citizenship, distinct from British subjecthood, and when immigration and census officers abandoned the Victorian way of classifying migrants and inhabitants by racial origins, a method that refused to acknowledge the possibility of an individual being a Canadian and nothing else. From the British side the situation was formally recognized some years later when new immigration laws for the United Kingdom finally deprived Canadians of the right without question to enter and live on British soil in the same way as those who were British-born.

At last, almost a century after Confederation, we were recognised — and were hesitantly recognizing ourselves — as legally Canadians and no more than Canadians. But having accepted the end of an age when Canadian patriotism implied an unquestioning loyalty to Britain, a willingness to serve the Empire whenever called upon, Canadians — and during the Cold War age this included even many French Canadians — were still doubtful whether their country was militarily strong enough or

In a rather dramatic way **Goldwin Smith's** career combines two opposing trends in Canadian views of the national destiny. Smith had already a distinguished historian's career in Britain before, at the age of 45 in 1868, he went to teach at Cornell, and gravitated to Canada, settling in Toronto in 1871, marrying money, living the life of a gentleman intellectual, and often partly subsidizing the periodicals — *The Nation, The Bystander, The Week* and *The Weekly Sun* — in which he wrote his polished and provocative articles under the *nom-de-plume* of 'A Bystander'. In his early days in Canada, Smith was associated with Canada First, a proto-nationalist movement hostile to American influence and inclined to see the role of Canada as an autonomous nation within an Empire that would be a confederation of equals. Eventually Smith dissociated himself from Canada First, and if he never actually advocated the annexation of Canada by the United States, he came to regard it as Canada's eventual political destiny to be absorbed into a North American union. This view, which earned him much unpopularity, Smith put forward most forcefully in *Canada and the Canadian Question*, published in 1891.

prosperous enough or even distinctive enough to stand on its own.

Continentalism — the belief that Canada and the United States were necessary to each other and that at some time in the future they were destined to merge into a single giant North American super-nation — had flourished in the nineteenth century as a counterpoise to imperialism. Canada's leading Victorian man of letters, the former Oxford history professor Goldwin Smith, had presented in *Canada and the Canadian Question* (1897) a closely and eloquently reasoned argument for the inevitable submersion of our politically and economically weak Canadian provinces into the expansive structure of a United States, vitalized by the concept of "manifest destiny," which had already swallowed large parts of Mexico. But despite Goldwin Smith's forebodings and his plausible arguments for accepting annexation, and despite its own inner contradictions as a political structure uniting two highly different traditions, Canada struggled through as an independent entity, even though it has remained less a nation than a huddle of regions growing together into a country. It survived also the age of latter-day continentalists like the late Clarence Decatur Howe, the powerful Minister of Trade and Commerce in the St. Laurent government of the 1950s, who seems quite sincerely to have seen nothing but benefit for Canadians in the process of developing our resources by attracting American capital, even if the eventual result might be the ownership of our key industries by foreign corporations. It was Howe's insistence on terminating discussion in the House of Commons on a grant to an American-controlled firm, Trans-Canada Pipelines Ltd., during the famous Pipeline Debate of 1956, which ensured John Diefenbaker's Conservative victory in 1957 and more than any other single incident alerted ordinary Canadians to the perils of foreign economic dominaiton.

There were many other Canadian politicians in the 1940s and even in the early 1950s who had not got used to the idea of Canada as a genuinely independent country, and their willingness to accept American financing and the political pressures associated with it was perhaps a natural development from the realization that Britain was no longer the dominant financial world power and was therefore unlikely to play a significant future role in Canadian economic growth. The archetypal Canadian corporations — the Hudson's Bay Company, the Canadian Pacific Railway — might continue to be largely British-owned, but they represented a dying era, and the only place where Canada could obtain sufficient additional capital for expansion from the 1940s onward seemed to be the United States. In the early years of reconstruction and expansion at the end of the Second World War we finally shook away the wreckage of the Depression, but it was at the cost — which few Canadians then recognized — of accepting so much American capital that one kind of colonialism was replaced by another, with, I believe, a permanent wounding of the Canadian collective pride, a wounding that is one of the reasons why we tend to agonize so much about our identity. The 1940s and the 1950s were the fatal decades; already, by the middle 1960s, the crucial point had been passed, more than 50 per cent of Canadian manufacturing industry was under American control, with far higher proportions in the key industries. "In the automobile industry," I said in *Canada and the Canadians* in 1968, "their control is as high as 97 per cent, in rubber products 91 per cent, in the electrical apparatus industry 67 per cent, in petroleum and natural gas more than 60 per cent, in chemicals 54 per cent, in mining and smelting 52 per cent, in agricultural machinery 52 per cent, and in pulp and paper 35 per cent." After such a record one can only share the astonishment implied in the historian J. Bartlet Brebner's remark: "Perhaps the most striking fact about Canada is that it is not part of the United States." (1960)

The disposal of so much that was economically vital to Canadian independence was not motivated entirely by a desire for material gain. Few Canadians consciously sold the pass. It was much more a question of the failure of mental fortitude. Only a few courageous and long-sighted Canadians had begun, in that crucial post-war decade, to envisage the possibility that they might be developing into a people whose individuality would find not only material shape but also an increasingly vital cultural expression. The confusion that existed among politicians and industrialists afflicted intellectuals and creators as well, with a very few exceptions; Hugh MacLennan, who, in novels like *Barometer Rising* (1941) and *Two Solitudes* (1945), set out to give fictional expression to a national myth, was one. It was more usual for writers and painters who had formerly looked to London and Paris for their models to turn their attention to New York and San Francisco. The attitude still existed that nothing vital could originate in Canada, and the few critics who talked of distinctive Canadian movements in the arts, the few artists who stayed at home to create them, were for the most part either mocked or disregarded. There seemed an extraordinary unsureness among Canadians, an extraordinary urge to manifest their identity according to the first of the OED definitions, by striving for an "absolute or essential sameness" with the older cultures from which their forebears had originally come.

Not until the 1950s were courses in Canadian literature very hesitantly offered in our universities. Not until the 1960s did critics begin to take our writers and painters seriously enough to study them as deeply as they studied British and French and American visual and literary artists. The 1950s was a time of great upsurge in artistic production, and there was, in particular, such a spate of books that in various ways could be classed as Canadiana that by 1967, the year of the Centennial and of Expo, it was difficult to realize that the sense of Canadian nationality on a mass scale, embracing large numbers of ordinary people and sweeping writers and scholars and even politicians in its flow, was a relatively new phenomenon. Only now, late in the twentieth century, can we begin to

Hugh MacLennan is the Canadian national novelist in much the same way that Balzac is the French national novelist. More than any other writer he has conscientiously examined the Canadian *condition humaine*: the way we live as individuals in parallel communities he has called the "two solitudes", the way our personal, social and political lives intermingle and create the national organism of Canada, he has charted in a series of novels beginning with *Barometer Rising* (1941) and ending with *Return of the Sphinx* (1967), since when he has published no further novels. MacLennan is a Cape Bretonner, bred with a sense of Scottish tradition and of Calvinist moral rigidities. Halfway through life he moved to Montréal, and since then has lived in the other Canada of Québec. In structure and in their controlling myths MacLennan's novels derive much from his classical education and especially from Homer's *Odyssey*; in other ways they are didactic works so clearly written to express opinions on our national destiny that many critics regard MacLennan as an essayist who happens to write fiction.

say that our conception of a Canadian identity has finally shifted its connotation from "the quality of being the same" to that of "individuality," of "individual existence."

Having reached the conclusion that at last Canadians do see their identity as something that distinguishes them from rather than identifying them with others, it is necessary to consider what that "individual existence," which so many of us now seem anxious to preserve for ourselves as Canadians, really consists of.

As will have become amply evident in the course of this book, I have always hesitated to apply the word "nation" to Canada, partly because of the historically negative connotations of the word *nationalism,* but partly also because in the strictly political sense I do not think federalist Canada has become or should become a nation-state in the classic nineteenth-century mode, which implies not only political centralization, but also an exclusiveness towards people outside one's borders that can end very easily in xenophobia.

Even the relatively mild OED definition of a nation, which has been carefully purged of extremist over-tones, hardly seems to apply to Canada as it has so far existed. For we are told that the definition of a nation as merely "a country," which might just about fit Canada, is "rare;" the favoured definition is: "A distinct race of people, characterized by common descent, language or history, usu. organized as a separate political state and occupying a definite territory."

Canadians, of course, are a conglomeration of races and peoples; they have no common descent or language, and many of them have shared a history for only a very brief period. There seems no chance, however long Canadians remain together, that they will speak a single language or establish a homogenous culture. In these respects Canada fits the conventional definition of a nation as little as does Switzerland. But lack of homogeneity does not necessarily mean lack of unity; the example of Switzerland shows that a genuine confederation can exist as a country united by common interests and can prosper over centuries without its becoming in any ordinary way a nation-state.

It is true that collectively Canadians occupy "a definite territory," but, as we have seen, their regional differences are perhaps even stronger than those between the various cantons of Switzerland, and there are many Canadians, not merely in Québec, who would be quite willing to end the links between the regions. And though Canadians may be organized in what is nominally "a separate political state," there are once again many of them who claim that its *separateness* has not assured its *independence,* economically or even politically. There were many whose anger was mingled with an uneasy feeling of agreement when the Russian diplomat Andrei Gromyko once described Canada as "the boring second fiddle in the American symphony."

Furthermore, the fact that Canada is one of the last of the world's countries still accepting relatively large numbers of immigrants implies that its people are still willing, for the time being at least, to tolerate a great deal of social fluidity and mutability, the qualities of an open-ended society that not only welcomes strangers but also accepts all that they bring to enrich and change its structure. The post-1945 migration (which unlike earlier such movements consisted mainly of people who have *stayed* in Canada) has been one of the most potent factors in preserving our culture and our way of life from absorption into the general North American pattern. Paradoxically, if we remain Canadians rather than undifferentiated North Americans, we owe it largely to the millions from Britain and continental Europe, from Asia and the Caribbean, who in the years since the Second World War have made that alternative viable by accepting Canada as their country. Many of these immigrants were artists and intellectuals who helped to develop a culture distinct from that of the United States, and others, like the refugees from Hungary and Czechoslovakia and — as deserters and draft resisters given refuge during the Vietnam War — from the United States, have helped to stop Canadian political attitudes from becoming too rigid.

Yet, though it represents no single race, no united people, though economically it is not totally independent and seems to many of its inhabitants a political anomaly, and though it is in no ordinary sense a nation, Canada is still an international presence. Its inhabitants accept with increasing willingness — even passion — the fact of being Canadian and the consequent obligation to defend what remains of Canadian independence in what often becomes very physical and earthy way — protecting the soil against alien pollution for example — as well as in a more narrowly political sense. And if we can determine what brings Canada, on occasion, the kind of international recognition that enabled it, for example, to play a crucial role in the UN during the Suez crisis of 1956 or in the Commonwealth when John Diefenbaker forced South Africa to leave that organization; if we can find out why the *idea* rather than the *nation* of Canada can win a growing loyalty rather than commanding it, then, it seems to me, we shall have come very near to trapping that elusive creature, the Canadian Identity.

Essentially, I think we must say, the land and the events for which it acted as the stage (or to give them academic names, our geography and our history) have made us what we are, but always with the proviso that history is merely the record of what happens when many individual wills react to a set of given circumstances. Canada without Canadians would be Voltaire's acres of snow (somewhat expanded and with a green corner added in the far west) with nobody to give them even a name. Yet it is impossible to explain Canadians as they have acted in and formed their history without taking the land into account. We have been shaped, mentally as well as physically, by the climatic rigours of our land, by the oppressive presence of a cold and empty north pressing down towards

Donald Creighton, born in 1902, has moved steadily, from the time his classic *Commercial Empire of the St. Lawrence* appeared in 1937, into the position of Canada's leading historian. Like all great historians, he deals with more than the facts of the past; he extracts from them the myths of a people. Only Hugh MacLennan, in the different medium of fiction, has done as much as Creighton to forge a sense of nationality among Canadians. His thesis is that of a geographical east-to-west thrust through the St. Lawrence River system that carried the historical development of Canada westward with such impetus, in the journeyings of the fur traders and the thrust of the railway builders, that the north-south geographical formation of the plains and the western cordillera was counteracted. Canada, in other words, was not a political accident; it came into being as a nation through a combination of historical and geographical circumstances that profoundly differentiated it from the United States. His passionate interest in the formation of Canada led Creighton to the sources of that development, and, apart from more general historical works like *Dominion of the North*, his books include *The Road to Confederation* and the classic biography of John A. Macdonald, published in two volumes, *The Young Politician* and *The Old Chieftain*.

our frontiers, by the proximity of a wilderness which we have largely despoiled without taming, by the very distances that separate us and the geographical barriers of mountain and sea that make the extremities of our land — British Columbia and Newfoundland — perpetually conscious of their differences from the central provinces even when language does not enter the question. These factors have made us, in curious combination, cautious and self-deprecating in comparison with our neighbours to the volatile south, but also capable at times of the kind of stoical daring that in the very dawn of our country's existence could build a railway through thousands of miles of wilderness to reach a few scattered settlements on the distant coast where the Pacific tide breaks on the beaches.

Claude T. Bissell, formerly President of the University of Toronto, expressed it well:

> Canadians move slowly, but when they are aroused they move with remarkable speed. Someone suggested recently that our way of life is "puritanism touched by orgy." Our history is a record of stolidity broken by bold imaginativeness.

We have been shaped equally by history, by the fact that for almost two centuries Canada has provided an alternative in North America to what is commonly and arrogantly called the "American Way of Life." Indeed, it is probably a good basic definition of Canadians to say that they are the descendents of those North Americans who deliberately chose a harsher and less dramatic way of existence rather than become citizens of the United States. That kind of choice recurs throughout our history. There were the *canadiens* who decided to stay in Québec in 1760 rather than return to a more constricted life in Old France, and their descendants who remained at home during the nineteenth century rather than join the exodus to the south that filled whole towns of New England with emigrant French Canadians. There were the Loyalists who, without being fervent Royalists, preferred something closer to the English political system than the new forms that were being created in the rebel colonies, and who often endured considerable hardship during the process of migration and settling in a raw land. There were the Canadians of all races who in the American War of Independence and later, in the War of 1812, passively or actively rejected the American invaders and their ideologies. There were the groups of immigrants during the nineteenth and early twentieth centuries who chose not to respond to the attractions of a more prosperous and a more expansive society, and who remained in Canada while the majority of their compatriots moved on into the American west. And finally, in more recent years, there have been the thousands of Americans in flight from the perils of megapolitics who have chosen Canada as their adoptive homeland.

Each of those who made a choice to remain in Canada did so as a responsible individual, and there must have been many occasions on which personal circumstances overrode all other considerations. Yet one is aware of an underlying unity of preference which in political terms meant that people who remained in Canada would rather live under a parliamentary system based on responsible government than under a republican system based on an irresponsible executive power. Nevertheless, the British model was inevitably modified by Canada's geography and by the various histories of the component colonies that became provinces. A hierarchy of legislatures developed rather than a single parliament, an example of the way in which tradition in Canada is always modified by local circumstances. Canada's very size and the different histories of its regions made federalism an appropriate political form. And federalism implies decentralization, as Pierre Trudeau emphasized in his independent youth, before political life turned him into something of a centralist in action. True decentralization, Trudeau remarked in 1951, "will involve giving real powers to local governments, and leaving as much responsibility as possible within easy reach of the people. It will also encourage the principle of self-government in semipublic bodies: unions, parish corporations, student associations and the rest." In this direction Canada's peculiar political destiny seems to point.

Yet tradition has remained a potent influence, since those who elected to stay in Canada, whether British or French or members of the other component races, were inclined to remain a more formal people, a people more willing to accept hierarchies and ancient ceremonial than were their neighbours to the south of the border, which is one reason why no move to transform Canada into a republic has succeeded or is likely to do so in the foreseeable future. That so many Canadians, doggedly if not enthusiastically, cling to monarchy implies more, however, than a reverence for the past. It illustrates the political cautiousness which is a part of the Canadian national character, and hence a part of that elusive "identity" which we are seeking. There are advantages to having a head of state removed entirely from the business of government and to having that head of state living, as it were, in the voluntary exile of Buckingham Palace with a mere deputy at Rideau Hall; it eliminates the temptation which inclines all republican executives to dream secretly of Napoleonic glories. George P. Grant, that pessimistic Tory, remarked in his *Lament for a Nation* that Canadians have attempted "a ridiculous task in trying to build a conservative nation in the age of progress, on a continent we share with the most dynamic nation on earth." But the English writer V. S. Pritchett tended to see Canadian attitudes in a more positive light, and I agree with him.

> The Canadian spirit is cautious, observant and critical where the American is assertive; the foreign policies of the two nations are never likely to fit very conveniently, and this, again, is just as well, for the

If Donald Creighton sounds the triumphant note in the history of Canadian nationality, **George P. Grant** can best be described as its threnodist. The grandson of George Munro Grant, the famous Victorian-age principal of Queen's University, Grant has specialized academically in philosophy and religion, yet he is best known for books with a distinctly political bearing. His *Lament for a Nation: The Defeat of Canadian Nationalism* appeared at a crucial time, 1965, when Canadians were becoming intensely conscious of the extent to which American economic and cultural imperialism had replaced British political imperialism as a shaping element in Canadian life. Though Grant's own tone was essentially pessimistic — that of a man who sees the battle lost — his book did in fact have an inspiring effect on nationalist intellectuals because it stated so starkly what was being lost and how. Grant tends to represent the conservative wing of Canadian nationalism, as became evident in his second book, *Technology and Empire: Perspectives on North America*, in which he discussed how technology and liberal politics as developed in North America tended to interact in a way that diminished the quality of existence.

peace of the world depends on a respect for differences.

The same cautiousness has resulted in a political pattern that allows for a great deal of socialism in transport, communications, and other fields in the theoretically non-socialist country of Canada, without bringing avowed socialists to power in Ottawa. Thus we have the gadfly benefits of a doctrinaire opposition, the NDP, without suffering the impositions of a doctrinaire administration. Canada indeed is one of the few countries in the world that appears to have benefitted rather than otherwise from its periods of minority government, when varying political philosophies interact within the power vacuum in a way that usually leads to beneficial legislation. Perhaps that is another way of stressing what I have already pointed out, that Canada is not a national state in the usually accepted sense, but a mutable and often dynamic political continuum suited to the varied historical roots of its peoples and to the broken patterns of its geography. Any attempt to tidy it up into a centralized nation-state would bring its immediate disintegration.

Nowhere is a country's identity, if by that word we have finally decided to mean its *individuality,* more deeply exemplified than in its culture, *i.e.*, its whole characteristic and customary way of life, but more especially the sum of its arts and its literature. The development of a characteristic literature and of characteristic styles of visual art are the first reliable signs that a people is becoming conscious of its real nature and hence its identity, for they are the signs of changes that are internal as well as external, changes in the mind as well as in the environment. As has already been mentioned, the emergence half a century ago of the Group of Seven, with its style of painting deliberately intended to capture the essential qualities of Canadian landscape; and the emergence in the years between the world wars of poets and novelists not content with a colonial literature that followed British and American models, were crucial events in the development of an inner sense of independence among Canadians. Today we can often trace more clearly in what our writers show us of ourselves than we can in the acts and vague statements of our politicians, the true outlines of a vision that can be no other than Canadian.

To expound the Canadian identity in merely political or sociological terms is, in the last resort, to talk in abstractions; if we want to feel concretely and imaginatively what it is, we must turn to our writers and artists. And here I do not mean only those who, like Hugh MacLennan, have used their fiction to tell us rather didactically about the *problems* of Canadian nationality. I mean equally those others — novelists like Morley Callaghan and Margaret Laurence and Sheila Watson, and poets like Earle Birney and Al Purdy and Margaret Atwood — who have given mythic form to our experience of the land and have put Canada and its people in our minds as living imaginative entities. I mean also painters like Jack Shadbolt and Alex Colville, sculptors like the Inuit Tiktak, and architects like Arthur Erickson, whose work shows a poetic apprehension of what it is, physically and mentally, to live in the twentieth century in our land, existing uneasily between the climatic rigours of its north and the political storms of its south.

Tension produced by outside threats is an element in the Canadian identity that we should not forget, any more than we should forget the more creative tensions that operate between us as people of different regions with different traditions. Without such tensions we should not have come to a dim sense of our common interests in 1812, we might never have been united in 1867, and we might have drifted apart long before the late 1970s in which I am writing.

The existence of such tensions mean that the Canadian tends to be less of an optimist than the American. It is true that for us the 1960s was a decade of almost uncharacteristic euphoria. It was a time when, as Robert Fulford said in his book on Expo, we had a feeling "not only of accomplishment in hand, but of even greater achievement to come." For Fulford, the 1960s "seemed . . . to mark the end of Little Canada . . . . We discovered ourselves." It was the decade when our standard of living was the second highest in the world; when our Centennial made us aware of the richness of our history; when Expo revealed creative qualities we had not imagined we possessed; when, by remaining in contact with Cuba and China and loosening our ties with NATO, we were showing our independence in foreign affairs to the world; when we carried Canadian flags on our packs and our suitcases as we travelled abroad to show how proud we were of our land and ourselves. Economic setbacks, changes in global conditions, threats to our precarious unity, have changed that mood to a more anxious one in which we recognize our true place in the world. But then, we never felt in our hearts that the decade of Expo and Trudeaumania and the flower children was quite real. In part it *was* a dream, yet it left its permanent effects on Canadian society: the threat of absolute destitution was removed through widespread welfare programmes; a far greater respect than had ever before existed was established for the rights of hitherto unprivileged minorities — native people, women, homosexuals, students, the unemployed, to name a few, are far better off than they were before the 1960s. And, if today we are facing critical circumstances in many directions, I think we face them with a difference. We have understood what Norman Angell perceived as long ago as 1914, when he said that "God has made Canada one of those nations which cannot be conquered and cannot be destroyed, except by itself." We have emerged so far from the colonial mentality that we no longer expect other people to save us. We know we must stand on our own, and perhaps, as the poet Alden Nowlan has said, "the question is not 'Who are we?' but 'What are we going to make of ourselves?'" If we have reached the point of asking such a question, perhaps we have at last found our identity.

Index

Aberhart, Wm., 183, 187
Acadia, 28, 96-100, 102, 103, 115
Acadians, 50, 77, 120
Adam of Bremen, 27
Aitken, William Maxwell (see Beaverbrook)
Alberta, 161-166, 181, 182, 187
Alexander, Sir Wm., 97
Allan, Sir Hugh, 104
Amundsen, Roald, 230
Anderson, Patrick, 72
Annapolis Valley, 77, 97
Argall, Samuel, 97
Athabaska, L., 33
Atwood, Margaret, 160, 217, 269, 271

Baffin Is., 28, 228
Baker Lake, 220
Baldwin, Robert, 65
Barbeau, Jacques, 276
Barker, 'Billy', 208
Barren Lands, 23, 222, 231
Battleford, 171
Bay of Fundy, 97, 104
Beaverbrook, Lord, 108, 114
Begbie, Matthew Baillie, 205, 208
Beckwith, John, 274
Bennett buggy, 186, 189
Bennett, R.B., 108
Bennett, W.A.C., 197
Bering Strait, 16
Birney, Earle, 217, 218, 269
Blackfoot Confederacy, 25, 170
Blais, Marie-Claire, 134, 273
Blanchet, M. Wylie, 217
Bloore, Ronald, 263
Boothia Peninsula, 223
Borden, Sir Robert, 100, 108
Borduas, Paul-Emile, 261
Bompas, Bishop William Carpenter, 225, 228
Bourassa, Henri, 68, 128, 241
Bourget, Bishop Ignace, 122
Bowering, George, 269
Brant, Joseph, 136
Brébeuf, Jean de, 117
Brewster, Elizabeth, 108
British Columbia, 59, 187, 193-218, 278
BNA Act, 68, 186
Brock, Sir Isaac, 51, 59
Brooke, Frances, 256
Brown, George, 67
Brûlé, Etienne, 28
Burke, Edmund, 102-3
Butler, Wm. Francis, 7
Bytown, 145, 149

Cabot, John, 27, 75, 95
canadiens, 54, 56, 61 124-5, 298
Canadian Northern, 175
Canadian Pacific Rly., 172, 175, 210
Callaghan, Morley, 131, 160, 269, 280
Calvert, Sir George, 48, 80
Campbell, Robert, 125
Cape Bona Vista, 96
Cape Breton Is., 48, 95, 98, 104
Carrier, Roch, 134, 273
Carleton, Sir Guy, 128
Carman, Bliss, 111, 210
Carmichael, Frank, 261
Carr, Emily, 217, 253, 261
Cartier, Jacques, 13, 14, 27
Chambers, Jack, 263
Champlain, Samuel de, 14, 96
Charlottetown, P.E.I., 110
Coaker, William, 85
Cobbett, William, 138
Cobden, Richard, 106
Cohen, Leonard, 131, 255, 269
Cohen, Matt, 271
Columbia R., 36, 37
Colville, Alex, 108, 263, 276
Confederation, 65-71, 90, 146, 170, 208
Cook, Michael, 276
Cook, Cpt. James, 26, 193, 200
Coppermine R., 43, 44
Cosmos, Amor de, 207, 293
Coulter, John, 276
coureurs de bois, 28, 31, 49, 117, 244
Crawford, Isabella, 159
Creighton, Donald, 297
Crémazie, Octave, 134, 256
Crowfoot, 173
Cunard, Samuel, 105
Cupids, Nfld., 77, 78

Davies, Robertson, 271, 274
Davies, Thomas, 259
Davis, John, 228
Dawson City, 219, 230
Deighton, 'Gassy' Jack, 210
Depression, The, 246,
  in Nfld., 90
  in Prairies, 183, 186-7
Diderot, Denis, 223
Douglas, Sir James, 201, 206, 207-8
Drake, Sir Francis, 200
Dudek, Louis, 133, 269
Dufferin, Lord, 71
Duley, Margaret, 93
Dumont, Gabriel, 71, 169, 172
Dunlop, William 'Tiger', 138, 140
Duplessis, Maurice, 131
Durham, John George Lambton, Earl of, 55, 63, 123

Eaton, Timothy, 147
Edmonton, Alta., 166, 189
Elgin, James Bruce, Earl of, 55, 144
Ellesmere Is., 7
Engel, Marian, 271
Erickson, Arthur, 196, 267, 268
Ericsson, Leif, 11, 95
Ericsson, Thorvald, 11
Eric the Red, 11

Family Compact, The, 61, 144
Fishing Admirals, 80, 81
Forts:
  Chipewyan, 34
  Edmonton, 167
  Franklin, 224
  Frontenac, 137, 150
  Garry, 168, 169
  George, 34, 201
  Good Hope, 224
  Langley, 203, 206
  Liard, 224
  Norman, 224
  Prince of Wales, 40
  Rae, 224
  Simpson, 203, 224, 225
  Vancouver, 201
  Victoria, 202, 203, 204
  William, 37
Franklin, Sir John, 44, 229
Fraser Canyon, 34
Fraser R., 23, 37
Fraser Valley, 49, 215
Fredericton, N.B., 110
Fréchette, Louis, 134, 256
Freydis, 11, 12
Frobisher, Martin, 74, 228
Frye, Northrop, 7, 49

Gallant, Mavis, 131
Garneau, François-Xavier, 123
Garneau, Hector de Saint Denys, 134, 271
Garner, Hugh, 271
Gaspé Peninsula, 27
Gastown, 210
Gelinas, Gratien, 276
Grant, George P., 299
Giguère, Roland, 271
Gilbert, Sir Humphrey, 31, 75
Godbout, Jacques, 273
Gokstad ship, 12
Grainger, Martin Allerdale, 217
Grand Banks, 27, 75, 79, 80
Grande Hermine, La, 13
Grand Pré, 98
Grant, Cuthbert, 224
Great Lakes, 30
Great Slave Lake, 32, 34, 223, 225
Greenland, 12, 79
Grenfell, Wilfred, 85
Gropius, Walter, 263
Groseillers, Medard Chouart, Sieur des, 30
Grove, Frederick Philip, 189, 269
Gulf of St. Lawrence, 13, 27, 47, 95, 115
Gurick, Robert, 276
Guy, John, 77

habitants, 28, 47, 49, 54, 61, 116, 117-20, 244
Haig-Brown, Roderick, 193, 215, 217

Haliburton, Thomas Chandler, 107, 109, 250
Halifax, N.S., 100, 101, 102
Hant's Harbour, 93
Harris, Lawren, 261
Harris, Robert, 108
Hearne, Samuel, 40-2, 44, 45, 259
Hébert, Anne, 134, 271
Hébert, Louis, 28
Helluland, 11
Helwig, David, 271
Henday, Anthony, 22, 40
Herbert, A.P., 89-90
Herbert, John, 276
Herjolfsen, Bjarni, 11
Hiemstra, Mary, 178
Hind, Henry Youle, 166
Hochelaga, 13, 14, 47
Hood, Hugh, 271
Hopkins, Frances Anne, 38, 39
Horne, William van, 210-11
Horwood, Harold, 76, 85, 93
Houde, Camillien, 134, 244
Howe, Clarence Decatur, 294
Howe, Joseph, 65, 107, 108
Hudson, Henry, 228
Hudson R., 30
Hudson's Bay Company, 30, 32, 36, 38, 39, 45, 166, 201, 220, 225, 231
Hulme, T.E., 162
Hurtig, Mel, 270

Indians (see Native Peoples)
Ingstad, Helge, 10, 11
Inuit (see Native Peoples)

Jackson, A.Y., 261
Jakitars, 78
James, Cpt. Thomas, 228
Jameson, Anna, 154
Jefferson, Thomas, 53
Johnston, Francis Hans, 261

Kane, Paul, 166, 259
Kamloops, B.C., 193
Kelsey, Henry, 39
King, Mackenzie, 184
Kingston, 137, 151
Kirke, David, 48, 80, 117
Klein, A.M., 133, 255, 268
Klondike gold rush, 219, 226

Labrador, 11, 27, 82, 93
Lacombe, Father Albert, 167, 168
Lafitau, Joseph, 30
Lafontaine, Hippolyte, 65
Lahontan, Baron de, 115
Lalemant, Gabriel, 22
Lambton, George, (see Durham, Earl of)
Lampman, Archibald, 160, 260
L'Anse aux Meadows, 11, 287
Larsen, Henry, 230
Lasnier, Rina, 271
Laurence, Margaret, 186, 187, 191, 271
Laurier, Sir Wilfrid, 70
Laval, Bishop François Xavier, 116, 117
Law, Bonar, 108, 114
Layton, Irving, 133, 255, 269
Leacock, Stephen, 160, 260
Leduc, Ozias, 261
Lescarbot, Marc, 96
Lévesque, René, 131, 242
Levine, Norman, 255
Lismer, Arthur, 261
Livesay, Dorothy, 217, 218, 268
livyers, 83
Longfellow, Henry Wadsworth, 99
Louisbourg, 48, 98, 289
Louisiana, 99
Lower Canada, 49, 55, 61, 65, 146
Lowry, Malcolm, 217
Loyalists, 55-6, 61, 104, 111, 122, 137, 298
Ludwig, Jack, 255
Lunenberg, 102

Macdonald, Sir John A., 60, 67, 149
Macdonald, J.E.H., 261
MacEwen, Gwendolyn, 269
Mackenzie, Alexander, 34, 47, 224, 227
Mackenzie R., 37, 224, 227
Mackenzie, William Lyon, 61, 63
MacLennan, Hugh, 108, 111, 112, 131, 295
Maclure, Samuel, 216
Maillet, Antonine, 110
Manitoba, 68, 161-2, 169, 175, 182
Markland, 11
Massey, Geoffrey, 267
Masterless men, 80, 82
May, 'Wop', 227
Maynard, Fredelle, 179
McClelland, Jack, 270
McClung, Nellie, 184, 242
McCulloch, Thomas, 107, 111
McDougall, George, 167
McLachlan, Alexander, 154
McLuhan, Marshall, 162, 291
Meares, Cpt. John, 200
Métis, 45, 168, 220
Milne, David, 261
Mitchell, W.O., 191
Montcalm, Louis-Joseph, Marquis de, 126
Montgomery, Lucy Maud, 108
Montreal, 45, 97, 115, 117, 123, 125, 126-7
Moodie, Susanna, 138, 143, 154, 258
Moody, Richard Clement, 207, 208
Monts, Pierre, Sieur de, 96
Moriyama, Raymond, 268
Morrice, James Wilson, 261
Morton, W.L., 291
Munk, Jens, 228
Munro, Alice, 271
Murphy, Emily, 184
Murray, Gnl. James, 120

Nakamura, Kazuo, 263
Native Peoples:
- Assiniboine, 170
- Beothuk, 12, 22, 25, 78
- Blackfoot, 25, 40
- Chipewyan, 40
- Coast Salish, 25
- Coast Tsimshian, 25
- Copper Eskimo, 12
- Cree, 25, 45, 170
- Dené, 220, 222, 223, 225
- Dorset culture, 78, 254
- Gitksan, 19
- Haida, 25, 200, 206
- Huron, 22, 28
- Inuit, 18, 23, 220, 225
- Iroquois, 13, 14, 20, 22
- Kwakiutl, 18, 19, 206
- Malecite, 22, 95
- Micmac, 13, 22, 79, 95
- Montagnais, 88
- Nascopie, 79
- Nootka, 17, 23
- Ojibway, 18, 243
- Sarcee, 25, 46
- Saulteaux, 46
- Thule culture, 12, 78
- Tlingit, 25, 225

Nelligan, Emile, 134, 260
New Brunswick, 50, 55, 95-114
New England, 59, 98, 99
Newfoundland, 11, 27, 48, 75-94, 115, 255
New France, 22, 27, 28, 47, 48, 54, 55, 117, 119, 133
New Westminster, 208
Northwest Company, The, 31, 32, 34, 166, 168, 201
Northwesters, 36, 37, 39
North West Mounted Police, 170, 176, 232, 233
North West Rebellion, 167
North West Territories, 181, 219-232
Nova Scotia, 27, 48, 65, 95-114, 242
Nowlan, Alden, 108, 111, 269, 301

O'Grady, Standish, 49
Okanagan Valley, 193, 214, 215
Onderdonk, Andrew, 210, 212
Onley, Toni, 263
Ontario, 50, 137-160
Ontario, Lake, 28
Ottawa, 151, 152
Ottawa R., 145, 149
Ostenso, Martha, 186, 190
Ouelette, Fernand, 271

Page, P.K., 133, 217, 269

Panneton, Philippe, (see Ringuet)
Papineau, Louis-Joseph, 61, 128, 131
Parry, Sir Edward, 83
Peguis, 25, 26
Pei, Mario, 267
Pellan, Alfred, 261
Perez, Juan, 200
Petty Harbour, 92
Phillips, R.A.J., 225
Pilon, Jean-Guy, 271
Pinsent, Gordon, 93
Pollock, Sharon, 276
Pond, Peter, 32
Port Royal, 28, 96
Poundmaker, 71
Prairies, The, 22, 39, 161-193, 278
Pratt, E.J., 89, 93, 94, 268
Prince Edward Is., 68, 95-114
Priestley, J.B., 291
Purdy, Al, 160, 217, 269

Québec Prov., 13, 115-137, 242, 271
Quebec City, 28, 32, 45, 97, 115, 116, 123, 126
Québec Conference, 68, 108
Queenston Heights, 51

Radisson, Pierre-Esprit, 30
Rae, Dr. John, 44, 230
Rattenbury, F.M., 216
Reaney, James, 274, 276
Rebellion Losses Bill, 54
Red River, 167
Red R., Valley, 69
Red River Valley Settlement, 167-8
Remittance men, 214
Richler, Mordecai, 131, 271, 155
Riel, Louis, 71, 168-9, 171
Riopelle, Jean-Paul, 261
Rindisbacher, Peter, 81
'Ringuet', 134, 271
Roberts, Charles G.D., 108, 111, 112, 260
Roberval, Jean-François, Sieur de, 75
Roche, Mazo de la, 160
Rohe, Mies van der, 263
Ronald, William, 263
Rosenblatt, Joe, 255
Ross, Sinclair, 191
Royal Canadian Mounted Police, 220
Roy, Gabrielle, 134, 271
Rupert's Land, 165, 220
Ryga, George, 276

Safdie, Moshe, 268
Salaberry, Col., Charles de, 59
Salle, Rene-Robert, Sieur de, 31, 38, 39
Salverson, Laura Goodman, 190, 186
Saint John, 104, 105
Saskatchewan, 161-193
Scott, Duncan Campbell, 160, 260
Scott, F.R., 133, 268
Scott, Thomas, 168
Secord, Laura, 50, 59
Selkirk, Thomas Douglas, Earl of, 49, 165, 167
Seven Oaks Massacre, 49, 168
Shadbolt, Jack, 253, 263
Shediac, N.B., 101
Sifton, Clifford, 172, 178
Simcoe, John Graves, 137
Simons, Beverley, 276
Simpson, Sir George, 201, 225
Skeena R., 19, 23
Skraelings, 11, 12, 78
Smallwood, 'Joey', 83, 89, 90
Smith, A.J.M., 131, 268
Smith, Donald, Lord Strathcona, 210
Smith, Goldwin, 247, 294
Smith, Gordon, 263
Souster, Raymond, 269
Stadacona, 13, 47
St. Croix R., 96
Stead, Robert, 190
Stefansson, Vilhjalmur, 13, 45
St. John's, Nfld., 75, 79, 82, 84
St. Lawrence R., 28, 30, 47, 49, 54, 115, 116, 120, 124, 126, 149
St. Lawrence Valley, 22, 72
Strachan, Bishop John, 147
Superior, Lake, 28

Tadoussac, 28
Tecumseh, 49, 59
Thériault, Yves, 273
Thom, Ron, 267
Thompson, David, 36-7
Thomson, Tom, 261, 285
Tiktak, 238
Tonnancour, Jacques de, 261
Toronto, 63, 145, 151-2
Town, Harold, 263
Traill, Catharine Parr, 139, 154, 258
Tremblay, Michel, 134, 276
Trois Rivières, 115, 117, 123
Trottier, Pierre, 271
Trudeau, Pierre Elliott, 196, 242

Urquhart, Tony, 263
United States of America, 53
Upper Canada, 47, 49, 55, 59, 61, 65, 137, 140, 144, 145, 247
Utrecht, Treaty of, 48, 75, 81

Vancouver, B.C., 193, 210, 211, 217
Vancouver, George, 46
Varley, Frederick, 261
Vérendrye, Sieur de la, 31
Verigin, Peter, 175
Victoria, B.C., 193, 207, 211, 218
Vinland, 11, 12, 27
voyageurs, 31, 32

War of 1812, 56
Watson, Sheila, 217, 271
Webb, Phyllis, 269
Whitehorse, Y.T., 220
Wilson, Ethel, 217
Winnipeg, 31, 161, 168, 170, 182, 189
Winslow, Col. John, 98-9
Wiseman, Adele, 186, 190, 255

Yale, B.C., 212
Yellowknife, N.W.T., 222, 227
York, 140
York Factory, 167
Yukon Territory, 219-239

Picture Credits

We would like to thank all the individuals, and staff of public institutions who made the pictorial material available to us, and who gave us permission to reproduce it. We have made every effort to appropriately identify and credit the source of each illustration and any further information would be appreciated and acknowledged in subsequent editions. The illustrations are listed as they appear on the page, from left to right and from top to bottom, and are separated by semi-colons. The following abbreviations are used:

AGO	Art Gallery of Ontario
GQMT	Government of Québec, Ministry of Tourism
HBC	Hudson's Bay Company
JRR	John Ross Robertson Collection, (MTL)
MDB	Multi-Cultural Development Branch, Ontario Ministry of Culture and Recreation
MTL	Metropolitan Toronto Library
NGC	National Gallery of Canada
NMC	National Museums of Canada
OA	Archives of Ontario
OMIT	Ontario Ministry of Industry and Tourism
PAC	Public Archives of Canada
RBL	Rare Books Library (PAC)
ROM	Royal Ontario Museum

/ 10 Parks Canada / 12 Universitetes Oldsaksamling, Oslo / 13 GQMT / 14 PAC C8029 / 15 PAC, RBL / 16 PAC C21115 / 17 NMC J2840; NMC J2426 / 18 PAC, RBL; ROM / 19 ROM 954.157.1 / 20 PAC L5309 / 21 PAC, RBL C92239 / 22 PAC, RBL L5312; PAC C9894 / 24 MTL / 25 ROM 75 CAN 919 / 26 PAC C65530 / 27 South Kensington Museum, London / 28 PAC, RBL / 29 MTL 912.71 B67 / 30 PAC, RBL / 31 MTL, JRR 54 / 32 PAC C42419 / 33 PAC C1026; PAC C19041 / 34 MTL, JRR 2753 / 35 PAC C16859; MTL, JRR 2086 / 36 ROM 75. CAN 925; HBC / 37 MTL, JRR 2351 / 38 PAC L5336 / 39 PAC C2773 / 40 PAC C20053 / 41 PAC C7300; MTL, JRR 2368 / 42 PAC / 43 PAC C25012 / 44 PAC NL5482 / 45 PAC NL5478 / 46 MTL, JRR 4677; MTL Map Room / 48 PAC National Map Collection / 49 MTL, JRR 3358 / 50 PAC C10717 / 51 OA S1431; MTL, JRR 229 / 52 OA S1439 / 53 OA S4381 / 54 PAC L6729 / 55 MTL X66-27; MTL, JRR 2268 / 56 PAC / 57 MTL, JRR; GQMT / 58 MTL, JRR 2087; PAC / 59 OMIT / 60 OA S280 / 62 MTL; Govt. Manitoba / 63 GQMT / 64 PAC; PAC / 66 PAC; PAC / 67 Parks Canada / 68 PAC C5110 / 69 Parks Canada / 70 MTL / 71 Govt. Alberta / 74 PAC L4863 / 76 PAC C15607 / 77 MTL, JRR 2252 / 78 PAC C2508; PAC C74897 / 79 MTL, JRR 42 / 80 MTL, JRR 2258 / 81 MTL, JRR 2281; PAC C1912 / 82 PAC C25700 / 83 PAC L7162 / 84 PAC C3686 / 85 PAC; PAC C22876 / 86 Parks Canada; PAC L4865 / 88 MTL, JRR 3244 / 89 PAC PA117105; Pratt Library, University of Toronto / 91 MTL, JRR 2262; MTL, JRR 2284 / 92 Parks Canada; MTL, JRR 45 / 93 George Draskoy / 96 PAC C76118 / 97 PAC / 98 MTL, JRR 2437 / 99 PAC C786 / 100 PAC C8107 / 101 MTL, JRR 2246; MTL Map Collection / 102 MTL, JRR / 103 PAC C2001; PAC C30870 / 104 MTL; PAC C13287 / 105 Public Archives, Nova Scotia / 106 OA S13598 / 107 Govt. Nova Scotia Information Centre / 108 Public Archives, Nova Scotia / 109 PAC C7163 / 110 MTL, JRR 2218; Public Archives, Nova Scotia / 112 MTL / 113 Govt. Nova Scotia / 114 PAC / 116 MTL, JRR 2059 / 117 PAC C34199 / 118 ROM 960.178; MTL, Map Collection / 119 PAC C2921 / 120 MTL, JRR 1659 / 121 MTL, JRR 1870; NGC 6278 / 122 GQMT; PAC C15876 / 123 MTL, JRR 1986-7 / 124 MTL, JRR 2084 / 125 MTL, JRR 2082 / 126 MTL, JRR 3430 / 127 MTL, Map Collection / 128 PAC; PAC C18541 / 129 OA S1144; GQMT / 130 MTL, JRR 87; GQMT / 131 MTL, JRR 1675 / 132 NGC 6272; PAC / 133 MTL, JRR 2851 / 134 PAC / 135 City Montreal P.R. / 136 NGC 5777 / 137 MTL, JRR / 138 PAC / 139 PAC C19353; MTL / 140 MTL, JRR 3612 / 141 OA S7550; OA ST43 / 142 PAC C1805; OA S7567 / 143 MTL / 144 OA S12666 / 145 PAC; OA S13363 / 146 Eaton's Archives / 147 OA L197; Eaton's Archives / 148 PAC C44625; OA S13287 / 149 PAC C2776 / 150 PAC / 151 MTL / 152 MTL 970-7-2; MTL, JRR / 153 MTL 192 / 154 PAC / 155 MTL, JRR 1407; OA / 156 MTL, JRR (both) / 157 MTL, JRR / 158 Eaton's Archives / 159 General Motors of Canada, Ltd. / 162 NGC / 163 PAC C19970 / 164 PAC; PAC C33612; PAC 164 / 165 PAC C1934; Manitoba Archives / 166 PAC C1901 / 167 PAC / 168 Public Archives of Alberta / 169 MTL, JRR D2-48a / 170 PAC / 171 Manitoba Archives / 172 Historical Society of Montana / 173 PAC / 174 McCord Museum; PAC / 175 Manitoba Archives / 176 MTL / 177 PAC C30621 / 178 PAC; PAC PA 28125 / 179 Canadian National / 180 PAC; Saskatchewan Archives; PAC / 182 PAC PA 21460 / 183 PAC / 185 Eaton's Archives / 186 PAC C80883 / 187 Eedie Steiner / 188 Manitoba Archives; PAC PA 19628 / 189 PAC C623 / 190 Gulf Oil Corp. / 192 MTL, JRR 13 / 193 Provincial Archives, B.C. / 194 MTL, JRR / 195 MTL; NMC J2426 / 196 PAC C20848 / 197 NMC C34788 / 198 PAC / 199 NMC J18807-3; NMC 72-2977 / 200 NMC J3360; PAC C16855 / 201-2 Hudson's Bay Company; Provincial Archives, B.C. / 203 McCord Museum M470 / 204 MTL / 205 PAC C10379; Provincial Archives, B.C. / 206 Provincial Archives, B.C. 13328 / 207 MTL / 208 PAC / 209 PAC; PAC / 210 McCord Museum / 211 Canadian Pacific / 212 PAC; PAC / 213 PAC PA 10033 / 214 McGill University / 215 PAC / 216 McGill University; Museum of Greater Victoria / 217 PAC / 218 Gulf Oil Corp. (both) / 219 PAC, RBL L6639 / 220 PAC C42854 / 221 PAC C1906; PAC C1913 / 222 PAC C1045 / 223 PAC C38856 / 224 MTL, JRR 3598; MTL, JRR 3593 / 225 PAC C23580 / 226 PAC C2771 / 227 PAC C16572 / 228 Public Archives of Alberta / 229 MTL, JRR 21; PAC C23538 / 230 MTL, JRR 180; PAC C6648 / 231 PAC; PAC C46599 / 232 PAC C17252; Eaton's Archives / 233 PAC / 234 Eaton's Archives / 234-5 PAC C8160 / 236 PAC C37125 / 237 all PAC / 238 Gulf Oil; Canadian Eskimo Arts Council / 241 PAC PA28932 / 242 MTL / 243 PAC PA56391; PAC / 244 United Church Archives; OA S9400 / 245 PAC PA29788; OA S9113 / 246 Mark Mietkeiwicz, MDB; Liza Linklater-Wood, MDB / 247-50 Maureen Allmen, MDB / 252 Jack Shadbolt / 253 AGO / 254 (middle) Don Summerhayes / 255 (top) David Lawrence; (lower) Toronto Arts Productions / 256 AGO / 257 NGC; AGO / 260 PAC / 261 Leacock Memorial Home; NGC; AGO / 262-5 AGO / 266 AGO; NGC; OMIT / 268 (top) Schiffer / 269 (lower) Betty Fairbank / 272 (top left) MTL / 274 National Ballet of Canada; Royal Winnipeg

Ballet / 275 Robert Ragsdale / 276 Alain Masson; Theatre Passe Muraille / 278 MTL; NGC; Toronto Maple Leafs / 279 PAC PA58045 / 280 MTL / 281 MTL / 282 MTL; OA / 284 OMIT; Govt. Alberta; Parks Canada; GQMT / 285 Malak; OMIT; OMIT / 286 OMIT; OA L1237 / 287 OMIT / 288 City Montreal P.R. / 289 Govt. Nova Scotia / 290 MTL / 294 PAC / 297 Alain Masson

Colour Illustrations

Morning Snow, Ivan Eyre; MIRA GODARD GALLERY. *Heina,* Emily Carr; *A View of Chateau Richer,* Thomas Davies; *Behind Bonsecours Market, Montreal,* William Raphael; NATIONAL GALLERY OF CANADA. *A Loggers' Camp on Vancouver Island,* E. Sandys; PUBLIC ARCHIVES OF CANADA. *Red River Carts on a Prairie Road,* Adrian Neison; ROYAL ONTARIO MUSEUM. *Le Chant de la Pierre,* Paul Emile Borduas; *Winter Sun,* A.J. Casson; *January,* Alex Colville; *Trans-Canada,* Jean-Paul Lemieux; *Homage,* William Ronald; *Red Square,* Michael Snow; TORONTO DOMINION BANK COLLECTION OF CANADIAN ART. *Snap No. 12,* Harold Town; HAROLD TOWN.